# Finnish Film Studios

**Global Film Studios**
Series Editor: Homer B. Pettey

The *Global Film Studios* series examines European, North American, South American, African, and Asian film studios and their global influence. Taking a multifaceted analysis, each volume addresses several studios representing an era, a regional intersection of production, a national cinema or a particular genre.

Titles in the series include:

*The Other Side of Glamour: The Left-wing Studio Network in Hong Kong Cinema in the Cold War Era and Beyond*
Vivian P.Y. Lee

*Finnish Film Studios*
Kimmo Laine

edinburghuniversitypress.com/series/gfs

# Finnish Film Studios

Kimmo Laine

Edinburgh University Press is one of the leading university presses in the UK. We publish academic books and journals in our selected subject areas across the humanities and social sciences, combining cutting-edge scholarship with high editorial and production values to produce academic works of lasting importance. For more information visit our website: edinburghuniversitypress.com

© Kimmo Laine 2023, 2024

Edinburgh University Press Ltd
The Tun – Holyrood Road
12(2f) Jackson's Entry
Edinburgh EH8 8PJ

First published in hardback by Edinburgh University Press 2023

Typeset in 12/14 Arno and Myriad by
IDSUK (Dataconnection) Ltd

A CIP record for this book is available from the British Library

ISBN 978 1 4744 4680 8 (hardback)
ISBN 978 1 4744 4681 5 (paperback)
ISBN 978 1 4744 4682 2 (webready PDF)
ISBN 978 1 4744 4683 9 (epub)

The right of Kimmo Laine to be identified as the author of this work has been asserted in accordance with the Copyright, Designs and Patents Act 1988, and the Copyright and Related Rights Regulations 2003 (SI No. 2498).

# Contents

| | | |
|---|---|---|
| List of figures | | vi |
| Acknowledgements | | viii |
| 1 | Introduction | 1 |
| 2 | Majors | 13 |
| 3 | Minors and independents | 30 |
| 4 | Professionals | 70 |
| 5 | Genres, cycles and series | 95 |
| 6 | House styles | 129 |
| 7 | Film politics and censorship | 149 |
| 8 | Epilogue | 170 |
| References | | 178 |
| Select filmography | | 186 |
| Index | | 188 |

# Figures

All images are courtesy of the National Audiovisual Institute.

2.1 Erkki Karu (centre) filming *War Profiteer Kaiku's Disrupted Summer Vacation* (1920). Interiors were shot on outdoor sets. 15
2.2 Risto Orko. 18
2.3 T. J. Särkkä. 22
2.4 Mauno Mäkelä (centre) with the author Mika Waltari (left) and the director Matti Kassila. 26
3.1 Still from *The Wide Road* (1931). 41
3.2 Still from *Stolen Death* (1938). 56
3.3 Still from *The White Reindeer* (1952). 63
4.1 Suomen Filmiteollisuus's sound recording department. 72
4.2 Suomi-Filmi's set construction department in 1945. 72
4.3 Suomi-Filmi's studio canteen in the 1920s. 73
4.4 Suomi-Filmi's wardrobe department. 79
4.5 Suomen Filmiteollisuus's Film School. 85
4.6 Still from *A Summer Night's Waltz* (1951). 88
5.1 *Activists* (1939): a rail built for an elaborate diagonal tracking shot. 101
5.2 Still from *The Vagabond's Waltz* (1941). 107
5.3 Still from *Song of the City Outskirts* (1948). 117
5.4 Severi Suhonen gets acquainted with high culture in *Hei, Trala-lala-lalaa* (1954). 119
5.5 *Hit Parade* (1959): producer Mauno Mäkelä and director Hannes Häyrinen with their backs to the camera, cinematographer Esko Töyri at the extreme left of the image. 120

| | |
|---|---:|
| 5.6 Still from *Inspector Palmu's Error* (1960). | 124 |
| 6.1 *The Fisherman of Storm Island* (1924): modern adventure film. All exterior scenes were filmed with two cameras to be on the safe side. | 133 |
| 6.2 Playing with urban neon lights in Valentin Vaala's *The Substitute Husband* (1936). | 140 |
| 6.3 Close-up of Regina Linnanheimo in *The Cross of Love* (1946). | 142 |
| 6.4 Noir lighting in *Northern Express* (1947). | 144 |
| 7.1 Still from *The Women of Niskavuori* (1938). | 158 |
| 7.2 Stereotype of a Soviet soldier, with a portrait of Stalin in the background in *Yes and Right Away* (1943). | 163 |
| 8.1 *Swinging Youth* (1961): Suomi-Filmi's attempt at a youth film. Valentin Vaala (centre) prepares for a motorcycle rear projection scene. | 174 |

# Acknowledgements

Way back when I started doing research on Finnish studio history, I never dreamed that someday a major academic publisher would be interested in bringing out a single volume in English on the subject. I am grateful to Edinburgh University Press for launching the wonderful Global Film Studios series, edited by Homer B. Pettey. I would like to offer my gratitude to Homer for his most constructive and encouraging comments, as well as to Sam Johnson, Gillian Leslie, Fiona Conn and Robert Tuesley Anderson for their kind and smooth professional guidance throughout the editing process. I am also thankful to Pietari Kääpä for suggesting me as the author of this volume in the first place.

I have had the pleasure of being involved with several other projects simultaneously with the writing this book. Many of them overlap with the contents of the book, and collaborating with friends and colleagues has contributed to this book immensely. The first of these projects resulted in the book *Unelmatehdas Liisankadulla* (2019), on the history of the Suomen Filmiteollisuus company, co-edited with Outi Hupaniittu, Minna Santakari and Juha Seitajärvi. The second was the monograph *ReFocus: The Films of Teuvo Tulio* (Edinburgh University Press, 2020) with Henry Bacon and Jaakko Seppälä. The third one is an ongoing project with Outi Hupaniittu, Heidi Keinonen, Tommi Römpötti, Minna Santakari, Juha Seitajärvi and Jaakko Seppälä on the history of the Fennada-Filmi company. Working with you all was been and will continue to be a delight.

The Universities of Turku and Oulu have provided a supporting and stimulating environment for doing research, and I would like to offer my gratitude to all my colleagues and students in Media Studies and Literature and Film Studies, respectively.

The National Audiovisual Institute in Helsinki has, in addition to being my former employer, always been helpful in providing knowledge and research material, including the production stills used in this book. Thanks to Jorma Junttila, Antti Kalliola, Matti Lukarila, Timo Matoniemi, Tommi Partanen, Olavi Similä and many others.

Kalevi Koukkunen and Kari Uusitalo have generously shared their incomparable knowledge about Finnish film history over the years. I am also grateful to Heta Reitala for interesting conversations about parallels between film history and theatre history.

Much of the actual writing of the book took place during the COVID-19 period, with limited and mainly virtual contacts with the outside world. This would have been a lonely time indeed had it not been for the regular SUAW ('Shut Up and Write') sessions organised by Anders Marklund. These online sessions include concentrated writing with phones and email turned off, as well as chatting and discussion about research-related issues, or whatever comes up. Without these sessions, sometimes taking place around the Baltic Sea region and sometimes extending to transatlantic dimensions, the manuscript would probably never have been finished. At any rate, working on it would have been significantly duller. My warmest thanks to Anders and all the others who have taken part in the SUAW sessions, including Ben Bigelow, Amanda Doxtater, Tobias Hochscherf, Åsa Jernudd, Arne Lunde, Anna Mrozewicz, Andrew Nestingen, Eva Näripea, Tytti Soila, Caper Tybjerg and Per Vesterlund.

Finally, I would like to thank my family, Silja, Jalmari, Verna and Lauri, for encouragement, company, patience, for watching and discussing movies together (even an occasional old Finnish film), and, most important, for being there.

# Chapter 1

# Introduction

Finnish cinema is a typical European small-nation cinema.[1] According to the twelve-volume *Finnish National Filmography*, 1,128 feature films were produced between 1907 and 2000. In addition to feature films, thousands of short films were made, partly due to the demand for newsreels, actualities and other topical material and partly because of a tax reduction system (1933–64) that made it economically lucrative for cinema owners to include a domestic short film as part of a screening.

Production of feature films has been relatively steady over the decades, with a few low points and a few high points. Among the low points were the years between 1916 and 1919, when first a filming prohibition imposed by the Russian authorities and then, after Finnish independence in 1917, the fierce civil war of 1918 caused a break in film production; the early 1930s, when worldwide recession, the coming of recorded sound and the internal crisis within the leading production company, Suomi-Filmi, temporarily decreased production volume; and the early 1970s, when film attendances radically dropped while the film subsidy system was still at a rather modest level. The major high points have been the mid-1950s, when studio-based production overheated just before collapsing, and the 2000s, when domestic cinema saw a new rise in popularity. With the exception of these anomalies, a typical yearly production volume has varied roughly between ten and twenty feature films.

As a small-nation cinema, Finnish film culture is in many ways comparable to that of other Nordic countries, despite some apparent differences. Unlike Denmark in the 1910s and Sweden in the late 1910s and early 1920s, Finnish cinema has never experienced an internationally acknowledged 'golden age'. No international film stars in the league of Greta Garbo or Ingrid Bergman have come from Finland, nor has the country produced internationally recognised auteurs like Carl Theodor Dreyer or Ingmar Bergman, at least not before Aki Kaurismäki's festival and art house success in the late 1900s and 2000s. Yet the similarities between Nordic countries are significant. Despite periods of international success, most Nordic films have been produced mainly for domestic markets. The mutual closeness of the Scandinavian languages has made it easier to distribute Swedish, Danish and Norwegian films to neighbouring countries than Finnish ones, since the Finnish language is totally incomprehensible to other Nordic peoples. Nonetheless, each Nordic country has produced numerous films that, despite their success in the domestic market, have not made it elsewhere.

On the other hand, regardless of the language difference, Scandinavian markets have been lucrative for Finnish producers. Especially from the 1930s to the late 1950s, Finnish films were exported most systematically to Scandinavian countries, in particular to Sweden.[2] Although there were few major successes, export appears to have been profitable enough to become a habit. From the Swedish point of view, it obviously helped that, since Finland is a bilingual country, films were often already provided with subtitles or at least with ready-made Swedish text lists. One common feature between Nordic countries is that, in all of them, subtitling instead of dubbing became a standard practice after the coming of sound. This evidently eased the export of Finnish films into Nordic markets. Yet for cinemagoers to hear a familiar language on screen was a bonus. Therefore, a number of dual-language versions, in Finnish and in Swedish, were made over the years, as will be discussed in Chapter 3.

Typical for small-nation cinemas with a limited production volume is that there is great demand for imported films. This means that film culture in Finland as well as in other Nordic countries has always been thoroughly transnational. In comparison with the three Finnish films that premiered in Finland in 1930, there were 306 imported films. For 1940, the respective figures were 23 and 104 (despite the ongoing war); for 1950, 15 and 376; and for 1960, 19 and 329.[3] Nonetheless, the significance of domestic films cannot be disregarded. Finnish films and their makers enjoyed remarkable media publicity, and the market share of domestic productions was generally high. While exact figures from the studio era are lacking, it can be estimated that, for example, in 1939 the market share of domestic films was approximately 37 per cent.[4]

The indisputable popularity of domestic films gave the producers credibility in their constant pushing and defending of the cause of national cinema. The industry's rhetoric about domestic cinema was characterised by the trinity of ideology, art and money, epitomised in the name of the biggest production company, Suomen Filmiteollisuus

(Finnish Film Industry). The three were seen as inseparable: nationalist ideology was considered a fertile breeding ground for raising the standard as well as the status of film art, which would lead to the industry's profitability; and conversely, a prosperous industry was the prerequisite for making high-quality films with a nationally relevant content. Such rhetoric was directed partly towards general filmgoers, especially during the nationally charged years before and during World War II, and partly towards policymakers. As we shall see in Chapter 7, from the perspective of filmmakers and producers, the attitude of state officials towards cinema was mainly negative. A typical complaint from the industry was that film was treated either as an object of taxation or censorship. Tax concessions favoured domestic production from time to time, but this was seldom enough to keep the film industry content.

## The Finnish studio system

Despite all the talk about a national mission, making feature films in Finland remained a purely commercial private enterprise until the introduction of state subsidies in the 1960s, when it gradually began to evolve into a hybrid system, combining private and public funding. The decades before the introduction of subsidies are the subject of this book. From the beginning of the 1920s to the early 1960s, Finnish feature film production was dominated by a few major studios – Suomi-Filmi (1919–), Suomen Filmiteollisuus (1933–65) and Fennada-Filmi (1950–82) – accompanied by dozens of minor and independent companies. This period is here referred to as the studio era of Finnish cinema.

Why should filmmaking in Finland between the 1920s and the 1960s be considered in terms of a studio industry? What were the prerequisites for a studio system? First, films were literally made in studios. The major – and most of the minor and independent – companies operated in their own filming studios, be they permanent or makeshift, and here most of the filmmaking process was concentrated. Exteriors were usually (if not always) shot outside of studios, but otherwise, the studios were at the centre of the process, from planning to post-production. The majors were 'full-service houses' with filming equipment and costume and props departments, with the best-equipped laboratories in the country, and with permanent staff on a monthly payroll. Each studio was thus the centre of a 'dream factory'.

Second, the studios operated on a hierarchic basis. The division of labour might have been more flexible than in big film industries, but the operations were nonetheless divided into departments each with its own manager, and the general mode of operation was producer-led. At the top of the hierarchy were the studio moguls, who in many ways embodied their companies: Erkki Karu, followed by Risto Orko, at Suomi-Filmi; Toivo Jalmari Särkkä at Suomen Filmiteollisuus, and Mauno Mäkelä at Fennada. The staff included, for example, directors, actors, technical experts, electricians, dressmakers, caterers, carpenters and office workers, and while there was some movement between some of these occupations and the potential for individuals to work their way up in the hierarchy, the basic operational structures of the film factories were relatively stable. The hierarchy was clearly visible in the companies' wage ladders, with the studio bosses and leading stars on the highest rung and most female-dominated occupations on the lowest.

Third, the major studios were diversified companies. The power of the classic Hollywood studios is considered a product of a system of vertical integration, concentrating all key sectors of film business, production, distribution and exhibition, in the same companies.[5] In Finland, two of the three majors, Suomi-Filmi and Fennada, were vertically integrated, which not only benefitted them at the expense of smaller production companies with potential distribution or exhibition problems, but also secured their existence at the times when feature film production was not profitable. Suomen Filmiteollisuus proved to be more vulnerable, since it was profiled mainly as a production company. Yet, the majors had also other means of securing their leading position. For example, many of the minors were dependent on their laboratories, or had to rent shooting equipment from them.

The fourth defining factor of the studio system was that mutual competition between the studios characterised many aspects of film business and culture. While the majors cooperated to a degree, for example in film organisations, as long as it was in their shared interest, the more dominant factor was constant competition between them. The competition was partly centripetal and partly centrifugal. The centripetal logic means that the companies kept a constant eye on their rivals, and borrowed, stole or copied whatever and whenever they could, starting with the company names, as will be discussed in Chapter 6. A similar kind of centripetal logic can be seen, for example, in poaching stars or technical staff from other companies, or in forming cycles out of the successful films of rivals. A prime example of the latter is the enormous success of the war epic *The Unknown Soldier* (SF 1955),[6] which was followed by a number of war films by other producers, even though practically no combat films had been made during the first decade after World War II.

The centrifugal logic of studio competition is seen in the urge of the studios to differentiate themselves from their rivals. The central factor in this differentiating process was to create a recognisable studio image for the company and a house style for the films. As we shall see in the forthcoming chapters, the studio image was an all-encompassing feature that covered everything from the visual style of the films to the public appearances of the studio bosses.

## A Finnish Hollywood?

The major production houses operated in many ways as smallish or middle-scale factories, combining creative practices in the handicraft tradition with efficient and functional factory-like working methods. In several ways, the modes of operation and the studio practices resembled those of the Hollywood studios. Indeed, for a long time historical film studies took it for granted that Hollywood provided a model for national cinemas around the world.[7] While there is no denying the global influence of Hollywood in general, let alone the dominance it had in the film markets, there is a great deal of variation in the actual influence of Hollywood in different countries. The Finnish film industry is a case in point: while Hollywood films were seen in Finland through the studio decades and while there was constant interest in Hollywood stars, I suggest that with regard to Finnish studios, Hollywood was not necessarily the most relevant point of reference, especially in the formative years before and during World War II.

First, even if American films dominated Finnish film markets in quantity from 1923 on,[8] the overall view of the film programme was relatively diverse. Whereas Hollywood imports included numerous programme fillers that were screened only for a week, European imports were usually quality films that had a long run. There were remarkable exceptions though, mainly after the World War II, like *Gone with the Wind* (1939), which premiered only in 1950 and had a record-breaking forty-week run in Helsinki.[9] As for the audience, a 1957 survey shows that while domestic and imported films were approximately as popular in general, Hollywood films were now favoured over others, especially by young audiences.[10]

Second, even if Hollywood provided the majority of imported films, they were seldom among the most valued. Especially during the 1930s and 1940s, both critics and film professionals looked up to French cinema in particular. While critics praised the sophisticated charm of French films, from the point of view of the film companies French cinema set the standard for filmmaking practices and professional skills.[11] This is evident in the eagerness of the studios to hire professionals from Central Europe, especially from France. In the post-war years, French cinema retained some its critical standing, although in part overtaken by the new Italian cinema, as neorealism served as a new model for socially conscious filmmaking.[12] The rise of new Swedish directors like Ingmar Bergman and Alf Sjöberg was also closely followed from early on. Hollywood films were undoubtedly appreciated, but, I would argue, rather as individual achievements emerging in spite of and not because of the Hollywood production system.

Third, while Finnish production companies had little or no direct contacts with Hollywood, they were familiar with European methods of filmmaking. Both studio bosses and employees visited French, German, British and Swedish studios in order to learn new working methods, purchase filming equipment, make contacts or hire new staff. Risto Orko even visited Soviet studios in Moscow and Leningrad in 1935, despite the political tensions between Finland and Soviet Union.[13] During the post-war years, contact and collaboration with the Soviet film industry became frequent. Therefore, to the extent that Hollywood influenced the Finnish film industry, this was indirectly, rather than directly, modified by European film production centres.

Fourth, English was not widely spoken in Finland, either among filmmakers and producers or among the filmgoing audience. In addition to Finnish and Swedish, Särkkä and Orko spoke German and Russian; Särkkä even had a Master's degree in Russian philology. There was a slight change in this respect during the post-war years with the emergence of directors such as Armand Lohikoski, William Markus and Jack Witikka, all of whom were fluent in English. Witikka's first feature film, *Arctic Fury* (1951), was even co-produced by Michael Powell, with whom he had become friendly when getting acquainted with the British film industry in London.

Moreover, not all influences on the Finnish film studios came from the bigger film-producing countries, or even from the film industry at large. Because many of the filmmakers, including the founders of Suomi-Filmi, were trained in theatre, it is likely that they adapted some of their working methods straight from there. At any rate, in many ways the production companies operated just like any other middle-scale business, with no need to shape everything after the model of overseas film companies.

## The rise and decline of the Finnish studios

This book focuses primarily on the four decades between the early 1920s and early 1960s that can be characterised as the core of the studio era. This was the time when feature films were made in studios and when the field was dominated by diversified, hierarchically organised production companies that competed with one other. For most of this period, cinema was among the most popular pastimes, if not the most popular, and making films was at least a potentially profitable business.

However, I am not aiming at a precise temporal definition of the studio era. Film production history involves continuities as well as ruptures, even if filmmakers, producers and critics have often been eager to emphasise total breaks from the past. In 1936, the critic and future film director Roland af Hällström began his survey of Finnish production history with these words:

> The history of Finnish cinema, if such a fine word ought to be used in the first place in connection to a young and underdeveloped branch like domestic cinema, really only begins in 1920. This is when Suomi-Filmi, founded by a group of young actors, began its activities. For a long time, it was the dominant and only brand in domestic film production. Obviously, there had been attempts to make 'moving pictures' before that, but all that is left of most of these attempts is a number of tragicomical anecdotes and rumours; not that it would not be worth it to collect and sift through these anecdotes.[14]

A few decades later, in 1972, the cinematographer Lasse Naukkarinen expressed another break from the past, this time from the studio years:

> I have never had anything to do with any Finnish film tradition. When I became interested in the cinema the 'new' Finnish cinema had already been born and I have always worked in it. Of course I have seen a lot of traditional Finnish cinema but I was never specially interested in it and I doubt if it has had any influence on me.[15]

In af Hällström's case, the loss of evidence was indeed a reality: most of the films made in Finland before 1920 had already been lost. Although discussions about the need for preserving films had begun much earlier,[16] the Finnish Film Archive was founded only in 1957. Regarding the studio decades, the proportion of preserved films is high, mainly because the production companies or at least the distribution companies survived and preserved the material themselves until the Finnish Film Archive started collecting films. Therefore, for Naukkarinen, it was not so much a question of the disappearance of the cinematic past – although the availability of film copies was indeed limited at the time – but rather an ideologically and aesthetically perceived break with tradition.

While both af Hällström and Naukkarinen sought to distance themselves from the cinematic past, for the former, the disdained past was represented by pre-studio filmmaking, and for the latter by studio filmmaking. For both, film history manifested itself as a gradually progressing series of ruptures.

If one were to approach film history as a dialectic between continuity and rupture, both the beginning and the end of the studio era would appear more flexible. Regarding the starting point, Outi Hupaniittu has argued that af Hällström's view was biased in the sense that it backed up and consolidated Suomi-Filmi's own version of film history where nothing that preceded the founding of the company was worth serious consideration. At the same time, af Hällström's view also followed the typical logic of nationalistic history writing in implying that a state's gaining of independence necessarily caused a break in all branches of activity.[17]

The studies on the early decades of Finnish cinema by Hupaniittu[18] and Hannu Salmi,[19] as well as Jari Sedergren and Ilkka Kippola's history of Finnish documentaries and short films,[20] have indicated that both the film trade and film production were much more systematic and consistent than af Hällström's summary implies. About 300 short films were produced before the gaining of independence,[21] and the *Finnish National Filmography* lists twenty-five feature films for the years 1907–16.[22] Several companies, including Atelier Apollo, Lyyra-Filmi, Nordiska Biograf Kompaniet and Finlandia-Filmi, produced films on a regular basis, and Finlandia-Filmi even built a glass-enclosed studio in 1916. The primary focus of all these companies was, however, on importation, distribution and exhibition. Hupaniittu aptly refers to the early decades of Finnish film trade as 'the reign of the biografi business', implying that, while these early companies were diversified, none of them invested in feature film production to the same extent as the major production companies of the coming decades.[23]

Since the focus of this book is on the studio-based production of feature films, it is appropriate to concentrate on the decades from the 1920s on. At the same time, it is important to keep in mind the critique Hupaniittu directs at the biased and nationalistic view of a total break in Finnish film history in the late 1910s and early 1920s. Even if the companies that produced feature films during the years of political autonomy all went out of business by the early 1920s, there were other concrete continuities between the periods. Several of the filmmakers at Suomi-Filmi, including Teuvo Puro, Karl Fager and Konrad Tallroth, had been actively involved in the making of early feature films. Tallroth had also directed eight films in Sweden at Svenska Bio in 1916–17.[24] The company roots of one of the major studios, Fennada, can also be traced back to 1912, when Adams-Filmi was founded as an import, distribution and exhibition firm, even if it started producing feature films only much later.

The endpoint of the studio era can also be perceived as flexible. On the one hand, as will be seen in the conclusion of this book, a sense of crisis prevailed even before the 1960s. On the other hand, two of the three major studios, Suomi-Filmi and Fennada, carried on making films years after that. Moreover, many of the filmmakers and the staff of the studios continued working in new companies and especially in television. Yet, in practice, the early 1960s can be seen as a turning point in feature film production. Suomen Filmiteollisuus ceased making feature films in 1963, and the other two majors drastically cut down their production, no longer employing full-time feature film professionals. Filmmaking was no longer studio-centred in any sense of that expression. Therefore, the main focus of this book will be on the period between the early 1920s and early 1960s, albeit with an open eye to what happened before and what came after this period.

## The structure of this book

Attention in this book is paid both to the major and the minor production companies, as they were all essential parts of the studio system. Chapter 2 focuses on the three majors, Suomi-Filmi (founded in 1919), Suomen Filmiteollisuus (founded in 1933) and Fennada-Filmi (founded in 1950). The aim of this chapter is to relatively briefly outline the history of these three majors and to tentatively investigate the strategies with which they maintained their dominant position.

Despite the dominant position of the majors, the boundaries between major, minor and independent studios were never stable or self-evident. On the one hand, the majors started small, and on the other hand, there was much variation in the modes of operation in the minors. Chapter 3 charts the challenges and the benefits of making films outside of the major studios, with a focus on Komedia-Filmi (late 1920s), Fennica (late 1920s to early 1930s), Jäger-Filmi (late 1930s to early 1940s), Fenno-Filmi (1940s) and Veikko Itkonen (late 1940s to early 1960s). Case studies will be provided on four individual productions, all momentous in their differing ways: *Stolen Death* (1938), *The Way You Wanted Me* (1944), *The White Reindeer* (1952) and *The Glass Heart* (1959).

The major studios labelled themselves 'full-service houses', implying that they were self-sufficient in their operations and that everything from pre-production to laboratory work could be handled within the company. Chapter 4 investigates how these full-service houses operated and what everyday work at a film studio was like. How was the filmmaking process organised into hierarchically ordered units? With no film schools, routes to a career in the film industry were varied. Therefore, the further objective of this chapter is to discuss the ways in which employees ended up with a career in cinema.

With the usual output of ten to twenty feature films of various kinds a year, it hardly makes sense to speak of genuinely Finnish genres, with the possible exception of lumberjack films and vagabond films. Indigenous interpretations of transnational genres such as the crime film, musical or screwball comedy were common, but these were seldom labelled as genre films either. Chapter 5 explores the strategies employed by film studios to plan their output in terms of not only genres but also production levels (A, B and C films), sequels, cycles and series.

An essential factor in the mutual competition between production companies was the creation of a recognisable image for each studio. This was an all-encompassing notion that covered a wide area – from the public appearances and attitudes of the studio bosses to the kinds of films the studio put out. In Chapter 6, the films are discussed in terms of a house style, from the perspectives of subject matter, visual style and audience differentiation.

Even if filmmaking during the studio era was a private enterprise, it was not unaffected by either national or international politics. Chapter 7 will discuss the relations of the state authorities and cinema from four perspectives: film as an object of taxation, film as an object of censorship, film as propaganda, and film as a means of doing national and international politics, concerning at times the USA and Nazi Germany and at other times Soviet Union.

Finally, in the concluding Chapter 8, I shall discuss the running down of the studio era. What happened to the big, diversified studios, and how were films made after their reign had ended? I shall suggest that, whereas the subsequent decades favoured modes of production that differed considerably from those of the studio era, since the late 1990s, certain characteristics of studio filmmaking have re-emerged. This is at least partly due to the new strategies adopted by the Finnish Film Foundation, which is a state-funded organisation responsible for distributing film subsidies, with an emphasis on the importance of strong production companies and continuity in feature film production.

## Notes

1. On the concept of small-nation cinema, see Hjort and Petrie 2007: 1–17.
2. Lehtisalo 2016: 123.
3. Uusitalo 1965: 109.
4. Laine 1999: 71.
5. Gomery 1986: 1–25.
6. In this book, SF will be used as an abbreviation for Suomen Filmiteollisuus, and SuFi for Suomi-Filmi.
7. See Nowell-Smith 1996: xx–xxi.
8. Seppälä 2012: 33–44.
9. 'Ensiesitysten pituus H:gin elokuvateattereissa', *Kinolehti* 5/1951: 36–7.
10. Janne Hakulinen: 'Kuinka käydään elokuvissa ja mitä elokuvia katsotaan?', *Kinolehti* 2/1957: 6–7.
11. Laine 1999: 323–5.
12. See Terttula 1957: 24–41.
13. Uusitalo 1999: 80–1.
14. Af Hällström 1936: 221. All translations in this book are by the author, unless otherwise stated.
15. Hillier 1972: 42.
16. R. Ö.: 'Filmi historiallisena arkistona', *Filmiaitta* 8/1923: 88.
17. Hupaniittu 2018: 14–18; see also Salmi 2002: 328.
18. Hupaniittu 2013.
19. Salmi 2002.
20. Sedergren and Kippola 2009.

21. Uusitalo 1972a: 148.
22. Uusitalo et al. 1996. It should be noted, however, that the concept of the feature film here is flexible, since the earliest films included in the Filmography are, in fact, one-reel films.
23. Hupaniittu 2013.
24. See Salmi 2002: 301–12.

# Chapter 2
# Majors

Finnish feature film production during the studio era was dominated first by one, then by two and finally by three companies. The first was Suomi-Filmi (founded in 1919), the second, Suomen Filmiteollisuus (founded in 1933), and the third, Fennada-Filmi (founded in 1950). While there was always competition not just among but also beyond these three, and while there was sometimes a thin line between the majors and other production companies, in the long run these three stand out as the most powerful and long-lasting. In terms of feature film production, their share was almost 70 per cent of the whole output of films between 1920 and 1963. Of the 619 feature films made during these years, Suomen Filmiteollisuus produced 237, Suomi-Filmi 142 and Fennada 53. This leaves a total of 187 films to the dozens of other, smaller and usually short-lived companies.

Unlike in Hollywood, the vertical integration of production, distribution and exhibition was not an absolute necessity for a major company. Of the three majors, Suomi-Filmi and Fennada-Filmi were fully integrated, whereas Suomen Filmiteollisuus concentrated mainly on producing and distributing its own films. This, however, proved to be the weak point for Suomen Filmiteollisuus, when the profitability of feature film production decreased in the late 1950s.

During the heyday of the studio era, however, the majors had other means to secure their oligarchy besides integrating vertically. For example, the majors controlled many of the trade organisations, such as the Finnish Film Producers Union, for which Suomen Filmiteollisuus's CEO, T. J. Särkkä, acted as the chair from 1945 to 1963, with Suomi-Filmi's Risto Orko as the vice chair and Fennada's Mauno Mäkelä as his successor. Most other powerful film organisations, like the Finnish Film Chamber and the Finnish Cinema Owners' Association had representatives from the majors, too. This means that, even if competition between the majors was harsh and the relations between the chief executives, especially between Orko and the other two, distant at best, it was in their common interest to pull together when necessary.

Vertical integration was thus an important if not entirely necessary means of achieving and maintaining power in film production. Generally, it was useful for a company to spread its tentacles everywhere, be it in production, distribution and exhibition, or laboratory services, film organisations, importing film equipment and making short films. Overall, one can say that the majors were majors simply because they were ... big. On the one hand, their sphere of operations was wide, which means that they had compensating sources of income even at times when filmmaking was insufficiently profitable; and, on the other hand, their output of feature films was large and regular enough for one successful film to compensate for the losses of another. For a minor or independent company, one box-office failure was often enough to put an end to its filmmaking.

The object of this chapter is to outline the history of Suomi-Filmi, Suomen Filmiteollisuus and Fennada, and to investigate the strategies with which they managed to achieve and maintain their dominant position. The main focus of this first chapter is on the structures and modes of operation of the majors, and detailed discussion about the crews and their working practices, as well as genres and house styles, will follow in later chapters.

## Suomi-Filmi

Suomi-Filmi is by far the most long-lasting Finnish film studio. Founded in 1919 as Suomen Filmikuvaamo, it changed its name to Suomi-Filmi two years later. More than a century later, the company still exists, although it has not produced any feature films since 1980 nor short films since 1991.

The company was founded by four persons: Erkki Karu, who had experience as an actor and backdrop painter on theatrical tours; Martti Tuukka, who was an actor and set designer; Karl Fager, who was a set designer at the National Theatre; and Teuvo Puro, who was one of the best-known actors of the National Theatre. All had some experience in filmmaking. Puro and Fager had been involved in the first Finnish fictional film, *The Moonshiners* (1907), and the first feature film, *Sylvi* (1913), and Karu and Tuukka had shot two short comedies in the summer of 1919 (Figure 2.1). According to the articles of association, the purpose of the

**Figure 2.1** Erkki Karu (centre) filming *War Profiteer Kaiku's Disrupted Summer Vacation* (1920). Interiors were shot on outdoor sets.

company was to 'prepare and shoot domestic motion pictures and to manufacture theatrical props'.[1] In practice, this meant painting backdrops for theatres. This proved to be a wise combination, not only because the founders were more experienced in scene painting than in filmmaking, but also because they began with a modest start-up capital and stage work provided them with a steady income right from the beginning.[2]

Thus, the key to Suomi-Filmi's success was that it centred on diverse areas of operation from the outset. In 1921, Karu, who was the CEO of the company, travelled to Germany with Fager in order to explore the filmmaking practices in that country's studios and especially its film laboratories. They also had the outspoken objective to hire a German expert to develop and supervise a modern film laboratory for Suomi-Filmi.[3] They found Kurt Jäger, who was not only to run the Suomi-Filmi laboratory, but also to serve as the company's main cinematographer. First at Suomi-Filmi and then in his own companies, Jäger was to be one of the central figures in film production and technology during the next quarter of a century.

Suomi-Filmi became by far the biggest production company of the 1920s, producing about thirty feature films between 1920 and 1933. These included four documentary features, the most notable of which was

*Finlandia* (1922), an account of Finnish nature, industry and culture that had a wide international distribution organised by the Foreign Ministry, which had been the initiator of the project. In addition, Suomi-Filmi was also the biggest producer of short films in the 1920s.

During the first years of its operation, Suomi-Filmi's films were distributed by Suomen Biografi Oy, but in 1923, a better contract was made with Adams-Filmi,[4] and a year later the company started not only to distribute its own films but also to import and distribute foreign films.[5] The growth of Suomi-Filmi was rapid. The annual report of 1922 stated that rental expenses of the studio were so high that the company needed to extend its operations.[6] The expansion strategy clearly succeeded.

A more radical step was taken in 1926, when Suomi-Filmi became a fully integrated company. The annual report of 1926 recounts:

> The past year has been the most remarkable in the activities of Suomi-Filmi, since the company has at last created an immediate connection with theatres by purchasing the share majority of the biggest cinema firm Suomen Biografi Oy. A supplementary association meeting made a decision about the deal on 18 April 1926, after continuous negotiations that had lasted for months.[7]

Suomen Biografi was an import, distribution and exhibition company that had been founded in 1918. At the time when Suomi-Filmi purchased the share majority, Suomen Biografi had twelve high-quality cinemas in the biggest cities, Helsinki, Turku, Tampere, Viipuri and Kuopio.[8] These included the Helsinki Kino-Palatsi, which was to become the premier venue of Suomi-Filmi for the next four decades.

The effects of the Suomen Biografi sale was twofold. On the one hand, it strengthened Suomi-Filmi's position compared to its rivals and sealed its standing as a fully integrated major film company for the coming decades. The company could now distribute both its own productions and imported films without a middleman and have premieres in the best cinemas. On the other hand, the Suomen Biografi deal was expensive; Suomen Biografi was a big company, in fact bigger than Suomi-Filmi itself. As Suomi-Filmi's capital was limited, a remarkable part of the purchase money had to be paid with a bank loan with an interest rate of over 10 per cent.[9] The annual report of 1929 thus announced that the year had been loss-making because of the debt interest payments. Moreover, the newest feature films, *The Supreme Victory* (1929) and *Between Two Dances* (1930), had been disappointments at the box office.[10]

Despite the obvious economic obstacles, Suomi-Filmi had further investment plans. The most notable of these, initiated in 1927, was building a high-rise office building in the centre of Helsinki. This was planned as an eighteen-storey block with the biggest and most glamorous cinema not only in Finland but in the whole Nordic area, with restaurants, cafés, offices and a hotel. As the highest building in Helsinki, this was known as a 'skyscraper project', and as soon as the plan was made public, it set off a heated debate for and against the new landmark. For some, it represented a positive development in the name of modernity; for others, it was an unsuitable addition to the relatively low Helsinki skyline, or was too commercial with its large display windows and neon lights.[11] It took several years, until 1931, for the controversial project to get a construction licence. By this time, Suomi-Filmi had drifted deeper into economic crisis, and the plan was never realised.

Suomi-Filmi's crisis was partly external and partly internal. The worldwide recession had hit Finland even before the October 1929 crash, and after the economic boom of the 1920s, unemployment was high and film attendances low. The coming of synchronised sound involved both uncertainties and investments, even if the advent of the native language in Finnish cinema proved to be a major asset for domestic film production in later years. The internal tensions in Suomi-Filmi increased not only because of the financial situation, but also because Karu had put much of his time and energy into the skyscraper. Despite the generally difficult situation, his salary was high, which raised objections among the board members. Although Karu's position as the head of Suomi-Filmi had been unassailable for over a decade, the shareholders now took more control over the company, and the clout of the KOP Bank was stronger than ever because of the debts. As a result, Karu finally resigned in August 1933.[12]

The film journal *Elokuva-Aitta* commented on Karu's resignation in its editorial:

> This is in a way the most remarkable piece of news that has ever concerned domestic cinema. Erkki Karu has had much to say in this field, and whatever one thinks about the results, he cannot be blamed for the lack of initiative. He has led domestic film production as a dictator. He has held all the portfolios in the film business ... The new management of Suomi-Filmi has announced that it will employ domestic directors and screenwriters and that it is open to proposals. No strict decisions has been made about the future of the firm, but let us hope for the best.[13]

At the moment of his resignation, Karu was working on a fictional public information film about tuberculosis, *Those 45,000* (1933), produced in cooperation with the Finnish Anti-Tuberculosis Association and supervised by Risto Orko (Figure 2.2), who had a background in anti-tuberculosis activism. The film project was finally finished by Orko as an independent production. Together with Karu, he was considering founding a new company, when Suomi-Filmi's board offered him a position as the production manager in the autumn of 1933.[14] Orko accepted the offer, after having first negotiated with Karu, according to his own recollection. Another version of the course of events is recounted by, for example, Karu's daughter, who claims that his father was extremely bitter and never spoke to Orko again.[15]

Possibly in order to avoid any new concentration of power, Suomi-Filmi decentralised its management. Orko was to direct films and be in charge of film production and the laboratory, Nils Dahlström took responsibility for import, distribution and the theatres, while Matti Schreck, who was a representative of the KOP Bank, became the CEO and the chair of the board. Of the three, Dahlstöm, a second-generation cinema owner, was the only one with substantial film-related experience. By 1936, the three

**Figure 2.2** Risto Orko.

were not only members of the board, but also the biggest shareholders of the company, each holding about one-quarter of the shares.[16]

The power struggle within the company went on, however, and Dahlström was forced to leave and sell his shares to Orko and Schreck in 1940.[17] Finally, after World War II, Orko was able to buy out Schreck, becoming both the CEO and the major shareholder of Suomi-Filmi. After that, Suomi-Filmi remained practically a family business for the Orkos.[18]

Suomi-Filmi had come out of the early 1930s crisis by 1935–6. Generally, the recession was over sooner than in many other countries, and the Finnish economy prospered again, even if it was only in 1937 that film attendances reached the figures of 1928.[19] The company invested in improving its theatres and purchasing new film equipment. Especially important was the Aga-Baltic sound-recording device that was brought over from Sweden, along with the sound engineer Georg Brodén in 1934. A mixing device was purchased a year later.[20] The significance of sound technology was decisive. Once the technical problems of the early sound films, recorded with homemade devices, were overcome, the popularity of domestic films rose to new highs. Concerning the continuity of Suomi-Filmi, the unforeseen success of the romantic comedy *Superintendent of the Siltala Farm* (1934) was crucial: it has been estimated that the attendances were close to one million,[21] guaranteeing that 1934 became the first profit-making year for the studio since 1928, if only marginally so. Moreover, after purchasing a second Aga-Baltic recording device, Suomi-Filmi was now able to increase its production volume and have two shooting groups working simultaneously.

During its first fifteen years of operation, Suomi-Filmi had actively worked mainly on one feature film project at a time. This meant that the shooting of the next film usually began, at the earliest, when the previous one was in post-production. In 1935, Suomi-Filmi changed this practice by hiring Valentin Vaala as a second director. Despite his youth, Vaala was already an experienced director, having made four feature films in collaboration with Theodor Tugai and two more independently. Furthermore, unlike most other potential candidates, Vaala had not learned his skills in the theatre but in filmmaking. He had not only proved to be an efficient director capable of shooting quickly and with low budgets, but he also had an eye for comedy, urban life and international cinematic phenomena, which fitted perfectly with Suomi-Filmi's new house style that tended towards modernity and internationalism.

Working with two units also allowed for some specialisation within the studio. While Orko was responsible for the big historical projects like *A Yager's Bride* (1938) and *Activists* (1939), Vaala specialised in urban comedies starting with *Everybody's Love* (1935) and *Surrogate Wife* (1936). In 1937, yet another shooting crew was set up, and the production volume kept increasing, reaching an average five to seven feature films a year.

After World War II, lack of material resources and the post-war political situation hampered Suomi-Filmi's operations, especially filmmaking, as will be discussed in detail in Chapter 7. The production volume remained somewhat lower than during the late 1930s and early 1940s, running at between two to five feature films a year. While production costs were on a constant rise, attendances decreased. According to a Suomi-Filmi chart dated to 1958, typical attendances in the 1950s were between 150,000 and 300,000, whereas previous figures were seldom less than 300,000. As a result, of the twenty-seven feature films listed between 1950 and 1958, twelve made losses, some of them of quite a substantial kind. None withstanding a few highly successful exceptions like the musical semi-biopic *The Summer Night's Waltz* (1951), the profitability of feature films was in constant decline.[22]

Suomi-Filmi started collaborating with the Soviet Mosfilm on its first full-length colour film *The Village Shoemakers* (1957), receiving colour film stock, which was otherwise difficult to obtain, in exchange for distribution rights of the films in the Soviet Union.[23] Even though *The Village Shoemakers* was a success and made a profit despite its high production costs, this was not enough to cover for the losses of the other films released in 1957–8. Finally, starting from the spring of 1958, there was a two-year total break in Suomi-Filmi's feature film production, with the exception of the large-scale Finnish–Soviet co-production *Sampo* (1959). Many studio employees were either discharged or moved into other departments of the company. Even Vaala, who had in many ways embodied the quality tradition of Suomi-Filmi for a quarter of a century, was finally given notice in 1963. This, however, earned the company so much bad publicity that he was given work in the documentary department. In 1957, producing short films and documentaries had, for the first time, become more profitable than making feature films. By this time, it was evident that Suomi-Filmi could only survive because it was a diversified company. The profitability of theatres decreased along with the feature films, but distribution, short film production and laboratory work kept the company going. The laboratory in particular prospered, since Suomi-Filmi was for several years the only company in Finland that had invested in colour film equipment.[24]

Suomi-Filmi continued producing feature films on an irregular basis until 1980. From the early 1960s on, these were, however, one-off productions, since the company no longer had neither regular staff nor a permanent studio for making feature films.

## Suomen Filmiteollisuus

Suomen Filmiteollisuus was by far the biggest feature film production company in Finland. It was founded by Erkki Karu in the autumn of 1933, shortly after he had left Suomi-Filmi. The initial capital stock was only 30,000 FM (Finnish marks), a nominal sum, as is clear when compared with the production costs of the company's first feature film, *Our Boys in the Air – We on the Ground* (1934), which were more than 650,000 FM. The starting point was all the more difficult, since Karu had neither a studio, nor shooting equipment, nor staff. His plan was to invest in a tried-and-tested subject. At Suomi-Filmi, he had scripted and directed two successful, comedy-oriented films about the army, *Our Boys* (1929) and *Our Boys at Sea* (1933). The third part of the trilogy was more serious in tone, at least partly for practical purposes. As the opening credits reveal, the film was made 'with the assistance of the General Stuff, the Air Force, Finnish Gas Defence Organisation and various military units'. What Suomen Filmiteollisuus gained was military experts, extras, shooting locations, uniforms and props. The Gas Defence Organisation also screened the film on its own tours.[25] The first issue of the company's journal *SF-Uutiset* introduced the film in a serious tone:

> *Our Boys in the Air – We on the Ground* is a propaganda film, but at the same time, it is also an art film. It is a wake-up call to the Finnish people; it seeks to clarify those matters of life and death that every nation needs to face. It attempts to make people realise the great dangers that are imminent, unless issues concerning air defence and civil defence from the threat of gas attack are cleared up.[26]

On the other hand, Karu hired the newly elected Miss Europe, Ester Toivonen, for a supporting role, and widely exploited her popularity in advertisements. Part of the funding for the film was provided by

Adams-Filmi, in exchange for first-run rights. Karu had collaborated with Abel Adams on many occasions for a decade, but, as Outi Hupaniittu remarks, this was a business deal for Adams and not just a gesture of goodwill: potential losses would be covered from Suomen Filmiteollisuus's share. Moreover, the deal also secured Adams-Filmi exclusive first-run rights for the production company's future films. With the growing popularity of domestic films, this was important to Adams-Filmi, since so far it had mostly represented independent companies. After the second film, *The Scapegoat* (1935), proved successful, Suomen Filmiteollisuus negotiated a better deal with Adams-Filmi.[27] Over the years, cooperation between the two companies turned out to be profitable for both and essential for Suomen Filmiteollisuus.

Even though *Our Boys in the Air – We on the Ground* made a loss, Suomen Filmiteollisuus was able to have a second chance. Hupaniittu explains this partly by the fact that the organisations backing the first project were happy with the propaganda boost and not looking for profit, and partly owing to the help of T. J. Särkkä (Figure 2.3).[28] Särkkä was a former bank manager and now the CEO of Domestic Production, an organisation whose mission was to promote Finnish industry and trade. In Domestic Production, he had shown growing interest in cinema,

**Figure 2.3** T. J. Särkkä.

writing critical articles about Finnish films for the organisation's journal. According to Särkkä's recollection, Karu had contacted him and asked for help. At first, Särkkä probably assisted with the new company's bank loans and also invested his own money. In the summer of 1934, he became one of the three members of the board.[29]

The success of the next two features, *The Scapegoat* and *On the Roinila Farm* (1935), guaranteed that the company could carry on making films and build up a studio. For *The Scapegoat*, a comedy about a new employee of a department store, no studio was needed, since settings were, again, provided by a collaborating partner. This time, the partner was Stockmann, the biggest and most glamorous department store in the country. Suomen Filmiteollisuus had the whole store, as well as the staff, at its disposal for the shooting. Stockmann even paid an additional sum of money for the positive publicity it received.[30]

After Karu's sudden and premature death at the end of 1935, Särkkä took over the company, becoming the CEO, the chair of the board and soon also the main director, at first co-directing with Yrjö Norta, who had initially provided shooting and sound-recording equipment for the company. During all of its three-decade run, Suomen Filmiteollisuus remained in the hands of Särkkä, who as the primary shareholder was responsible for all major decisions. After a modest start, Suomen Filmiteollisuus's production volume increased even faster than Suomi-Filmi's, and by the end of the decade, it had become the biggest feature film company in the country. Having started with one shooting crew and one or two films a year, by 1939 the company had four shooting crews and nine opening nights.

During and after the war period (Winter War, 1939–40, and Continuation War, 1941–4), Suomen Filmiteollisuus, too, was hit by material shortages and political tensions, albeit to a lesser degree than Suomi-Filmi. Filmmaking continued with only minor interruptions during the war years, and in fact, domestic films were more popular than ever, as the number of imported films decreased and as many competing forms of entertainment, like dancing, were restricted or banned. The success climaxed with the costume drama *The Vagabond's Waltz* (1941), which broke all previous records with its more than 1.2 million spectators.

After a short decline in production between 1945 and 1947, due especially to the unavailability of raw film stock, Suomen Filmiteollisuus increased its production volume again. The high point was reached in 1954 and 1955 with fourteen new feature films each year. Films were ever more sharply divided into different categories, depending on the production values. Occasional prestige films (like the historical romance *The Dance over the Graves*, 1950), were accompanied by middle-range crime films (the semi-documentary police film *The Price of One Night*, 1952), melodramas (the rural melodrama *The Milkmaid*, 1953) and quality comedies (the small-town comedy of errors *Hilma's Name Day*, 1954) and numerous low-cost farces like the 'rillumarei' films discussed in Chapter 5, often based on a quickly drafted, sketchy script and shot and post-produced in a few weeks.

In early 1955, Suomen Filmiteollisuus managed to buy film rights for *The Unknown Soldier*, a war novel by Väinö Linna about a Continuation War machine-gun company. Having been published just a few weeks earlier, the novel was already on its way to becoming a bestseller and a definitive Finnish war narrative. Work on the adaptation started right away, and despite the magnitude of the project, the film premiered in December 1955. At that point, *The Unknown Soldier* was by far the longest (at three hours) and most expensive Finnish film made. The production cost was more than 45,000,000 FM, roughly five times as much as an average Suomen Filmiteollisuus film at the time. Yet, the box-office returns exceeded all expectations. With more than 2.5 million attendances, the film brought in over 200,000,000 FM during the first year.[31]

Paradoxically, the unforeseen success of *The Unknown Soldier* proved to be a turning point for Suomen Filmiteollisuus. In order to avoid a heavy tax bill, the huge returns of the film were immediately invested in new productions. This led to considerable overproduction, even to what became known as 'storage films', films that were made in 1956 but released only gradually over the next five years. At the same time, constantly rising production costs and declining attendances pushed Suomen Filmiteollisuus along with the rest of the production companies into deepening problems.

Unlike Suomi-Filmi and Fennada-Filmi, Suomen Filmiteollisuus had always concentrated mainly on feature film production, which made it more vulnerable whenever there were obstacles to production. Särkkä had always been aware of this potential weakness, which is evident in his memo from May 1945, promoting the raising of ticket prices in a situation where production costs and salaries had increased more than returns:

> A company that benefits neither from cinemas that have been truly profitable during the last few years, nor from distributing foreign films, but is simply a production house for domestic films has lately only been

able to meet engagements and cover for the losses of recent films with the aid of older films. Admittedly, conditions have been favourable enough for even the oldest of domestic films to have several reruns in a same area. However, now we have reached a point when these old pictures have 'worn out', and the increased supply of foreign films has its effect as well.[32]

The late-1950s crisis therefore hit Suomen Filmiteollisuus even harder than the other major companies. In 1958, it laid off half of its staff, whereas the lay-offs of the other majors were somewhat more moderate, a quarter of the staff for Suomi-Filmi and a third for Fennada.[33] Suomen Filmiteollisuus managed to keep on making feature films until 1963, helped by the stabilising of production costs. Some encouragement was also offered from the state, with the launching of the first subsidies in 1961 in the form of a state prize for cinema. The prizes, however, were modest at the start, and only one film by Suomen Filmiteollisuus, the home-front war film *The Boys* (1963) by Mikko Niskanen, who was to become a central figure in the 1960s new cinema, received the prize.

Film producers and exhibitors had found the coming of television mainly as a threat to cinema, and television screenings of domestic films were strictly regulated at first. In 1963, Särkkä shocked the film industry by selling the television rights of all of Suomen Filmiteollisuus's films to the Finnish Broadcasting Company. He excused himself by claiming that this had been the only way to keep the company going.[34]

Suomen Filmiteollisuus produced only a few more feature films, and after 1963, it focused on making advertising films. Two years later, Suomen Filmiteollisuus petitioned for bankruptcy, and Särkkä retired from the film business, at the age of seventy-five.

## Fennada-Filmi

Unlike the two other majors, Fennada-Filmi was an integrated, financially sound company right from the beginning. It was established in 1950 as a merger between the production units of two existing companies, Fenno-Filmi and Adams-Filmi; thus the name Fennada (Fenno plus Adams).

Fenno-Filmi, a minor production company established in 1942, was on a way to growing into a major with a permanent, reasonably well-equipped studio, steady output of films and a distribution and exhibition branch (see Chapter 3). After a promising start, however, the feature films

**Figure 2.4** Mauno Mäkelä (centre) with the author Mika Waltari (left) and the director Matti Kassila.

made between 1948 and 1950 were box-office disappointments, which encouraged the new CEO of the company, Mauno Mäkelä (Figure 2.4), to try something else, especially since Fenno-Filmi's filming equipment needed upgrading and new investments. Merging with Adams-Filmi provided an opportunity for taking the next step.[35]

Adams-Filmi was primarily an import, distribution and exhibition company with one of the most remarkable theatre chains in Finland. It had previously produced one feature film in 1926 and a series of short documentaries, as well as backing several feature film productions with advance payments, as in the case of Suomen Filmiteollisuus.[36] In the late 1930s, Adams-Filmi invested in its own feature film production more seriously than before with the first films by Teuvo Tulio as a director: *The Fight over the Heikkilä Mansion* (1936), *Silja – Fallen Asleep When Young* (1937) and *Temptation* (1938). Adams even provided Tulio with a studio, but as the cooperation ended, the studio was rented out to Erik Blomberg. A decade later, Adams-Filmi made a third effort at feature films, this time with Hannu Leminen, an experienced director, who had worked both for Suomi-Filmi and Suomen Filmiteollisuus. Leminen directed four very divergent films for Adams-Filmi between 1947 and

1949, including the problem film *Ruined Youth* (1947), the melodrama *Play for Me, Helena!* (1948) and the swashbuckler *Rob the Robber* (1949). Having no permanent studio at this time, Adams-Filmi rented Fenno-Filmi's and Suomen Filmiteollisuus's studios in turn for these films.

According to Mauno Mäkelä's memoirs, the merger was initially his idea.[37] Eventually, it benefitted both parties: while Fenno-Filmi had facilities for making films but limited financial resources and little success with recent films, Adams-Filmi had a more stable economic position but no means for making feature films on a permanent basis. Both were able to handle distribution, and it was agreed that each successive film made at Fennada would be distributed alternately by Fenno and by Adams. The films also had a possibility for an excellent opening run, since both Adams and Kinosto, a family business owned by the Mäkeläs, had an extensive theatre chain. Thus, Fennada was able to break into the same league and same markets as Suomi-Filmi and Suomen Filmiteollisuus right from the beginning.

Soon after the merger, Fennada set up a studio in an old tennis hall in the Kulosaari suburb of Helsinki, giving up the old Fenno studio. Part of the studio was reserved for use by the independent producer-director Teuvo Tulio. According to the initial contract, both Fennada and Tulio were to make two films a year. However, it soon proved to be impossible for Tulio to keep to his part of the contract, and he ended up owing rent money to Fennada. Fennada, for its part, had to increase its production volume in order to cover the fixed expenses and keep the studio going.[38] From 1952 to 1958, Fennada produced five to eight films a year, and it was only during the 1958 crisis that the numbers started to decrease. In addition, Fennada produced about 250 short films over the years, as well as hundreds of advertising films through a separate unit called Fennada Junior, established in 1958.[39]

Since the original intention of making fewer but better feature films proved impossible, Fennada had to adopt a production strategy similar to that of Suomen Filmiteollisuus, if on a smaller scale, making low-cost farces in addition to the initially planned prestige films and middle-range social problem and crime films. From the company's perspective, the production costs of the prestige films were higher than those of the farces, but both were designed with audiences in mind. Fennada's prestige films were usually literary adaptations of canonised Finnish novels such as Joel Lehtonen's *Children of the Wilderness* (1954) and Ilmari Kianto's *Joseph of Ryysyranta* (1955). Both had already been tried and tested as adaptations on the popular stage, and production decisions were made only after Mäkelä and Fennada's main director, Roland af Hällström, had witnessed their success in a summer theatre.[40]

Fennada's span as a major production company was intensive but obviously much shorter than that of Suomi-Filmi or Suomen Filmiteollisuus. In 1958, Fennada too had to lay off part of its staff. According to the set designer Ensio Suominen, Mäkelä acted as humanely and sensitively as possible in this situation: he let go the most skilled workers for whom it would be easy to find new jobs, and kept the rest.[41] Indeed, many of the young Fennada workers ended up as key forces in television during the forthcoming decades.

In general, Fennada's path after the crisis in film production intertwined closely with television. Mäkelä reveals in his memoirs that he negotiated already in the early 1960s about selling Fennada to the Finnish Broadcasting Company. The talks broke down, however, after Suomen Filmiteollisuus's television deal, as the Finnish Broadcasting Company was unable to make yet another large-scale transaction at the time.[42] Yet, Fennada collaborated with the Broadcasting Company in many ways, most notably when filming the historical epic about tenant farmers during the late nineteenth and early twentieth century, *Here, beneath the North Star*. Based on the best-selling trilogy by Väinö Linna, the film was released in cinemas in two parts (1968 and 1970) and as a serialised television version. The Broadcasting Company covered part of the production costs in exchange of the television rights. This was the first attempt at such collaboration between a film production company and a television company. During the subsequent years, this became a standard procedure.

Like Suomi-Filmi, Fennada kept on producing feature films through the 1960s and 1970s, albeit on an irregular basis, and by the early 1970s, most of the staff involved in feature film production had been laid off. In 1974, Mauno Mäkelä was replaced by his younger brother as the CEO, and as Fennada had become a burden rather than an asset to the Mäkelä family, the company was finally sold to the Finnish Broadcasting Company in 1982.[43]

## Notes

1. *Rekisterilehti* 753 (1920): 279.
2. Uusitalo 1994: 24–7.
3. 'Pieniä tietoja', *Kauppalehti* 28 April 1921.
4. Suomi-Filmi's annual report 1923. Suomi-Filmi Collection, Helsinki: National Audiovisual Archive.

5. Suomi-Filmi's annual report 1924. Suomi-Filmi Collection, Helsinki: National Audiovisual Archive.
6. Suomi-Filmi's annual report 1922. Suomi-Filmi Collection, Helsinki: National Audiovisual Archive.
7. Suomi-Filmi's annual report 1926. Suomi-Filmi Collection, Helsinki: National Audiovisual Archive.
8. Uusitalo 1988: 43–4.
9. Ibid.: 102.
10. Suomi-Filmi's annual report 1929. Suomi-Filmi Collection, Helsinki: National Audiovisual Archive.
11. Laine 2011: 236–45.
12. Hupaniittu 2019a: 21–31.
13. 'Tähdenlentoja', *Elokuva-Aitta* 1/1933: 293.
14. Uusitalo 1994: 111–15.
15. Von Bagh 1993a.
16. Uusitalo 1994: 126–7.
17. Uusitalo 1999: 110–11.
18. Ibid.: 137–41.
19. Keto 1974: 64.
20. Kuusela 1976: 22–3.
21. Uusitalo et al. 1996: 598.
22. Suomi-Filmi's chart on attendances, costs and profits of feature films 28 March 1958. Suomi-Filmi Collection, Helsinki: National Audiovisual Archive.
23. Mäkinen 1999.
24. Uusitalo 1994: 283–90.
25. Uusitalo et al. 1996: 605.
26. 'Meidän poikamme ilmassa – me maassa', *SF-Uutiset* 1/1935: 22.
27. Hupaniittu 2019a: 37, 42–3.
28. Ibid.: 39–40.
29. Uusitalo 1975: 56–7.
30. Uusitalo et al. 1996: 617.
31. Uusitalo et al. 1989: 418–19.
32. T. J. Särkkä's memo on the profitability of domestic film production 31 May 1945. Suomen Filmiteollisuus Collection, Helsinki: National Audiovisual Archive.
33. Uusitalo 1981: 17.
34. See Hupaniittu 2019b: 326–8.
35. Uusitalo 1992: 30
36. Uusitalo 1972b: 20–1, 33.
37. Mäkelä 1996: 87–8.
38. Ibid.: 92–3.
39. Uusitalo 1992: 34.
40. Mäkelä 1996: 115.
41. Von Bagh 1993b.
42. Mäkelä 1996: 184–5.
43. Uusitalo 1992: 34.

Chapter 3

# Minors and independents

Effective as it was, the dominance of the major studios was never total. Despite the difficulties in working outside the big companies, some of the minors and independents managed to achieve a relatively considerable output, and, in fact, some of the established classics of the studio era were made outside of the big studios (for example *Juha*, 1937, *The White Reindeer*, 1952, as well as all the films by Teuvo Tulio). While some of the competing minor and independent companies were established specifically for producing feature films, others were distributors or short-film producers, who tried their luck in feature film with varying success. Still others, like Teuvo Tulio, were independent producer-directors.

Some of the difficulties encountered by non-majors were obvious. While the majors had permanent studios with permanent, professionally skilled staff and up-to-date technology, the independents often had to rely on old cameras, ad hoc studios, small crews and overall small budgets. Also, just as in Hollywood, distributing and exhibiting films was always more difficult for the independents than it was for the majors, and the deals made with distributors and exhibitors rarely favoured the independent producers.[1] This chapter charts the challenges (lack of money and facilities) as well as the benefits (creative freedom) of working on the outskirts of studio production. Case studies include the production histories of the experimental adventure film *The Stolen Death* (1938) by Nyrki Tapiovaara, the characteristically excessive melodrama *The Way You Wanted Me* (1944) by Teuvo Tulio, the poetic fantasy film *The White Reindeer* (1952) by Erik Blomberg and the modernist 'walking film' *The Glass Heart* (1959) by Matti Kassila.

## Major, minor, independent, amateur

There was often a thin line between major, minor and independent studios. As we have seen in the previous chapter, vertical integration was not always a necessary requirement for a major company. Of the three majors, Suomi-Filmi and Fennada-Filmi were fully integrated with production, distribution and exhibition branches, whereas Suomen Filmiteollisuus concentrated mainly on producing and distributing its own films. However, the long-term contract with Adams-Filmi ensured that high-quality venues were always available for Suomen Filmiteollisuus, too.

The majors had other means to secure their oligarchy besides integrating vertically. In addition to dominating many of the trade organisations, the majors also either owned or at least controlled the most modern and best-equipped film laboratories. As a result, the independents had to count on their services or otherwise have their films developed in substandard laboratories or abroad, which was not only slower but usually also much more expensive. A case in point is *The Little Bride of the Garrison* (1943), a military comedy by Karhu-Filmi, a minor company established in 1935 mainly for producing short films. The film ran into various kinds of problems with the censorship office, due mainly to ideological issues – it was considered disrespectful towards the military forces – but also to the technical quality of the film.

During World War II, film censorship was compulsory, and special attention was paid to films that concerned the ongoing war or the army, including military comedies that had met with no censorship difficulties before the war. As was usual in potentially problematic wartime cases, two officers from military headquarters were present at the censorship screening of *The Little Bride of the Garrison*. The film was banned in June 1943,[2] after which a lengthy process of correspondence and re-editing began. *The Little Bride of the Garrison* finally passed the examination and premiered in December 1943, shortened by several minutes, almost a year and a half after the shooting first began.

Karhu-Filmi's problems did not end with the release of the film: *The Little Bride of the Garrison* was given the highest 'penalty tax' rating of 35 per cent. The highest rating was rather rarely used for domestic films, and when it was, it was usually for films made by minors and independents. As with *The Little Bride of the Garrison*, the use of the penalty tax was often justified by both the content and the technical quality of the film. After hearing the tax decision, Kurt Nylund, the head of Karhu-Filmi, wrote to the censorship board, asking for mercy:

> Post-production of the film began at Suomi-Filmi before the film dispute, but after the breaking of the film dispute, Suomi-Filmi was no longer willing to finish the film; we had to change companies and cut the film

into 60-meter long strips, which in its own way weakened the film and will cost a huge amount of money.³

In the case of *The Little Bride of the Garrison*, it seems that all the main obstacles encountered by Karhu-Filmi resulted from its minor studio status. Especially during the war years, it was even more difficult than before for a small production company like Karhu-Filmi, operating outside the German-minded Film Union, to find the facilities necessary for feature film production. The State Office of Film Censorship was, arguably, inclined to be critical of films by minor studios to begin with, let alone of films that lacked technical polish. Moreover, after the censorship office punished the film with a penalty tax, the company had even less chance of covering the post-production costs. Thus, a vicious circle was established. Although Karhu-Filmi kept on producing short films on a relatively regular basis, it had to wait almost for three years before trying its luck with another feature film, a ghost comedy *What a Night!* (1945). With decent reviews but poor attendances, this proved to be the last of Karhu-Filmi's attempts at feature film production.

The line between Finnish majors, minors and independents could be drawn in various ways. Here, majors refer to diversified companies with long-running and continuous feature film production, mainly Suomi-Filmi, Suomen Filmiteollisuus and Fennada. By minors, I mean companies that had a relatively steady output of feature films by more than one filmmaker, at least for a period of time. While the majors had several units operating simultaneously, the minors concentrated on one production at a time. Most of the minors operated in other branches of the film industry, too, besides feature filmmaking, which kept them going even when feature films were not profitable. It should be noted that not all minors were minors in terms of the size of the company, only in relation to feature filmmaking. Adams-Filmi, for example, owned a nationwide chain of cinemas (fourteen theatres in 1938),⁴ and as an import and distribution agency it was the second biggest during the studio years, second only to Suomi-Filmi.⁵ Yet, it produced only a handful of feature films between 1926 and 1949, before its production branch merged with Fenno-Filmi into Fennada-Filmi.

Independents refer here to individual producers who produced mainly their own films, be they directors, cinematographers or in some other role. Once again, there was a thin line between independents and minors. Veikko Itkonen, for example, started as a producer-director in 1945, but produced also several films directed by others between 1945 and 1960.

Furthermore, the status of a company often changed during its period of activity. Of the three majors, only Fennada was a major right from the start, since both Adams-Filmi and Fenno-Filmi were already diversified companies at the time of the merger. As we have seen, both Suomi-Filmi and Suomen Filmiteollisuus had a modest start, and it took a while to make feature filmmaking into a profitable business. Even the line between professionals and amateurs was often ambiguous. When starting Suomen Filmiteollisuus in 1933, Erkki Karu was obviously an experienced professional filmmaker, but at the time Suomi-Filmi was established fourteen years earlier, the key personnel, including Karu, had much more experience in theatre and backdrop painting than in filmmaking. They were definitely performing arts professionals, but more or less amateurs in filmmaking. The same goes for many minors and independents, too: since there were no film schools before the late studio era, many of them started with very little or no experience in filmmaking. An extreme example is Fennica. Valentin Vaala and Theodor Tugai were still in their teens and barely out of school, when they started their first film experiments that resulted in the feature film *Dark Eyes* (1929).

## Minors and independents

The rest of this chapter will focus on some of the most prominent minor and independent film production companies. First, I shall outline the histories of five companies or individual producers that are representative of the whole studio era: Komedia-Filmi (late 1920s), Fennica (late 1920s to early 1930s), Jäger-Filmi (late 1930s to early 1940s), Fenno-Filmi (1940s) and Veikko Itkonen (late 1940s to early 1960s). Second, I shall offer case studies of four individual productions: *Stolen Death* (1938), *The Way You Wanted Me* (1944), *The White Reindeer* (1952) and *The Glass Heart* (1959). All of these films and their production histories are, I suggest, representative in their specificity: while they have much in common, they also illustrate that there was no one way of working outside of the majors and that an amount of improvisation and creative thinking was always involved in minor productions.

### *Komedia-Filmi*

Komedia-Filmi was, or at least could have been, the first serious threat to Suomi-Filmi's dominance in the 1920s. The founding of the company was initiated by Kurt Jäger, a German-born cinematographer who had worked for Suomi-Filmi since 1921. Having fallen out with Karu, he left Suomi-Filmi in 1925 and founded his first own company, Taide-Filmi, which focused mainly on laboratory services, especially shooting Finnish and Swedish intertitles for imported films. Taide-Filmi also made nearly sixty newsreels and short actualities as well as three feature documentaries.

It seems likely that Suomi-Filmi felt threatened by Taide-Filmi, since it bought the company from Jäger in the summer of 1926.[6] Taide-Filmi had not managed to start narrative film production, as it had meant to, but its substantial output of documentaries probably surprised Karu. In feature documentaries, Taide-Filmi evidently managed to beat the older firm. Two of the three feature documentaries by Taide-Filmi were about state visits by heads of state, and the latter of these two, *The King of Sweden in Finland* (1925), premiered just four days before Suomi-Filmi's documentary on the same subject, *Visit of the Swedish Royal Couple*, and was much more successful.[7]

If Suomi-Filmi's intention in buying Taide-Filmi was to eliminate competition, this proved to be unsuccessful. Jäger used the money from selling the old company to found a new one, Komedia-Filmi, almost immediately. Not only that, he also persuaded Karu's old partners, Teuvo Puro and Karl Fager, who had left Suomi-Filmi some time before, as his associates.[8] The first feature film by Komedia-Filmi, *Before the Face of the Sea*, a sea drama with mystical Gothic undertones directed and scripted by Puro, shot and edited by Jäger and set-designed by Fager, premiered as early as October 1926. Despite the film's wide distribution and apparent success,[9] Puro and Fager left Komedia-Filmi soon after and returned to Suomi-Filmi, likely because Karu had offered them a better deal than Jäger could afford.[10]

Soon after this, Puro explained the reasons for their return in an interview in the first issue of *Elokuva* magazine:

> I ended up working in Komedia-Filmi for a period of time ... It was our intention to continue this summer with two features, but that takes money, which we did not have. It should have been more than half a million. Mister Gustaf Molin would have financed them, but he demanded our shares and receivables as collateral. This is not an unusual custom, but still I was concerned about it. It also felt repulsive not to hear a word of Finnish at the firm. Therefore, as Karu had already in the winter talked about co-operation between domestic forces, both Fager and I moved back to Suomi-Filmi, and so be it. We cannot afford to disperse domestic forces.[11]

Puro's comment implies that there was much more at stake than just the undeniably important contribution of Puro and Fager. In 1926, while

Komedia-Filmi was working on *Before the Face of the Sea*, the Finnish film trade drifted into a conflict that was to be called the 'trust war'. At the centre of the conflict was Gustaf Molin, an importer and theatre owner, who indirectly soon became the biggest owner of Komedia-Filmi. Operating through several companies, Molin had during the 1920s become one of the most powerful players in Finnish film business.[12] In 1926, he had an interest in buying Suomen Biografi, the biggest cinema chain and distributor at the time, but lost the bidding contest to Karu and Suomi-Filmi. Instead, he managed to become the Finnish agent of the German-American distribution company Parufamet. Under the company name of Ufanamet, Molin thus had exclusive rights to all films produced and distributed by three of the biggest and most influential international companies, the German UFA and the Hollywood majors Paramount and MGM.[13]

As a result of this arrangement, the opponents, primarily Karu and Suomi-Filmi, attacked Molin severely. Since the leading film magazine *Filmiaitta* remained sympathetic to Molin, Suomi-Filmi launched *Elokuva* as its mouthpiece in a politically charged situation; in 1932, after the trust war was over, the two magazines merged into *Elokuva-Aitta*, which was to be the leading popular film magazine during the rest of the studio era.

Backed by Adams-Filmi, Suomi-Filmi rounded on Ufanamet, using two main arguments. First, right from the beginning, they had spoken of Ufanamet as a trust and of themselves as antitrust players. Rhetorically, this was projected as a United States versus Europe issue:

> Europe, the 'old world', has set out to oppose the trustified American film factories that with the power of the Dollar aim at conquering not only filmmaking but also cinemas around the world ... Obvious signs indicate that the trust has gained a hold here too, with willing help from certain foreigners who carry on business here, and even from a previous film magazine. This explains our emergence. Our stance towards the enterprise of film is thoroughly domestic and anti-trust.[14]

As Outi Hupaniittu has remarked, as anti-trust as Karu and Abel Adams claimed to be, they actually shared the same basic business model with Molin. They all ran a theatre chain, they all imported and distributed films, and they all were involved in film production – Karu more than the others. Molin had simply succeeded in making a better deal with the mighty German and American companies.[15] What is more, despite the strong anti-American rhetoric they favoured, both Suomi-Filmi and especially Adams-Filmi had imported Hollywood films for years;[16]

Adams-Filmi had even been the Finnish representative for Paramount and MGM.[17] Thus, the second argument against Ufanamet, built on ethno-nationalist rhetorics and aimed directly at the persons involved, was actually more important than the first one:

> The trust is backed by a fifth partner of the agency, the Swedish mister Gustaf Molin, who owns at least five remarkable cinemas in the capital ... A comrade-in-arms with the trust in its fight against domestic film distributors is Filmi-Keskus, led by the German cinematographer Kurt Jäger. Further assistance is provided by the 'Finnish' film production company Komedia-Filmi, headed by the one and same Kurt Jäger, and the mouthpiece for all of these is Filmiaitta. Here's 'nationality' for you ... On the one side is the trust with its assistants, and on the other side are domestic film distributors and those Finnish, nationally spirited cinema owners, who do not want to end up in the trust's net and let their cinemas become an easy prey for foreigners.[18]

Both Molin and Jäger were easy targets for verbal ethno-nationalist attacks: the former was a Swedish citizen born in Russia and the latter a German citizen born in Germany. The newly independent Finland offered a breeding ground for such rhetorics. One tendency of the nationalist movement of the interwar years centred on anti-Bolshevism and the aftermath of the 1918 Civil War, while the other tendency, partially intertwining with the first one, focused on language and ethnicity. Even though Finland was constituted as a bilingual country (Finnish and Swedish), the latter tendency, the 'True Finnishness' (*aitosuomalaisuus*) movement, demanded, for example, that teaching at the University of Helsinki should be only in Finnish and that the highest positions in the armed forces should be reserved for Finnish-speaking officers. An important factor in this endeavour concerned business life and industry. According to the 'True Finns', the numbers of Swedish-speaking Finns, and also Swedish citizens and banks, in Finnish commerce were excessively high.[19] In the polemics directed at Ufanamet, Karu and Adams shared these views and even cited the *Aitosuomalainen* ('True Finn') magazine on several occasions.

As concerns Komedia-Filmi's output, the most severe criticism was directed at the company's second (and last) feature film, *On the Highway of Life* (1927). It is a melodrama about an organ grinder who travels around searching for a daughter he has lost in the turmoil of war. The war in question is presumably World War I, and some of the details and the names allude to Italy, but neither time nor place is clearly specified.

The intention is obviously to remain ambiguous and tell an 'international' story that could take place anywhere and anytime.

*Filmiaitta* was, not surprisingly, sympathetic towards such aims: 'Judging from the script at least, the film blazes a trail in domestic film art; the action is utterly international.'[20] Not all reviewers shared this positive view. One critic of a right-wing newspaper wrote:

> What bizarre mess is this *On the Highway of Life*? Where does it take place? Not in Finland anyway, even if we are meant to believe so, and even if a Finnish city and nature and domestic faces are being shown! So strange is the form of this film that one cannot help but wonder whether the nice donkey in the film symbolises us viewers.[21]

*Elokuva* did not mince its words when discussing *On the Highway of Life*. Commenting on Jäger's intentions to find international markets for his film, *Elokuva* referred to the familiar notion that it is easier to conquer world markets with national than international films – even if Suomi-Filmi itself during the late 1920s and early 1930s produced a series of films that were inclined towards cosmopolitan tendencies:[22]

> Does our film production have to abandon the national ground it has built on so far; on this we differ with Mr. Jäger ... Films with national subjects, provided that the content is well thought-out, have one more advantage that those with international subjects Mr Jäger strives for do not have; they make our country and people known abroad, which is something Mr. Jäger, as might be expected, cannot value highly enough.[23]

The dispute went on in 1928, when Komedia-Filmi announced that it would make a feature documentary for international markets about the different regions of Finland. In denouncing the plan, *Elokuva* once again relied on Karu, 'the experienced film director and a *Finnish* man who knows our country and our people from every angle'.[24] Karu diminished Jäger's intentions by emphasising that to make a film like this one needed to have proper plans, which Jäger presumably did not have. What Karu left unmentioned was that Jäger was no novice in making such a film; he had been the director of photography in Suomi-Filmi's own feature documentary *Finlandia* in 1922. *Aitosuomalainen* was also cited in *Elokuva*'s article on Jäger's plans:

> When it comes to the filmmakers, one cannot help but get worried, since, as far as we know, not one Finn, not one person inspired by Finnish national spirit, is behind the proposition. If a picture about the finest and most sensitive issues of our people, seen through foreign spectacles,

entered the world markets, it would definitely do a disservice to the best endeavours of our rising nationalism.[25]

The documentary feature was never made, and Komedia-Filmi produced only a few more short films. Besides shooting intertitles, Jäger concentrated on building up a sound equipment as well as a subtitling system. In 1932, Suomi-Filmi once again bought Jäger's company, this time not because it felt threatened by Komedia-Filmi but rather because it needed Jäger's sound-recording equipment.[26]

## *Fennica*

Fennica emerged only two years later than Komedia-Filmi, but this time Suomi-Filmi did not seem to find itself as threatened as earlier, even though there was much in common between Komedia-Filmi and Fennica: both were run by immigrants, and both turned away from national subjects and strove for cosmopolitanism instead. The differences, however, were as obvious as the similarities. From Suomi-Filmi's perspective, Kurt Jäger's professional skills were well known, whereas the creative forces behind Fennica, Valentin Vaala and Theodor Tugai, were mere teenagers and definitely amateurs as filmmakers.

Vaala and Tugai had met in the German secondary school in Helsinki. Vaala, born Valentin Ivanoff in Helsinki, was of Russian origin, and he spoke Russian, Swedish and Finnish fluently. Tugai's family roots were Latvian, Polish and Turkish. Raised in Latvia in a multicultural and multilingual extended family, he could speak Latvian, German, English, Russian and some Yiddish and, having moved to Finland, became fluent in Finnish and Swedish.

Unlike the majority of Finnish studio–era filmmakers, Vaala and Tugai had no connection to theatre. Rather, they were of the first generation who grew up watching films. Tugai recalls in his memoirs, first published in the 1970s: 'Just like boys decide to make bombs with no idea as how to get hold of powder, we began to write a script, firmly believing that it would turn out fine, even if we had absolutely no money or other necessities.'[27] Their first completed film was *Dark Eyes*, which premiered in 1929 when Vaala was nineteen and Tugai sixteen. Before this, they had shot several 'practice films', the first one presumably with a homemade camera.[28] From *Dark Eyes* on, they would count as independents rather than amateurs: their films premiered in a public film theatre and were examined by the State Film Censorship Board, which, in practice, was a prerequisite of a public screening.²⁹ Yet, all of Fennica's productions remained predominantly self-made films. Vaala was the director, editor and set designer, while Tugai was the lead actor. Many of the other actors were their friends, among them two future film stars, Regina Linnanheimo and Hanna Taini. Ideas for the films were usually thought up between Vaala and Tugai.

Both *Dark Eyes* and its successor, *The Gypsy Charmer* (1929), were set in the world of Romani people, relying on 'gypsy romantic' tradition. They presented Tugai as the 'Finnish Valentino', openly emphasising both his ethnic and sexual ambiguity. The films' critical reception was relatively positive, especially among the young modernists who welcomed the exoticism of the films as a longed-for counterpoint to the presumably ethnographic mainstream of contemporary Finnish films.

Fennica's productions were financed mainly by private patrons. The first of these was Tugai's mother, who may have provided initial capital for the making of *Dark Eyes*,³⁰ and at any rate loaned furniture and props for the films.³¹ The principle financier was Armas Willamo, a businessman and a friend of Tugai's family, who also let Vaala and Tugai use the name of his agency, Oy Fennica Ab.³² All of Vaala and Tugai's four collaborations, as well as the first of Vaala's two solo efforts after breaking with Tugai, were produced under the name of Fennica. No data on costs and returns survive, but, according to Tugai, Willamo usually got back what he had invested, if not much more. However, Willamo's businesses were hit by the Depression,³³ and in 1934, Fennica went into liquidation.³⁴

For *Dark Eyes*, Vaala and Tugai needed a proper camera and asked Oscar Lindelöf, an experienced cinematographer and an owner of a film supply store, for filming equipment. Lindelöf agreed, provided that he himself would act as the cinematographer.³⁵ This was most convenient for the young filmmakers: not only did they get the equipment on favourable terms, but they also had their first opportunity to learn filmmaking from a professional.

For *The Gypsy Charmer*, Vaala and Tugai contacted the brothers Heikki Aho and Björn Soldan, since Lindelöf was unavailable. The brothers ran the production company Aho & Soldan, which specialised in modernist-oriented documentaries, and both were excellent cinematographers. Aho & Soldan also had a relatively well-equipped film laboratory, which enabled Vaala and Tugai to cut costs remarkably. Both Vaala and Tugai also worked in the laboratory in the early 1930s,³⁶ which, according to the cinematographer Esko Töyri, was the best way to learn filmmaking skills at the time.[37]

During their Fennica years, Vaala and Tugai adopted several means to cut costs and get by on small budgets. They were probably the first in Finland to use product placement. In their third and fourth feature films, *The Wide Road* (1931) and *The Blue Shadow* (1933), the product placement was rather explicit. In the former, the opening credits read: 'settings by the Stockmann Department Store, costumes by Maison Augusta', and so on. In the latter, the products themselves are openly displayed throughout the film, either as trade signs or posters, or referred to in the dialogue and songs. According to Vaala's memoirs, the attempt was to embed product references in the dialogue in a subtle way, so that the spectators would not quite be aware they were being advertised to. The income received through product placement was used for buying film stock,[38] which implies that Fennica's operations were often based on hand-to-mouth practices and that ad hoc solutions were an essential part of their way of making films.

Yet another way of raising money for *The Wide Road* was by making a short advertising film *Restaurant Patrons Seen through the Camera Lens* (1930). This film presents a group of people at a restaurant, including Tugai, introduced in an intertitle as 'the Finnish Valentino', as well as a Harold Lloyd lookalike and a party of women, introduced as 'the parade of future film stars'. The main focus of the film is on the luxurious products these characters use: fur coats, shoes, coffee, cream, cigarettes and so on, the labels and brand names of which are clearly on display in close-ups or in the intertitles.

The two first Fennica films were shot mainly outdoors; the few indoor sequences needed were made in makeshift studios that were built in restaurants or empty factory buildings. For *The Wide Road*, Willamo managed to make a deal with Suomi-Filmi for the use of its studio. As a result, the mise-en-scène of *The Wide Road* with its lavish art deco sets differs remarkably from that of the previous films (Figure 3.1).

Distributing their films was typically difficult for independent producers, let alone amateurs. Willamo's connections among the business world, however, were a benefit for Fennica, starting from their second feature. The first, *Dark Eyes*, had its Helsinki premiere in a medium-sized theatre named Pallas in the working-class district of Kallio, since Suomi-Filmi was at first reluctant to rent one of its downtown theatres.[39] For *The Gypsy Charmer*, Willamo made a contract with Suomen Biografi,

**Figure 3.1** Still from *The Wide Road* (1931).

which at the time was the exhibition end of Suomi-Filmi. According to the contract, the film would open in a downtown theatre, La Scala, in Helsinki, which was a remarkable improvement on the previous venue. Fennica would receive 30 per cent of the net proceeds in the city cinemas (which basically meant those owned by Suomen Biografi) and 50 per cent of the net proceeds in the rural cinemas.⁴⁰ For the next two films, *The Wide Road* and *The Blue Shadow*, the deal became still more favourable for Fennica: the films would premiere in Kino-Palatsi, Suomi-Filmi's flagship cinema, and for *The Blue Shadow*, Fennica's share would rise to 55 per cent for the opening week and 50 per cent for the remainder of the screenings.⁴¹

After departing, Vaala and Tugai went very different ways. Vaala directed two more independent films and also played the romantic lead himself in the second of these, *When Father Wants To* (1935), a comedy loosely based on George McManus's comic strip *Bringing Up Father*. After that, he was recruited to Suomi-Filmi, where his subtle melodramas and sophisticated comedies best epitomised the company's house style for the rest of the studio years. Unlike Vaala, Tugai never worked for the major production companies. Under the name of Teuvo Tulio he started directing films in 1936 and became, arguably, the most important producer-director of the studio era, specialising in over-the-top melodramas, quite different from those made by the major studios.

## Jäger-Filmi

After Komedia-Filmi's second feature, Kurt Jäger focused on constructing sound-recording equipment and a subtitling system. Generally, the Finnish film business converted to sound relatively slowly. The first sound cinemas opened in the autumn of 1929, and the first domestic feature films with recorded sound premiered in 1931.

The first sound features were recorded with home-built sound-on-film technology. Jäger's only rival in the beginning was Lahyn-Filmi, a small photograph company that had made a few short films and one feature film in 1924. Lahyn-Filmi's own *Say It in Finnish* (1931) was a revue film consisting of musical numbers, comic sketches and interviews. Lahyn also provided sound technology for Suomi-Filmi's comedy *Dressed Like Adam and a Bit Like Eve Too* (1931). This was intended as a silent film, but since there were rumours that several sound films were being made at this time, Suomi-Filmi decided to add a post-recorded soundtrack that comprised of background music, sound effects and a few songs.

Jäger, for his part, recorded several hybrid films made in 1931. The first of these was Fennica's *The Wide Road*, which was released both as a silent print and as a sound version with background music, songs and sound effects. *A Yager's Bride* (Sarastus), based on a highly popular adventure-musical stage play, was a similar kind of hybrid, too, but this time the songs recorded by Jäger were not just an added attraction, since songs had been an essential part of the play's success. Since Lahyn was involved in film projects in Sweden, Suomi-Filmi, too, approached Jäger, which indicates that the conflict between the two was, temporarily, over. *The Dean's Honeymoon Travels* (1931) was yet another comedy with a recorded musical soundtrack but no spoken dialogue. *The Lumberjack's Bride* (1931) had some expository intertitles, too, but the dialogue was now recorded and synchronised, making this 'the first 100 per cent sound film', as was advertised.[42]

After selling his sound-recording equipment to Suomi-Filmi, Jäger focused on importing and distributing films, on the one hand, and developing film subtitling, on the other. He had two separate companies that specialised in these activities. Jägerin Filmitoimisto ('Jäger's Film Office') imported films mainly from Germany but also from France and Scandinavian countries. In 1933, when a new tax reduction system came into effect, Jägerin Filmitoimisto started making short films, too. The company's documentary production culminated in the feature documentary *From the Land of the Kalevala* (1935), which presents Karelian landscapes, customs and rune singers celebrating the 100th anniversary of the publication of the Finnish national epic *Kalevala*.

The other company, Jägerin Filmilaboratorio ('Jäger's Film Laboratory'), specialised in subtitling technology. Translating imported films had been, arguably, the biggest challenge that related to the coming of recorded sound. Finland was a small language area, and a relatively small section of the people could understand any other language besides their mother tongue, be that Finnish or Swedish. In secondary schools, one was more likely to learn the basics of German than of English. Therefore, Hollywood sound films, in particular, caused problems.

Various solutions were tested out. If only for economic reasons, multiple-language versions were out of the question: no film manufacturer anywhere would have considered it worthwhile to make costly parallel versions of films in Finnish. The same goes for dubbing films: this, too, would have been too expensive for Finnish importers, considering the box-office proceeds of an average imported film. Besides, part of the audience spoke Swedish, not Finnish. Even the major Disney animations were not dubbed into Finnish until the 1960s; Swedish dubbings, however, would sometimes be shown in Finland, too.

Instead of multiple-language versions and dubbing, early solutions included summarising the film and translating part of the dialogue in the programme leaflet, or inserting silent film–type intertitles amid the dialogue. This, of course, had the obvious disadvantage of interrupting the soundtrack and was soon forbidden by foreign import companies.[43] On a few occasions, scenes with Finnish actors were also added into imported films (for example James Cruze's *The Great Gabbo*, 1929), but this served more like a temporary attraction than a lasting solution to translation problems.

After a short transition period, the final resolution proved to be subtitling, as in certain other small language areas, including the other Nordic countries. This did not mean that the transition to subtitles was entirely unproblematic. Various technological methods were tried out, including superimposing the subtitles and projecting them separately, before printing the titles directly onto a softened film strip became a standard practice.[44] Of course, technology was not the only issue involved. Reading subtitles demanded practice, and although literacy was very high, many people were not accustomed to reading at speed. Regarding this, the ideal length of a single subtitle was also discussed: how long does it take for the spectator to read the title? Should the dialogue be translated word by word or selectively? Should there be only one title per one shot, or is it possible to have the title run from one shot to the next without disorienting the spectator?[45] Does it make it too difficult and disturbing to print both the Finnish and Swedish titles onto the same film copy?[46]

In addition to such questions concerning the technology and practices of subtitling, there were legal issues to be solved. In 1933, Jäger had purchased the rights for the printing system developed by the Norwegian Leif Eriksen, and sued Suomi-Filmi for using the allegedly same system. Suomi-Filmi replied that it did not rely on Eriksen's system, but rather on the one developed by the Hungarian Oliver Turchányi in 1935.[47] Indeed, both systems were patented in Finland.[48] Jäger and Suomi-Filmi litigated over the printing patent for over a decade, which indicated that their relations were not very good, despite occasional cooperation.

In 1936, Jäger returned to producing fictional feature films under the company name of Jäger-Fimi. His first two films, both light adventure films and both now lost, were unsuccessful. According to the *Finnish National Filmography*, both were distributed rather widely, despite low attendances. This is because Jäger made a contract with several theatre owners and sold the exhibition rights in exchange for advance payment.[49] The third film, *The Log Drivers* (1937), based on a popular stage play with lots of songs, proved to be more successful. Unlike in the previous films, which were directed by actors inexperienced in filmmaking, Jussi Snellman and Tapio Ilomäki, respectively, the director of *The Log Drivers* was an established filmmaker, Kalle Kaarna. He would also cooperate with Jäger in the next three productions.

In 1936, Jäger built a new studio building on the outskirts of Helsinki; this was, in fact, one of the very few studios in Finland built specifically for filmmaking purposes. The location was convenient not only because building land was less expensive than in the city, but also because of proximity to various kinds of exteriors, be they city streets, seashores, fields or forests.[50] The studio included a sound stage, a recording room, a laboratory and a subtitling department. According to the cinematographer Esko Töyri, the last-mentioned was clearly the biggest section of the studio in terms of both the space and the number of employees: eleven permanent workers.[51] It seems probable that Jäger-Filmi's feature filmmaking was not very profitable, even if Jäger was known to be particular about costs.[52] More likely, filmmaking was financed through the constant and guaranteed proceeds from subtitling.

The best known of Jäger-Filmi's feature productions were relatively large-scale historical films, *The Slaying of Elina* (1938), *The Great Wrath* (1939) and *Simo Hurtta* (1940), the making of which would have been impossible without the facilities provided by a permanent studio. Interestingly, while the majority of Finnish historical films took place in the nineteenth or early twentieth century, Jäger-Filmi focused on earlier periods: *The Slaying of Elina* is set in the Middle Ages and the other two in the early eighteenth century. Yet, despite the difference in the period depicted, especially *The Great Wrath* had much in common with the late-1930s cycle of historical dramas that included films like *The Stolen Death* (produced by Erik Blomberg, 1938), *February Manifesto* (SF 1939) and *Activists* (SuFi 1939). Since all of these were about Finnish–Russian relations in various historical times, they can easily be seen as allegories of the contemporary political situation, the increasingly tense relations between Finland and Soviet Union.

With its eventful censorship history, discussed in detail in Chapter 7, *The Great Wrath* received a lot of publicity. Attendances, however, were low. It was the first of the two films that premiered during the 105-day-long Winter War, and even though cinemagoing later established itself as the most important form of entertainment during the war years, these first few months were turbulent. Jäger-Filmi produced one more historical film, *Simo Hurtta*, now lost, which was shot in the summer of 1939 and was supposed to open later that year. The premier was postponed until the following autumn, and its success was as modest as that of *The Great Wrath*.

In the late 1930s, Jäger was evidently optimistic about the future. The company published its own film magazine, *Päivän Elokuva*, between 1937 and 1939, and in 1939, it also announced a competition for finding suitable scripts for filming, as a token of its willingness to increase its production volume.[53] It seems likely, however, that the outbreak of war hit feature film production much more severely at Jäger-Filmi than at Suomi-Filmi or Suomen Filmiteollisuus. Jäger-Filmi produced only one more feature film, shot immediately after the end of the Continuation War in the autumn of 1944. *Love's Sacrifice* (1945), now lost, was the first of the short post-war cycle of 'syphilis films', problem films about venereal diseases. It was an ill-fated production with changing directors and cinematographers. Erik Blomberg, who was the third cinematographer hired for the project, called it afterwards a 'very odd production'. For example, because of Jäger's carefulness with money, the crew could seldom see the rushes. As a result, the image in the completed film appears to have been too dark.[54] The final deathblow to the company's feature film production came when Jäger was interned for a period after the war; he had remained a German citizen all through his long career in Finland.

## Fenno-Filmi

Fenno-Filmi was founded in 1942, with a relatively modest start-up capital. The purpose of the company was to 'manufacture, sell, distribute, exchange, export and import films and to import and sell film cameras, projectors, photographic cameras and accessories'.[55] The strength of the company lay in technological skill. The key founder was Theodor Luts, a cinematographer, who had worked for both Suomi-Filmi and Suomen Filmiteollisuus. He was joined by Yrjö Norta, an expert in sound recording who had his own sound equipment. Also involved was Eino Kari, a cinematographer and an editor who had a relatively well-equipped film laboratory. All the essential technical fields of filmmaking were thus well covered in Fenno-Filmi right from the beginning.

Fenno-Filmi started off with *The Secret Weapon* (1943), an espionage film that centres around a ring of spies trying to steal the blueprints for a secret military device, and a security police and a reporter who are in pursuit of the spies. An instant success, *The Secret Weapon* was followed by three other espionage films over the next two years, *Shadows over the Ishtmus* (1943), *Creeping Danger* (1944) and *On the Way to Adventure* (1945). The last-mentioned was a dual-language film, made in collaboration with the Swedish independent company Hamberg-Studio. Based on a script by the Swede Gösta Rodin, both versions were shot in Finland with a mainly Finnish crew. Rodin directed the Swedish and Yrjö Norta the Finnish version, and both versions featured main actors from the respective countries, while the supporting actors were Finnish. In exchange for the crew and the shooting facilities, Rodin brought raw film stock from Sweden; there was constant lack of film stock in Finland after the war, even though Fenno-Filmi did not suffer from this lack as much as those companies that had been more active in the pro-German Film Union of Finland.[56]

*The Secret Weapon* is estimated to have remained Fenno-Filmi's biggest success.[57] Yet, the company managed to put out seventeen feature films, usually two or three a year, thus becoming the biggest minor company of the 1940s, and, in fact, of the whole studio era. An essential factor in the relative success of Fenno-Filmi was that two distribution and exhibition companies became partners of the firm. In the spring of 1944, Bio-Kuva Oy obtained a partnership, and in the autumn, Emil Viljanen, the owner of Bio-Kuva, replaced Theodor Luts as the managing director of Fenno-Filmi; even though the Estonian-born Luts had been granted Finnish citizenship in 1940, he had to flee the country as the Soviet–Finnish truce was agreed upon. Bio-Kuva, which owned, for example, the largest cinema in Finland at the time, the 1,000-seat Metropol in Helsinki, distributed all of Fenno-Filmi's films until 1947.

Also involved with Fenno-Filmi from 1944 on were the father and son Väinö and Mauno Mäkelä. Väinö Mäkelä was the managing director of the Kinosto concern, an owner of a large cinema chain and, overall, one of the most powerful players in Finnish film business. In the 1940s, he was, for example, the president of the Finnish Film Chamber and the Finnish Cinema Owners' Association. Mauno Mäkelä, besides being on the board of Kinosto, was the managing director of the distribution company Väinän Filmi. In 1949, as the weight of the Mäkelä family grew within Fenno-Filmi, Mauno Mäkelä was appointed as the managing director of the company. Shortly after, when Fenno-Filmi merged with Adams-Filmi into Fennada, he went on to run the new company, too.

*The Secret Weapon* included a great deal of on-location shooting in Helsinki. As Aksella Luts, Theodor Luts's wife and one of the scriptwriters of the film, recollected decades later, this was partly in order to achieve suspense and authenticity in the contemporary spy narrative.[58] Another reason was, undoubtedly, that Fenno-Filmi initially lacked a proper studio. For the first films, a makeshift studio was built in the Great Hall of the Helsinki University of Technology that had served as a film studio several times before this, most notably for Teuvo Tulio and for Suomi-Filmi after its Vironkatu studio burned down in 1936.

In the autumn of 1944, when shooting its fifth film, *Creeping Danger*, Fenno-Filmi rented an unused tennis hall in central Helsinki as a permanent studio facility; this was one of several tennis halls used for filmmaking during the Finnish studio years. The studio was not large, but it had room enough for an office, staff facilities, a sound-recording studio and several interior settings. One of the challenges of the studio was that it was located on the fifth floor of the building. The cinematographer Esko Töyri later reminisced about the difficulties of, for example, bringing a horse on the set.⁵⁹ When asked by an interviewer about the new studio and the possibilities it opened for filmmaking, Luts commented:

> Obviously, we will be able to make more films each year than before. Shooting can go on almost without interruptions, because several interiors will be ready for shooting at any moment. However, we will keep up with our principle of not making films in an industrial and factory-like manner; rather, we want to work carefully and meticulously.⁶⁰

Luts's comment on factory-like filmmaking was undoubtedly directed at his previous employer, Suomen Filmiteollisuus, whose yearly output during this time was close to ten feature films. Fenno-Filmi, too, increased its production volume: four films by Fenno-Filmi premiered in 1945, which means that the productions at least partly overlapped. With its own studio, a steady output and a distribution and exhibition branch, Fenno-Filmi was thus on the verge of growing from a minor into a major production company. Yet, in some ways, it was still behind Suomen Filmiteollisuus and Suomi-Filmi. It had few starring actors under contract and occasionally had to borrow actors from the major studios. Examples of these are Esko Vettenranta, who starred in *King of the Village Streets* (1945), and Eino Kaipainen, who starred in *The Decoy* (1946), both on loan from Suomen Filmiteollisuus.⁶¹

Despite a good start and a few successful films like *The Northern Express* (1947), the production end of Fenno-Filmi did not prosper. None of the films made between 1948 and 1950 was profitable; this was the main reason for appointing Mauno Mäkelä as the managing director, and finally, for merging Fenno-Filmi with Adams-Filmi.⁶² One of the challenges after the war years was a constant lack of up-to-date equipment. Esko Töyri, who became the head cinematographer of Fenno-Filmi and later of Fennada, recalled that, when shooting *The Northern Express*, he had to use film stock of varying brand and date. The lighting equipment consisted mainly of large arc lamps attached high above, with no Fresnels. This meant that he had to rely on cardboard sheets and other ad hoc solutions in order to direct light straight to the intended object. Given that scarcely lit noirish style became one of the trademarks of Fenno-Filmi and, indeed, Töyri himself as a cinematographer, this proved to be a true obstacle. Furthermore, as much as Töyri valued Yrjö Norta as a colleague and as a mentor, Norta's camera that was in primary use at Fenno-Filmi for many years was a silent film camera from the early 1920s converted into a sound film camera, and thus quite inconvenient and outdated.⁶³ In 1947, a more up-to-date Debrie camera was purchased.⁶⁴

Technical expertise was one of the strong areas of Fenno-Filmi, but the company's first years of operation were marked by frequent change of directors and screenwriters. Of the principal persons involved with the company, only Yrjö Norta had notable experience in directing, mainly as the co-director with Särkkä at Suomen Filmiteollisuus, responsible for the technical side of film directing. Norta directed five films at Fenno-Filmi, including the only three comedies made by the company, but he had to devote much of his time to managing productions, editing and being in charge of, especially, the sound technology. Luts and Eino Kari also tried out directing, with little previous experience,[65] as did the actors Eero Leväluoma and Erkki Uotila. Temporary solutions were tried by hiring relatively experienced actor-directors Jorma Nortimo and Edvin Laine, both with a background in theatre, to direct one film each. Nortimo, who had worked for both Suomen Filmiteollisuus and Suomi-Filmi, as well as for the independent producer Veikko Itkonen, directed the rather traditional rural drama *King of the Village Streets*. Edvin Laine was a contract director at Suomen Filmiteollisuus and stayed in the company until the very end. *The Gold Candlestick* (1946), made on loan for Fenno-Filmi, was a mixture of Gothic horror and over-the-top melodrama about the haunting of the present by the past and a family curse, quite different from the social realism typical of Laine's films at Suomen Filmiteollisuus.

The problem was finally solved when Roland af Hällström joined the company in 1946 to write and direct the noirish fallen woman film *The Decoy*. Af Hällström, a critic who had previously directed two feature films and worked as an assistant director for Teuvo Tulio's *The Way You Wanted Me* (1944), soon became the head director at Fenno-Filmi, and remained in that position in Fennada until his death in 1956. His most remarkable films at Fenno-Filmi were, arguably, *The Northern Express* and *Halli's Johnny* (1950). The former was both a popular and a critical success, a noir-style 'network narrative'[66] drama about the interlocking fates of various characters on a night train. It won three Jussi awards, presented by the Film Journalists Association, including those for best direction and best script, and established af Hällström as a prominent filmmaker. *Halli's Johnny*, based on a nineteenth-century robbery and a part of a short-lived cycle of 'ballad-films' of the late 1940s and early 1950s, was a critical success as well, though it failed in terms of box-office returns.[67] It was the first film produced by Mauno Mäkelä, thus leading the way to the Fennada merger.

## Veikko Itkonen

According to Veikko Itkonen's memoirs, published as a series of magazine articles in 1974, his career as an independent film producer was, at least indirectly, a result of the casting policy of Fenno-Filmi. Itkonen's newly wed wife Eija Karipää had starred in three of Fenno-Filmi's films in 1943–4 and was promised a lead also in *Creeping Danger*. However, the role was suddenly given to Dolly von Alfthan. Itkonen claims that not only was she willing to do the part with a lower salary than Karipää, but also that her husband invested in the film in order to get the role for von Alfthan.[68] Be this as it may, as a result, Itkonen and Karipää decided to go their own way.

Itkonen had little experience in feature films, merely a few minor parts as an actor, but he had been the announcer for dozens of newsreels, besides being a popular announcer for radio and wartime live concerts. Therefore, he had a wide network of contacts, which helped him to get a start in the film business. He began by buying an existing company, Filmi-Kuva Oy, which had produced two short films in the early 1930s but had been inactive since. Itkonen was to use this company name until the early 1950s and again in the early 1960s. Meanwhile, he also produced films in his own name or under the company name Filmivalmistamo Oy. In practice, whatever the company name, all of Itkonen's films were independent productions.

A decisive stroke of good fortune was that Itkonen was able to buy a load of raw film stock at the end of the Continuation War. Because of the general lack of raw film, Suomi-Filmi let Itkonen use its shooting equipment and laboratory in exchange for raw film. For funding, he relied on his acquaintances. Since Adams-Filmi, having been active in the pro-German Film Union of Finland during the war years, was temporarily unable to import or distribute any American films, it offered to purchase distribution rights for Itkonen's films.[69] Thus, one of Itkonen's first two films was distributed by Suomi-Filmi and one by Adams-Filmi, and both premiered in the biggest downtown cinemas in Helsinki.

Furthermore, since Itkonen started producing feature films at the same moment that Fenno-Filmi moved to its new studio, he was able to shoot the interior scenes for his first films in the Great Hall of the Helsinki University of Technology. Itkonen and Karipää even lived in a backroom of the Great Hall for a while.[70] In the early 1950s, Itkonen rented Teuvo Tulio's end of the Fennada/Tulio studio for a few years. In 1955, he finally established his own studio in an unused youth association building in the Haaga suburb of Helsinki.

Despite a good start, feature filmmaking did not prove profitable at first, and after the two first efforts, the screwball-influenced *The Star Reporters Are Coming* (1945) and the noirish crime melodrama *Destiny Guides Our Way* (1945), Itkonen moved to producing short films and newsreels. These proved to be the backbone of his company, whereas the success of feature films varied from year to year. Drawing on his own popularity as a 'voice', he himself often acted as an announcer for the shorts and newsreels. He also tried his luck with two feature documentaries: *Thus Was the Present Day Born* (1951), a compilation film based on old film material by Suomi-Filmi and other companies, and *To the Dark Continent* (1952), a travelogue shot during Itkonen and Karipää's journey through Europe and Africa.

Itkonen returned to fictional feature films in 1952, producing fifteen films until 1962 and directing seven of these. The most notable among the other directors employed by Itkonen was Jack Witikka, an established theatre director, who had directed one independent film and three films for Suomen Filmiteollisuus before joining Itkonen in 1956. The most ambitious of Witikka's films at Suomen Filmiteollisuus was *The Doll Merchant* (1955), a stylised fairy-tale-like account of a totalitarian state, and an exceptional departure from studio realism. Witikka directed five films for Itkonen between 1956 and 1960, while working simultaneously for the Finnish National Theatre.

Witikka's *Silja – the Maid* (1956) was a readaptation of the Nobel Prize–winning author F. E. Sillanpää's novel (1931) about a young orphan woman caught in the middle of the changing social classes and the frontlines of the 1918 Civil War. Of all of Itkonen's productions, this was, arguably, closest to the kind of prestige films made at the major studios. *A Man from This Planet* (1958) was a prestige film of a different kind, moving towards new ways of filmmaking rather than relying on the traditions of studio realism. Even though initiated and sponsored by the state alcohol company Alkoholiliike, this film about a variety of characters with a drinking problem was subtle and non-tendentious. With its on-location shooting, open ending and grim grey-scale cinematography, *A Man from This Planet* can be seen, along with Matti Kassila's *The Glass Heart* (1959) and Maunu Kurkvaara's *The Queen of Spades* (1959), as an early precursor of the New Wave aesthetics and patterns of the 1960s.

Yet, despite critical recognition, neither *Silja – The Maid* nor *A Man from This Planet* was a box-office success. As a compensation, Witikka and Itkonen tried to develop a more saleable concept with *The Big Hit Parade* (1959). A compilation of topical popular songs with a very loose and self-reflective backstage frame story, it was an attempt to invest in the growing popularity of Schlager music. This attempt was soon followed by other production companies and thus initiated a cycle of Schlager films, as discussed in Chapter 5.

Itkonen's own career as a film director was as varied as that of Witikka, and for much the same reason. Although the dividing line was not always clear, it seems obvious that, while some of Itkonen's productions were first and foremost artistically motivated, others were put together out of an urgent need of money. Such duality, of course, was not unfamiliar among other companies either, be they majors or minors. Among Itkonen's successful attempts to invest in topical popular phenomena was *The Loveliest Girl in the World* (1953). The topical specialty of this film was that the lead was played by Armi Kuusela, the newly chosen Miss Universum of 1952, whose popularity in Finland was unforeseen. The film itself was a fairly standard romantic comedy, a story of an orphan girl who, by removing her eyeglasses, doing her hair and dressing up, turns from an ugly duckling to a beauty queen. Itkonen's plans for a follow-up film to *The Loveliest Girl in the World* fell through, as Kuusela got married and moved to the Philippines.[71] A less successful attempt to capitalise on popular performers was *Helter-Skelter* (1961), which aimed at reviving the rillumarei cycle of the early 1950s (see Chapter 5). As outdated as it was in the eyes of contemporary critics,[72] in retrospect *Helter-Skelter* can be seen as a transitional bridge between post-war forms of entertainment and new, more urban and youth-oriented forms emerging in the early 1960s; among the mainly old-school performers were Pertti 'Spede' Pasanen and Matti Kuusla, both of whom were shortly to become key television entertainers.

Itkonen's most ambitious films were *Eyes in the Dark* (1952) and *Dangerous Freedom* (1962). The former is a quintessential noir crime film, a story of an office robbery and the traumatic backgrounds of the individual members of the mob, including a failed marriage, loss of a child, wartime shell shock, and so on. Although a frame story reveals that both the robbery and the individual stories exist only in the imagination of a writer observing a group of men playing cards, the stories themselves and the bleak atmosphere were closely attached to post-war reality. *Dangerous*

*Freedom* is a politically explosive story of a Soviet Estonian defector who is helped by a group of ordinary Finnish people, to no avail. Since Finnish–Soviet relations were extremely delicate in the early 1960s, the opinion of an officer from the Ministry of Foreign Affairs was sought when the film was reviewed at the State Office of Film Censorship. He concluded that, while the film was politically disturbing, more harm would be done if it were banned. He closed his report by saying that the film 'skilfully undermines the official foreign policy of Finland'.[73]

*Dangerous Freedom* was to be Itkonen's last feature film in Finland. Interestingly, the end of his career paralleled that of Suomen Filmiteollisuus. Just like the major production company, and approximately at the same time, Itkonen got into tax debt and sold the rights for all of his films to the Finnish Broadcasting Company, along with his studio and shooting equipment.

## *Stolen Death* (1938)

Nyrki Tapiovaara was in many ways an exception among Finnish filmmakers of the studio era. While the major studios advocated national-bourgeois politics, Tapiovaara was an openly leftist intellectual, involved with several artist groups and organisations, including the modernist (and in the 1930s increasingly leftist-modernist) Tulenkantajat (The Torch Bearers). And whereas the usual way to become a filmmaker at a time when there were no film schools was to work one's way up by learning the occupation on the job, Tapiovaara became a film director by invitation at the age of twenty-five, with no previous practical experience. He had been given a chance to run the Helsinki Workers' Theatre in 1934 and directed several contemporary, politically oriented plays, under the constant observation of the security police, and it was probably his reputation as a nonconformist young theatre maker and intellectual that caught the attention of independent film producers, too.

Tapiovaara's career was short: he died in the Winter War in 1940 after directing only five feature films. Of these five films, *Juha* (1937) and *One Man's Fate* (1940) were rural (melo)dramas and adaptations of well-established novels, while *Two Henpecked Husbands* (1939) and *Mr Lahtinen Takes French Leave* (1939) were musical comedies, and *Stolen Death* (1938) was a political thriller. Although all of his films were recognisable genre films, none of them was a typical representative of its genre. Rather, Tapiovaara's specialty was to synthesise popular film genres with a variety of modernist and avant-garde devices.

Accordingly, the mode of production of Tapiovaara's films differed considerably from that of major studios. Tapiovaara's first film was *Juha* (1937), an adaptation of Juhani Aho's classic novel, produced by the author's sons Heikki Aho and Björn Soldan, whose company, Aho & Soldan, was at the time the most renowned Finnish firm specialising in short films. Aho and Soldan shared with Tapiovaara an interest in modernist and experimental cinema; all of them were, for example, members of the short-lived but highly influential film club Projektio that screened films like Luis Buñuel and Salvador Dalí's *Un chien andalou* (1929), Jean Cocteau's *Le Sang d'un poète* (1932) and László Moholy-Nagy's *Lichtspiel Schwarz-Weiss-Grau* (1930). Shot mainly on location in north-east Finland, *Juha* remained the only fictional film produced by Aho & Soldan.

Tapiovaara's second film, *Stolen Death*, was produced independently by the cinematographer Erik Blomberg, with financial backing from the documentary filmmaker Eva-Lisa Viljanen, who came from a wealthy family. For the last three films, Blomberg acted as the executive producer for Eloseppo, a short-lived company set up for producing alternative narrative films.

*Stolen Death* was initiated by Blomberg, who bought the rights for Runar Schildt's short story that it is based on, and co-wrote the first draft for a script. He planned to direct the film himself, but did not feel ready for the endeavour and turned to Tapiovaara, who, along with the author Matti Kurjensaari, fine-tuned the script.[74] As Blomberg realised that organising an independent production was a full-time job, he hired Olavi Gunnari for his co-cinematographer.

According to Blomberg, he had raised about 20–25 per cent of the budget by the time shooting began, and managed to come up with more as the project slowly proceeded. Costs were cut wherever possible: the amount of on-location shooting in the city was much higher than in an average studio film; many of the actors and extras were amateurs, often friends of Blomberg and Tapiovaara; and sets and props of many of the interiors were borrowed from relatives rather than constructed for the film.[75]

Blomberg and Tapiovaara did have a proper studio available, however. Teuvo Tulio had convinced Abel Adams to build a studio in the Katajanokka district of Helsinki, after the success of his first film for Adams, *The Fight over the Heikkilä Mansion* (1936). With technical help from Blomberg, who shot his first films, Tulio was able to provide the studio with relatively up-to-date technology. After the collaboration between Tulio and Adams ended in 1938, Blomberg rented the studio. He made a distribution contract with Adams, according to which the rent was paid out of the distribution fees.[76]

*Stolen Death* is set around 1904–5, during the Russo-Japanese War. The protagonists are Robert, a young member of the activist resistance movement against the Russian officials in Finland; Claesson, a cynical arms dealer; and Manja, Claesson's helper, who falls in love with Robert and turns into an activist herself. The action centres on a machine gun Robert and his companions first try to buy and then steal from Claesson.

Schildt's original short story takes place during the 1918 Civil War, when Helsinki was occupied by the revolutionary Red Army. In the short story, Robert is part of an underground movement trying to purchase guns for the White Army that is gathering outside of the city. This shift in the adaptation, suggested by Tapiovaara, is politically significant: while the short story focuses on the bourgeois counterrevolutionary forces, the film's emphasis is on national rather than class struggle, albeit with a much less pronounced nationalist ethos than found in such historical films by the majors as *February Manifesto* (SF 1939) or *Activists* (SuFi 1939). Because of the change of focus in the adaptation and the leftist or liberal inclination of the filmmakers, *Stolen Death* has sometimes been interpreted as an allegory of the underground struggles of the communist movement that was prohibited in the post–civil war Finland. As Sakari Toiviainen suggests, however, this allegorical interpretation is based on a fairly general feeling of the experience of freedom rather than on strictly narrative features.[77]

In terms of narrative and style, *Stolen Death* differed considerably from average studio films. It is characterised by striking angles and compositions, montage sequences, unmotivated camera movements and scenes shot from behind fences, curtains or houseplants (Figure 3.2). A prime example is a scene near the beginning that starts with a high-angle shot of two men under a lamppost. It is followed by a relatively fast-cut series of scarcely lit shots from various angles, accompanied only by background music. We see a man, whom we may recognise as the underground activist introduced in the opening scene, followed by two other men, presumably the two from under the lamppost. The activist is carrying some papers, which he hides just before the two other men halt him and frisk him. Meanwhile, we see an unknown woman grab the papers and merge with the darkness.

**Figure 3.2** Still from *Stolen Death* (1938).

One can grasp some narrative information from the scene, but it is only later that we get to know who the woman is, why she has taken the papers, and so on. What is at stake in this scene has at least as much to do with style itself as with narrative progression. The high angle is justified later, when we learn that it is a point-of-view shot from the arms trader Claesson's window, but at the same time, it gives the scene a formal structuring principle: we return to this angle several times during the scene, as well as later in the film. The gloomy shadows and the sharp backlights add to the atmosphere and serve the narrative by controlling the amount of information revealed to the spectator, thus heightening suspense, but they also create mysterious and effective compositions that have a value of their own, irrespective of the narrative.

Hence, while *Stolen Death* is a narrative adventure film, it stretches the limits of classical narration further than is usual in mainstream cinema. Whereas the typical forms of classical film narration tend to emphasise intelligibility and keep stylistic details within the boundaries of narration, *Stolen Death* contains elements that are not only 'unnecessary' in terms of narrative flow but may even hinder narrative comprehension. Indeed, when the film reopened in 1954, Blomberg had cut what he considered the 'worst frills', thus reducing the most experimental elements and editing the film more in line with classical filmmaking. Yet, even in this simplified form, *Stolen Death* proved to become probably the most influential and inspirational film for the post-war generations of filmmakers. In contrast to most studio-era filmmakers, Tapiovaara was looked up to as a model for new ways of filmmaking – as a rare example of an independent filmmaker capable of breaking out of the assumed limitations of studio production.

## *The Way You Wanted Me* (1944)

Teuvo Tulio debuted as a film director in 1936 with *The Fight over the Heikkilä Mansion*. It was a rural melodrama based on a story by Johannes Linnankoski, whose novel *The Song of the Blood-Red Flower* (1905)[78] had been filmed twice in Sweden and would be readapted by Tulio two years later. After departing with Valentin Vaala, Tulio joined forces with Adams-Filmi. Before this, Adams-filmi had produced only one feature film in 1926 and concentrated mainly on import, distribution and exhibition.

Adams-Filmi produced Tulio's first three films, which were successful enough to keep Abel Adams happy. For Tulio, the contract with Adams, though never anything more than an informal draft on a piece of paper,[79] was definitely rewarding. Adams was a rather generous producer: production values were high compared to just about any other minor or independent company, and Adams even established a studio near the centre of Helsinki; the films were broadly distributed throughout the country and premiered in Bio Rex, a brand-new Adams venue right in the centre of Helsinki.

Abel Adams died in 1938, and from his fourth film, *The Song of the Scarlet Flower* (1938), on, Tulio acted mainly as an independent producer-director. He got off to a flying start: according to the estimation by the *Finnish National Filmography*, *The Song of the Scarlet Flower* was the most successful domestic film in 1938,[80] which means that the attendances could have been close to a million.

During the Continuation War, Tulio served as a cinematographer in the Finnish army's information corps, which caused a four-year break in production. Consequently, Tulio's career as an independent producer-director never took off quite as well, economically speaking, as it seemed it might at the outset. Yet, according to Tulio's memoirs, none of his first ten independent productions, until *You've Gone into My Blood* (1956), made a loss.[81] A popular 1950 book on the Finnish film industry still introduced Tulio as a rare exception to the general rule that films could only be produced with any success within the major studios.[82] A few years later, however, he was no longer in such a position; in fact, Veikko Itkonen seems to have taken his place as the most successful independent producer. After *You've Gone into My Blood*, Tulio directed only two more films, both of which were critical and popular failures. Furthermore, for *In the Beginning Was an Apple* (1962), Tulio worked only as a hired director, and the disastrous project ended up being released only as a 37-minute half-finished version, accompanied by a self-reflexive parodic account of the filming process, *Stardom* (1962), directed by Armand Lohikoski.

The first film Tulio released after his war service, *The Way You Wanted Me*, was a success, however. He had started one film project in 1941, but that remained unfinished, not only because of his military service, but also because his star, Kille Oksanen, was killed in the war. For his next film, initiated in 1943, Tulio wanted to have as tried-and-tested ingredients as possible: with little capital, he had to operate economically and make sure that the film would bring in a profit. He returned, once again, to *The Song of the Scarlet Flower*, which includes a scene in which one of the women seduced by the protagonist returns as a prostitute and announces: 'Here I am. Just the way you wanted me.' *The Way You Wanted Me* tells a story of a young woman from the archipelago, who is abandoned by her fiancé and forced to become a prostitute without prospects of survival. In a sense, it is a response to *The Song of the Scarlet Flower* from a female point of view.[83]

Scarcity of raw film stock was a constant problem for Tulio, as it was for most producers. This meant, first, that it was difficult to keep up with the shooting schedule, since every now and then one had to wait for a new supply, and second, that retakes were next to impossible. Shortages of other materials caused problems, too. Tulio's old trusted man, Kosti Aaltonen, convinced him, however, that material obstacles could be overcome. The youth association house he had used as a makeshift studio for his previous films was still available, as were sets from these films. For Tulio, who worked with a very small crew, Aaltonen was a precious partner. A painter and a carpenter by trade, he served as set designer, props manager and general jack-of-all-trades and was able to reuse old sets over and over again to minimise the need for new materials. Aaltonen even provided catering for the filming crew, using his black-market connections.[84]

One of the arguments Aaltonen used to convince Tulio into making a new film was that there was a great demand for domestic films at the time. This was, indeed, true, since the number of imported films had dropped considerably during the war years: a total of 139 foreign films premiered in 1942 and a total of 154 in 1943, whereas in 1938 and 1939, the figures had been 296 and 252, respectively.[85]

Tulio soon had other ambitions as well that exceeded the domestic markets. Since the transnational exchange of films, film subjects and professionals between Nordic countries had been frequent since the early cinema era,[86] Swedish markets appeared attractive. Tulio was well aware of this background and the general cultural proximity[87] among the Nordic nations. His own realisation of the close cultural connections between Nordic countries and the economic potential stemming from them dates back to 1935, when he acted in a Danish–Swedish co-production directed by George Schnéevoigt, *Outlaw* (1935). He recounts that he had the idea for dual-language versions from this film, produced in both Danish and Swedish.[88]

Tulio first tried making two versions of his second film for Adams-Filmi, *Silja – Fallen Asleep when Young* (1937), one in Finnish and one in Swedish. From *The Way You Wanted Me* on, he made dual-language versions of almost all his films. While this, of course, increased production costs, Tulio learned to cut other costs wherever possible. The script, the sets, and the staff were the same in both language versions. For each scene, he shot first the Finnish takes and then the Swedish takes. Whenever possible, he used the same shot in both versions. This concerned mainly shots with no actors, or shots with the same actors in both versions and no lip-sync dialogue.

In order to complete the Swedish version of *The Way You Wanted Me*, he signed a new distribution contract with Väinän Filmi, a distribution company led by the then novice Mauno Mäkelä.[89] Väinän Filmi had been established in 1938 as a feature film production company, but only one film was ever completed. By 1944, Väinän Filmi was owned solely by the Mäkelä family and concentrated on distribution and exhibition. The theatres managed by Väinän Filmi were more modest than those of Suomi-Filmi, but proper enough to guarantee a successful first run for the film. When signing a contract with Väinän Filmi, Tulio also sold all rights to his previous films. Tulio seems to have been happy with the contract, even if it was even more profitable to Väinän Filmi than to him: while the contract price was 2,150,000 FM, *The Way You Wanted Me* alone made a profit of 4.5 million during its first run.[90]

Internationally, the phenomenon of dual-language versions had peaked in the late 1920s and early 1930s, until the practices of dubbing (in the large language areas) and subtitling (in the small language areas like the Nordic countries) became established as the standard ways of translating foreign-language films. The much more expensive multiple-language versions became relatively rare.[91] Thus, when Tulio began to make his dual-language versions, the phenomenon was no longer an obvious choice. A few other Finnish films were made as Swedish versions over the studio years, but Tulio was by far the most systematic in his efforts to conquer Scandinavian markets with different language versions.[92] Occasionally, this seems to have been an ad hoc survival tactic typical of him: for example, in exchange for the Swedish version of *In the Grip of Passion* (1947), Tulio received raw film stock from Sweden.[93] Generally, however, his aim was to extend the potential markets for his films.

In a sense, dual-language versions seem like a logical extension of Tulio's marketing strategies. From the beginning of his career as a director, he looked for stories that would appeal to audiences in other Scandinavian countries, too. This was actually a familiar strategy already from the 'golden age' of Swedish film in the late 1910s and early 1920s, when Victor Sjöström, Mauritz Stiller and others adapted novels and plays from all Nordic countries and remoulded them into a consistent body of Nordic culture. Among such cases was, of course, Stiller's *The Song of the Scarlet Flower* (1919), which was highly influential in Finland.

Tulio's first dual-language film, *Silja – Fallen Asleep when Young*, was adapted from the novel *The Maid Silja* by Frans Emil Sillanpää. By the late 1930s, Sillanpää had become a household name, especially in Scandinavia, and there were growing rumours that Sillanpää would be a winner of the Nobel Prize in Literature. This, of course, meant free publicity for the film, even if it was not until 1939 that Sillanpää won the prize. Subjects for many of Tulio's later films were also picked with cultural proximity and Nordic appeal in mind. *The Way You Wanted Me*, for example, was inspired not only by *The Song of the Scarlet Flower*, but also by the highly successful Swedish fallen woman melodrama *King's Street* (1943).[94]

In his first dual-language films, Tulio used mainly Finnish actors who spoke both Finnish and Swedish, many of them amateurs, since it was easier to find bilingual amateurs than professional actors. No doubt, using amateurs was also less expensive. After the war years, he relied partly on double casting, hiring professional Swedish actors for some of the most important roles in the Swedish version. Though not big stars, most of them were well-enough-known actors to be familiar to Swedish audiences. Only the bilingual Regina Linnanheimo, Tulio's principle leading actor and a frequent co-writer of his scripts, was always there for both language versions from 1946. When making *The Way You Wanted Me*, Linnanheimo, who had starred in Tulio's first three films, was still under contract with Suomi-Filmi. Hence, Tulio had to find a new leading actor. He ended up with Marie-Louise Fock, a Swedish-speaking Finnish actor, who, on this occasion, had difficulties learning her Finnish lines.[95]

While no figures exist for the Nordic sales of Tulio's Swedish versions, it seems obvious that making them paid off; Tulio was in no position to keep on making such economic experiments for long if they did not. His memoirs may not always be the most reliable source of information, but he recollects that *The Way You Wanted Me* was so successful that his Swedish colleagues turned against him and tried to impede his subsequent efforts in conquering the Swedish market.[96]

## *The White Reindeer* (1952)

*The White Reindeer* is a poetic fantasy film about a Sami woman who during the full moon turns into a lethal white reindeer, is hunted down while in her reindeer form and finally killed by her own husband. In terms of both production and expression, this film differed considerably from the usual studio realism of the period. It was shot by a small crew primarily up in Lapland, and it contained elements of fantasy and horror rarely seen in Finnish films.

The main creative forces behind *The White Reindeer* were the cinematographer Erik Blomberg and the actor-screenwriter Mirjami Kuosmanen. Both had experience for working at big studios as well as independent companies. During World War II, after collaborating with Teuvo Tulio and Nyrki Tapiovaara in the late 1930s, Blomberg served as a cinematographer in the information company and shot a few feature films for Suomi-Filmi, Fenno-Filmi and other companies. After the war, he worked in Sweden and shot, for example, three films for the director Ivar Johansson. In a retrospective interview, Blomberg looked back on his experiences in Sweden with respect: the Swedish film professionals he worked with were highly skilled, and productions were well organised.[97] Although Bolmberg does not say so explicitly, one can sense that his experiences with Swedish studios like Sandrew-Produktion and Monark Film were more positive than those he had with Finnish ones.

Kuosmanen's first major roles as an actor were in Tulio's *The Song of the Scarlet Flower* and Tapiovaara's *One Man's Fate*. During World War II, she also took starring roles with Suomen Filmiteollisuus (*The Sin of the Mistress of Yrjänä*, 1943), but by the post-war period, her roles got smaller. From the early 1950s on, she concentrated mainly on working with Blomberg, both as a screenwriter and the leading actor; the two had got married in 1939.

After returning from Sweden, Blomberg directed a series of well-received short documentaries from Lapland, and both he and Kuosmanen developed an interest in the northern landscape and Sami mythology. Their first attempt at a feature film in Lapland was *Arctic Fury* (1951), a tragic love story of a Sami woman (played by Kuosmanen) and a southern hunter. The project was initiated by Jack Witikka, with an aim at international markets. A managing director of Parvisfilmi, an import company that represented, for example, Rank Organisation's films in Finland, Witikka had become friendly with Michael Powell in London.[98] Powell visited Lapland at an early stage of the project in 1947[99] and was credited as a co-producer of *Arctic Fury*, but he was not actively involved with the production as such. Instead, he sent his trusted friend and editor Jon Seabourne to Lapland to supervise the project. Witikka debuted as a feature film director, but, according to Blomberg, the result was an unsuccessful compromise with nobody in charge,[100] and the film failed both artistically and commercially.

Disappointed in *Arctic Fury*, Kuosmanen and Blomberg started to outline a new script, inspired partly by Northern mythology and partly by werewolves and other stories of metamorphosis. They first approached Suomen Filmiteollisuus, but as Särkkä would have demanded to rewrite the script and keep the project under his control, they backed off.[101] Soon they found a new partner in Junior-Filmi, which had produced one feature film and was working on another.

Junior-Filmi was founded by Matti Kassila, who had left Suomen Filmiteollisuus for the first time to try out independent filmmaking, the cinematographer Osmo Harkimo, who had worked with Kassila on several films, and Aarne Tarkas, an advertising manager for Suomi-Filmi who was keen on getting into filmmaking. Tarkas's father-in-law was a wealthy banker, who helped raise funding for *The White Reindeer* project.[102] The three had collaborated in making *The Radio Commits a Burglary* (1951) for Suomen Filmiteollisuus. As successful as this adventure comedy was, both at the box office and among critics, winning three of the major Jussi awards, Kassila received an offer to direct *At the Rovaniemi Fair* as his next film instead of the sequel to *The Radio Commits a Burglary* that he wanted to make. Frustrated with the situation, he left Suomen Filmiteollisuus with Harkimo to join forces with Tarkas.

The young filmmakers, who had little material resources at hand, approached Teuvo Tulio for help. Tulio promised to provide financial aid, as well as his end of the studio he shared with Fennada, and he also edited the film, which was to be called *The Radio Goes Mad* (1952). According to Kassila, cooperation with Tulio went well, until it was time to count the proceeds of this relatively profitable film: all they had was a verbal contract, and Kassila claims that he and his partners never received any of the profits and that Tulio avoided meeting him for a long time.[103]

By the time Blomberg and Kuosmanen contacted Junior-Filmi, Kassila had already decided to return to Suomen Filmiteollisuus. Tarkas, however, stayed on and was, according to the initial plan, supposed to direct *The White Reindeer*. As it soon turned out that he had no aspiration to take responsibility for the actual shooting, Blomberg took over, and Tarkas acted mainly as head of production. Furthermore, Blomberg was not happy with Tarkas's intentions to turn the film into 'an erotic thriller of some sort'.[104] According to Kassila, financial management was not one of Tarkas's strengths either, despite his Master's degree in economics, as he was too much of a bohemian to take care of expenses and receipts. This was, presumably, the main reason for Junior-Filmi's bankruptcy soon after.[105]

Blomberg claims that he would have wanted to focus on cinematography and never aspired to becoming a film director. Of course, he was, along with Kuosmanen, involved with the story and Sami mythology, but his main interest was in the challenges of shooting with the northern light. The exteriors of *The White Reindeer* were shot during the spring of 1952, when there was already a lot of sunshine but the ground was still covered with snow. Blomberg's challenge was to control this 'most active light on Earth', using filters, for example, in order to create different variations of snowy landscape (Figure 3.3).[106]

**Figure 3.3** Still from *The White Reindeer* (1952).

Blomberg had remained on good terms with Särkkä and was able to shoot the relatively few interiors needed for the film at the Suomen Filmiteollisuus studio. *The White Reindeer* premiered in July 1952, with positive reviews but rather low attendances; the Helsinki Olympics, which opened the same week, presumably overshadowed the film. However, it received more attention afterwards, when it won three Jussi awards, including the best cinematography award for Blomberg and the best actress award for Kuosmanen. In 1953, *The White Reindeer* became the first Finnish film to be included in the official selection at the Cannes Film Festival, and it received several international awards, including a Golden Globe in the Foreign Film category in 1957.

Blomberg and Kuosmanen benefitted little from the subsequent success of *The White Reindeer*. Junior-Filmi produced one more film, a noirish crime film *The Night Is Long* (1952), scripted by Tarkas and Kassila and directed by Tarkas as his debut film. Since this failed at the box office, Junior-Filmi got into serious debt, not even being able to cover the costs of the laboratory work, which was done in the Suomi-Filmi laboratory. In the bankruptcy auction, Suomi-Filmi bought the rights for *The White Reindeer*, while Blomberg and Kuosmanen, who had owned a 48 per cent minority stake in Junior-Filmi, ended up with nothing.[107]

*The White Reindeer* soon established its position as an exceptional art film, demonstrating for the upcoming film generation that filmmaking was not only possible but also potentially more creative and productive outside of the studio system. Paradoxically, though, the screening copies were now appended with Suomi-Filmi's logo. The film has preserved its status as a classic, although since the millennium critical voices have arisen concerning the stereotyping of Sami characters in the film as well as the issue of cultural appropriation.[108]

## *The Glass Heart*

Matti Kassila was by any standard the most remarkable young director working during the last decade of the studio era. He began his film career as a props assistant and a continuity supervisor at Suomi-Filmi, while at the same time serving as an apprentice in the theatre. After showing his talents with several short films, he ended up as a feature-film assistant director at Suomen Filmiteollisuus, where he was given a chance to direct his first feature film, *The Head of the House Plays the Accordion* (1949), at the age of twenty-five. This was a standard rural comedy made after a shooting script assigned by Särkkä, but as Kassila proved to be a reliable and efficient director, he soon became one of the few trusted young employees at Suomen Filmiteollisuus.

Between 1950 and 1962, Kassila directed twenty feature films, never remaining loyal to any production company for a long time. He regularly negotiated his terms with Suomen Filmiteollisuus, Fennada and Suomi-Filmi, being able to realise one of his own ideas every now and then in exchange for the customised projects handed to him by producers. Several times during the 1950s, he broke out of studio filmmaking altogether, heading into either the theatre or independent film productions. His first attempt at independent filmmaking was *The Radio Goes Mad* with Junior-Filmi, discussed in the previous section. The second was *The Glass Heart* (1959), after Kassila's two-year period as the head of the Helsinki Folk Theatre, during which time he directed two films for Fennada with one-off contracts.

Produced by Kassila and his trusted cinematographer, Osmo Harkimo, *The Glass Heart* was a notable attempt to break out of the conventions of studio filmmaking. Portraying a successful but frustrated glass designer who wanders aimlessly in the countryside, it is an art cinema–influenced road movie, or a 'walking film' with a loose rather than classical structure, as Kassila has characterised it. 'The aim', he wrote, 'was to free oneself from the straitjacket of plot, to liberate the possibilities of image and sound through free association.'[109] Kassila has also added that *The Glass Heart* 'to a degree explored French New Wave'.[110]

Indeed, in the New Wave manner, *The Glass Heart* was shot mainly outdoors using lightweight equipment. The basic crew consisted of Kassila, Harkimo, one property man, one all-round assistant and the two main actors, Jussi Jurkka and Toivo Mäkelä; three private cars were used to transport the crew and the equipment from one location to another.[111] The film was shot with a silent Arriflex camera, and sound recorded using only a small tape recorder, to be used as a reference when post-recording the dialogue. This was necessary especially because the script was flexible and much of the dialogue was improvised on set.[112]

The project met with an unfortunate adversity: one of the cars crashed while returning from a shooting location and the assistant was killed. Harkimo suffered a concussion and had to be replaced by the Fennada cinematographer Esko Nevalainen for a few weeks. Yet, the project was completed on schedule and approximately on budget. The production costs were 4 million FM, whereas Kassila's previous film for Fennada, *The Red Line* (1959), had cost 25 million.[113]

*The Glass Heart* was made in a situation when the old studios were already clearly in crisis. Film attendances had been in decline since 1955, and all three majors were reducing their staff.[114] Rural–urban migration was accelerating, and since the popularity of domestic films had been especially high in the countryside and in small towns, the future of the film industry seemed insecure. Even though the majors, too, made their own attempts to reach young and urban audiences with, for example, youth films and international-type crime films,[115] Kassila and Harkimo's breakaway can be seen as a more radical step towards new directions.

According to Kassila's memoirs, *The Radio Commits a Burglary* and *The Radio Goes Mad* had already addressed students and other young urban audiences, while an average Suomen Filmiteollisuus film in the early 1950s was targeted at rural markets.[116] *The Glass Heart* was a new and more urgent attempt at this reimagining of the audience. Besides flirting with early New Wave narrative, Kassila aimed at modernising film music. During the 1950s, the Finnish popular music industry had been largely dominated by the Musiikki-Fazer record company, with Toivo Kärki as the head of production. As Kärki was also a regular composer for Suomen Filmiteollisuus, the sound of Fazer, considered by many as domestic and 'folksy', was also the sound of rillumarei films, Puupää films, lumberjack films and other popular film genres and cycles. In *The Glass Heart*, Kassila relied on Scandia-Musiikki instead, an upcoming rival of Fazer, differentiating itself with a more youthful, international and jazzy sound. The score by Jaakko Salo, the head of production at Scandia, was arranged for a small band instead of the typical full-scale orchestra, and it included improvisation as well as several jazz Schlagers, typical of the Scandia sound.[117]

*The Glass Heart* was well received by the critics, but its popular success was modest. Artistically, it may have anticipated new ways of filmmaking as well as new ways of cinematic expression, but in terms of finance it was an early example of the difficulties of making non-commercial independent films during the post-studio era. Kassila probably would not have managed to have the film released without the surprise help of Särkkä. Suomen Filmiteollisuus's laboratory was used for post-production, and the film was distributed by Suomen Filmiteollisuus almost for free. Later on, Kassila realised that Särkkä's help was not entirely altruistic: he subsequently persuaded Kassila to return to the company once more to direct *Inspector Palmu's Error* (1960).[118] This was to begin a film series that in many ways became the swansong of studio-era filmmaking.

# Notes

1. Hupaniittu 2015a.
2. 'Varuskunnan pikku morsian', Censorship decision document, 15 November 1943. State Board of Film Classification Collection, Helsinki: National Archives.
3. Kurt Nylund: Letter to the State Office of Film Censorship 16 December 1943. State Board of Film Classification Collection, Helsinki: National Archives.
4. Uusitalo 1972b: 30.
5. Uusitalo 1965: 111.
6. Hupaniittu 2015a.
7. Uusitalo et al. 1996: 294.
8. Uusitalo 1988: 106.
9. No exact figures exist, but *Finnish National Filmography* has estimated that *Before the Face of the Sea* was the most successful domestic film of 1926. Uusitalo et al. 1996: 320.
10. Hupaniittu 2015a.
11. 'Kohta 20 vuotta', *Elokuva* 1/1927: 4.
12. Hupaniittu 2015b.
13. Ibid.; Uusitalo 1988: 119–21.
14. 'Kantamme', *Elokuva* 1/1927: 1.
15. Hupaniittu 2011: 211–14.
16. Seppälä 2012: 265–79.
17. Uusitalo 1972b: 17.
18. Jurtikka: 'Niskavillat pörrössä', *Elokuva* 1/1927: 10.
19. Hämäläinen 1968: 160–1.
20. 'Elämän maantiellä', *Filmiaitta* 19–20/1927: 15.
21. Khti.: 'Saako kotimaisesta filmistä sanoa totuutta?' *Sisä-Suomi* 11 December 1927.
22. Seppälä 2017.
23. 'Millä pohjalla on kotimaisen elokuvatuotantomme työskenneltävä', *Elokuva* 2/1927: 3.
24. Jurtikka: 'Muukalaisetko "kansalliselokuvaa" tekemään', *Elokuva* 8/1928: 12. Italics in the original.
25. Asianharrastaja: 'Muukalaisetko "kansalliselokuvaa" tekemään!', *Aitosuomalainen* 2/1928: 2.
26. Hupaniittu 2015a.
27. Tulio 2002: 51.
28. Tykkyläinen 2004: 22–5.
29. Sedergren 2006: 15–21.
30. Klemola 2004: 286–7.
31. Tulio 2002: 64.
32. Uusitalo et al. 1996: 405.
33. Tulio 2002: 55, 64.
34. Uusitalo et al. 1996: 622.
35. Klemola 2004: 287; Tulio 2002: 52–3.
36. Töyri 1978: 57.
37. Töyri 1983: 252.

38. Klemola 2004: 290.
39. Ibid.: 287.
40. A contract between Suomen Biografi Oy and Oy Fennica 17 October 1929. Suomi-Filmi Collection, Helsinki: National Audiovisual Archive.
41. A contract between Suomi-Filmi Oy and Oy Fennica 22 October 1930. Suomi-Filmi Collection, Helsinki: National Audiovisual Archive; A contract between Suomi-Filmi Oy and Oy Fennica 15 March 1933. Suomi-Filmi Collection, Helsinki: National Audiovisual Archive.
42. –ka: '100%', *Elokuva* 18/1931: 6.
43. See Töyri 1978: 199.
44. Honka-Hallila 1996: 468–9.
45. Linssi: 'Ammatin alalta', *Suomen Kinolehti* 9/1934: 166.
46. 'Katsauksia', *Suomen Kinolehti* 12/1937: 464.
47. 'Patenttiriita', *Kauppalehti* 11 June 1936.
48. *Patenttirekisteri* 12/1932: 37; *Patenttirekisteri* 5/1937: 3.
49. Uusitalo et al. 1995: 139.
50. 'Jäger Filmin atelieri', *Suomen Kinolehti* 3/1937: 80.
51. Töyri 1978: 93–4.
52. See Toiviainen, Tykkyläinen and von Bagh 1980: 21.
53. 'Jäger Filmi toimeenpanee käsikirjoituskilpailun', *Suomen Kinolehti* 6–7/1939: 318.
54. Toiviainen, Tykkyläinen and von Bagh 1980: 21.
55. *Suomen Kaupparekisteri* 18/1942: 10.
56. Vaakamestari: 'Kotimaisen elokuvatuotannon vaiheet', *Elokuvateatteri* 9/1944: 2.
57. Uusitalo et al. 1993: 148.
58. Ibid.: 147.
59. Töyri 1983: 254.
60. Silmäpari: 'Fenno Filmin uusi studio', *Elokuvateatteri* 6/1944: 21–2.
61. A contract between Suomen Filmiteollisuus and Fenno-Filmi 30 June 1945; 31 October 1945. Fennada-Filmi Collection, Helsinki: National Audiovisual Archive.
62. Uusitalo 1992: 30–1.
63. Töyri 1983: 257.
64. Riimala 1998: 113.
65. Luts had directed a classic Estonian war film *Young Eagles* (1927), before emigrating to Finland, but his main occupation in Finland had been as a cinematographer.
66. See Bordwell 2008: 189–250.
67. Uusitalo et al. 1992: 266.
68. Veikko Itkonen: 'Elämäni filmi Aunuksesta Kaliforniaan 3', *Apu* 48/1974: 59–60.
69. Ibid.: 61–3.
70. Ibid.: 63–4.
71. Veikko Itkonen: 'Elämäni filmi Aunuksesta Kaliforniaan 4', *Apu* 49/1974: 65.
72. Uusitalo et al. 1991: 532–3.
73. Uusitalo et al. 1998: 142.
74. Toiviainen 1986: 55; Talvio 2015: 158.
75. Toiviainen, Tykkyläinen and von Bagh 1980: 15–17.
76. Ibid.: 17.
77. Toiviainen 1986: 58–9.

78. Linnankoski's novel is translated as *The Song of the Blood-Red Fower*, whereas the film adatations are usually translated as *The Song of the Scarlet Flower*.
79. Tulio 2002: 25.
80. Uusitalo et al. 1995: 314.
81. Tulio 2002: 151.
82. Toni 1950: 35.
83. Tulio 2002: 139.
84. Ibid.: 139.
85. *Suomen Kinolehti* 1/1939: 3; *Suomen Kinolehti* 1–3/1945: 126.
86. Soila 2019: 286–91.
87. See Straubhaar, LaRose and Davenport 2009: 504.
88. Tulio 2002: 77.
89. Ibid.: 144.
90. Mäkelä 1996: 84–5.
91. Garncarz 1999: 269.
92. Lehtisalo 2016: 123–4.
93. Tulio 2002: 124.
94. Ibid.: 139.
95. Ibid.: 140–1.
96. Ibid.: 144.
97. Toiviainen, Tykkyläinen and von Bagh 1980: 21.
98. Nevala 2018: 28–9.
99. Antreas Kälppäinen: 'Kameran tuolta ja tältä puolen', *Elokuva-Aitta* 17/1947: 268.
100. Toiviainen, Tykkyläinen and von Bagh 1981: 7–8.
101. Ibid.: 5.
102. Uusitalo 2006: 43.
103. Kassila 2004: 122–30.
104. Toiviainen, Tykkyläinen and von Bagh 1981: 6.
105. Kassila 2004: 117–18.
106. Toiviainen, Tykkyläinen and von Bagh 1981: 8–9.
107. Ibid.: 5–6.
108. Lahtonen and Teppo 2020.
109. Kassila 1995: 207.
110. Kirjavainen, Pensala and von Zansen 2013: 183.
111. Kassila 1995: 207.
112. Ibid.: 208.
113. Uusitalo et al. 1991: 309, 342.
114. Hupaniittu 2019b: 324–6.
115. Römpötti 2019; Seppälä 2019.
116. Kassila 1995: 109.
117. Juva 2008: 68–72.
118. Kassila 2004: 262.

# Chapter 4

# Professionals

In his fiftieth birthday interviews in 1940, T. J. Särkkä announced himself as 'first errand boy of the company [Suomen Filmiteollisuus]',[1] whose job was to 'do everything that is involved in a film studio: writing scripts, directing movies, overseeing the office etc. etc.'.[2] There is a touch of truth in what Särkkä said: indeed, besides overseeing the office, he was the most prolific director and screenwriter of Suomen Filmiteollisuus. However, the obvious goal of the statement was to emphasise the cosy and family-like atmosphere at the company, as if 'we are all in the same boat'. Compared with a Hollywood factory, Suomen Filmiteollisuus may, indeed, have looked like a cottage industry workshop, but it was still a biggish enterprise with hundreds of employees, a hierarchical structure and a considerable pay gap between different jobs as well as between genders.

This chapter focuses on the contribution and position of various work groups from the actors, directors, screenwriters and cinematographers to the carpenters, electricians, make-up artists and dressmakers. What was the division of labour like in the major film companies? How did one end up with a career in cinema? What was everyday work at a film studio like?

## Division of labour at the studios

In terms of labour, the majors operated basically like small-scale studios in Hollywood or the big European film production countries. The mode of production was producer-led, hierarchical and divided into specialised departments: the majors labelled themselves 'full-service houses', implying that the whole process of filmmaking from scriptwriting to post-production could be handled by their regular staff.

The size of these 'full-service houses', of course, varied throughout the studio years, with a modest start and a descending end. Exact figures and lists of the personnel are hard to find, as most surviving company papers are incomplete. However, Suomi-Filmi's archive, as well as Kari Uusitalo's company history of Suomi-Filmi, gives us a good picture of the scale of a major company from the 1920s to the 1960s. While knowledge about Suomen Filmiteollisuus and Fennada is much more sparse and fragmented, based mostly on articles in newspapers and film journals, these studios can be assessed and compared with what we know about Suomi-Filmi with more certainty.

In 1921, there were around ten employees at Suomi-Filmi, including three of the founders of the company, Erkki Karu, Martti Tuukka and Ilmari Mattson, the cinematographer Kurt Jäger, who had just been recruited from Germany with a salary that was higher than Erkki Karu's, one or two office workers and a few apprentices.[3] By 1924, the number of employees was close to twenty. Besides studio and office workers, the company now employed Waldemar Järvinen, a new head of distribution, whose monthly salary was the second highest in the company.[4]

The acquisition of a theatre chain in 1926 undoubtedly raised the number of the employees across the company considerably, but exact numbers from the late 1920s and 1930s are hard to find. In 1935, the company's own journal, *Suomi-Filmin Uutisaitta*, reported: 'During this summer, Suomi-Filmi has employed fifty-six of the first-rate performing artists in the country, twenty-two extras with speaking parts, about one hundred and fifty other extras and circa sixty members of the technical crew.'[5] While the actors at this point worked mainly if not solely on a freelance basis, the technical crew was probably on a monthly payroll. However, there is no mention in the article about office workers or the theatre crew.

A personnel list from 1941 counts 118 employees working at the studio and the laboratory, and 76 working at the theatres.[6] This number, however, includes neither office workers, actors, directors nor the management, which means that the size of the whole company at this point was probably around 300 employees. As for the studio, the 1941 list indicates that Suomi-Filmi had already developed into a 'full-service house' that employed not only cinematographers and their assistants, sound engineers (Figure 4.1) and their assistants, props managers, and members of the set and dress designing crews (Figure 4.2), but also a clapper loader, errand boys, cleaners, carpenters, painters, a canteen hostess (Figure 4.3), drivers and their assistants, metal workers, storage workers and electricians, as well as scores of people working in the laboratory and in the theatres.

**Figure 4.1** Suomen Filmiteollisuus's sound recording department.

**Figure 4.2** Suomi-Filmi's set construction department in 1945.

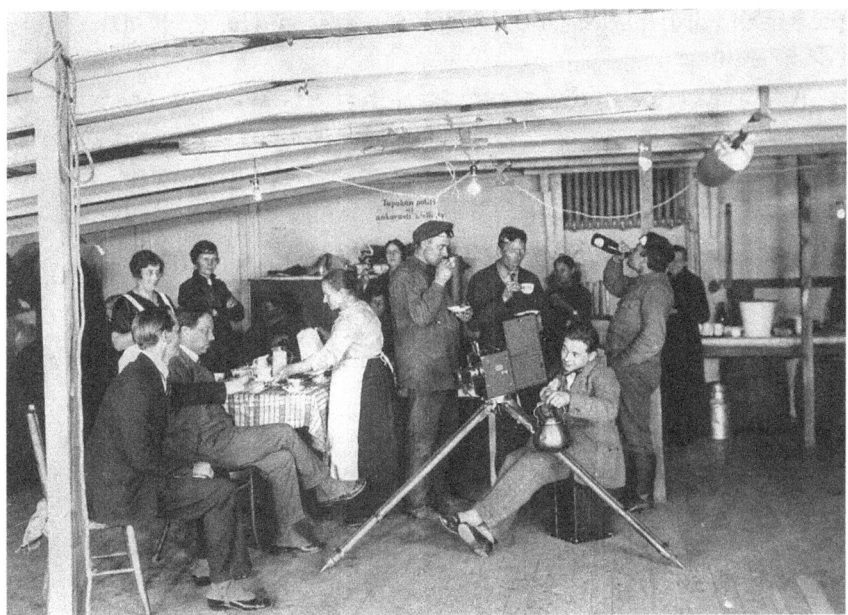

**Figure 4.3** Suomi-Filmi's studio canteen in the 1920s.

The number of Suomi-Filmi's employees kept on growing until 1957, when it reached its all-time peak of 438.[7] By 1966, the figure had dropped to 294. At this time, the company's feature film production had become sporadic, and the only studio professionals on the regular payroll worked for the short-film department. The main sources of the company's income were in import and exhibition, even though film attendances were in decline as well. Laboratory work, on the other hand, was increasing as Suomi-Filmi had invested in a colour film laboratory relatively early on.[8]

Since Suomen Filmiteollisuus never focused much on import or exhibition, it probably never employed quite as many people as its long-time rival, even if it was the biggest feature film production company from the late 1930s to the early 1960s. An article in its own magazine, *SF-Uutiset*. from 1944 reports that, while in the beginning the company relied on temporary workers, by the time of writing, it employed nearly 300 persons.[9] Presumably, the majority of these were more or less directly involved in making feature films. At the time of its bankruptcy in 1965, Suomen Filmiteollisuus employed about fifty people.[10] As for Fennada, it has been estimated that, in its heyday in the 1950s, it employed around sixty people.[11] This figure must refer to the studio employees, since the theatre and distribution sides of the business would have raised the figure considerably.

As Särkkä's description of himself as 'first errand boy of the company' suggests, the division of labour in Finnish studios was never quite as systematic and differentiated as in big film production countries. Besides the studio bosses, there were also many others who did multiple jobs. Ville Salminen, Hannu Leminen and Ossi Elstelä, for example, were set designers and directors, Lea Joutseno was an actor, a screenwriter and a translator, and Reino Helismaa was a screenwriter and songwriter as well as an actor. In addition, mobility within hierarchy was likely to be easier than in big film industries.

Yet, the mode of production in major companies was hierarchical and producer-led. As concerns the role of the producer, the Finnish system was somewhat similar to, and possibly influenced by, either directly or indirectly, the Hollywood central producer system that prevailed until the early 1930s: the producer, or production manager of the company, was primarily responsible for all the feature films made in the company.[12] Besides the volume of the output, the main difference between Hollywood central producers and Finnish producers was that both Orko and Särkkä not only supervised productions but also directed films. This, again, reminds us that specialisation of tasks was never as strict as in Hollywood.

The three majors differed from each other, though, regarding the actual role of the producer. Especially at Suomi-Filmi, there was also considerable change over the years. During the early era (1919–33), Erkki Karu's authority at Suomi-Filmi was indisputable, at least as far as actual filmmaking was concerned. He was not only the production manager and the most prolific director but also the CEO of the company, and of the five founding members, he was the only one working full-time for the company. As only one shooting unit was operating at a time, Karu was able to supervise every production, even those directed by others. Most major decisions concerning film productions seem to have been made by Karu. By the late 1920s and early 1930s, however, as the company fell into financial distress, other shareholders took more control of the company and finally forced Karu to resign.[13]

After the crisis, Matti Schreck, the representative of the KOP Bank, was appointed first as the chair of the board and then as the CEO of the company. The distribution and exhibition branch was headed by Nils Dahlström, and film production and the laboratory by Risto Orko. As we have seen, Orko's power and influence in the company increased over the years, as Dahlström was forced to leave in 1940 and Schreck in 1945. By the late 1940s, Orko was both the CEO and the major shareholder of Suomi-Filmi.

Until 1945, Schreck was usually credited as the executive producer and Orko the production manager of the company's feature films. It seems likely that Schreck had little to do with actual film work, as he carried on his banking career at the same time. The board of the company held regular meetings and made big decisions regarding, for example, property and salaries. The themes and subjects of feature films, as well as the acquisition of filming technology, were also discussed in board meetings, but, in practice, these discussions were usually based on reports made by Orko, and the board merely gave its approval to his plans.[14] A rare exception to this practice concerned the filming of *The Women of Niskavuori* (1938), based on a play by the well-known socialist playwright Hella Wuolijoki.[15] Initially, Orko was against the adaptation, presumably for political reasons, but the project was pushed through by Suomi-Filmi's office manager, Jaakko Huttunen, who adapted the script for the film, and the final decision for filming was made by Schreck, Huttunen's brother-in-law.[16] The film proved to be a success, and Orko seems to have changed his mind later, since Suomi-Filmi continued adapting Wuolijoki's work for years.

After World War II, having become the CEO of Suomi-Filmi, Orko gave up directing films and was more and more occupied with running the company. Yet, it appears that, even then, he wanted to be part of the daily work of filmmaking. In 1991, he recounted in an interview:

> I would like to add that I have probably been a tough production manager, because I've interfered with just about everything. I've tried to be as subtle as possible, but then again, I have specifically wanted to keep an eye on everything. Every script has been on my table, every discussion before the shooting starts has taken place in my office.[17]

The personal power of T. J. Särkkä at Suomen Filmiteollisuus was, arguably, even more comprehensive than that of Orko. With a background in banking, he started at Suomen Filmiteollisuus first as a sponsor and silent partner – an interested onlooker on the film set but not involved with the actual process of filmmaking.[18] After Erkki Karu's unexpected death in 1935, however, he took responsibility for running the company, becoming the CEO and production manager as well as a screenwriter and a director almost all at once.

Särkkä also acquired the share majority of Suomen Filmiteollisuus, and served as the chair of the board. The other regular members of the board were Särkkä's wife, Margarita, and Karu's widow, Elli, neither of whom took an active part in filmmaking.[19] This means that Särkkä indeed was responsible for all major decisions at Suomen Filmiteollisuus, and as the company mainly focused on feature film production, it seems plausible that he was able to control everything, at least up to a point.

Whether he was actively directing a film at the moment or not, Särkkä usually started his mornings by visiting the studios, before rushing off to the office. According to countless recollections of employees, Särkkä's visits to the studio were anything but subtle: he loudly and often crudely expressed his opinions about every possible detail from the set decorations to the dresses and make-up. 'The Master's morning devotion' was the nickname given to these visits by the studio employees.[20] Särkkä also watched all the daily rushes at the studio theatre, often sharply commenting on the day's outcome.

On the other hand, despite his controversial tendency for micromanaging, Särkkä's all-around attitude left room for company professionals, as long as they got along with him, and it seems that he did have a genuine trust in the skills of his long-time workers. Ville Salminen recounts that during his first year as a director at Suomen Filmiteollisuus, Särkkä kept a sharp eye on everything he did, often insisting on retakes, but after that he usually merely approved the daily rushes.[21]

Until 1939, Särkkä co-directed his films with the technology expert Yrjö Norta, who was mainly responsible for image and sound, while Särkkä concentrated on guiding the actors. According to the cinematographer Felix Forsman, Särkkä 'did not concern himself with cinematography, not even with set design or sound',[22] and the cinematographer Olavi Tuomi confirms that 'Särkkä was always busy, and sometimes the cinematographer had to direct the rest of the daily takes, when the Master went off somewhere'.[23] Every employee seems to agree that, unlike Orko, Särkkä had neither knowledge about nor interest in film technology. 'He didn't realise that it took time to change the camera angle and re-arrange the lights,' recollects the cinematographer Osmo Harkimo, who wondered whether Särkkä 'really knew what the difference between negative and positive film was'.[24]

Among the major company producers, Fennada's Mauno Mäkelä was the only one who neither directed nor scripted films, even if he, having a schooling and a background in engineering, had much more knowledge about film technology than Särkkä. Mäkelä, in fact, had wanted to become a professional engineer before entering the film business. Family pressure was an obvious factor in his final career choice: his father was Väinö Mäkelä, who was the founder and CEO of the large distribution and exhibition company Kinosto, and all three of Mauno's brothers ended up working in the film business, too. Mauno Mäkelä was appointed the CEO of Fenno-Filmi in 1949, and when Fenno merged with Adams-Filmi, he was the obvious choice for the president of the new company, Fennada, too.

Mäkelä's voice in production decisions at Fennada was more limited than that of Särkkä's or Orko's in their companies, since all decisions had to be confirmed by the board.[25] Therefore, decision-making at Fennada was sometimes slow and formal, especially compared with that at Suomen Filmiteollisuus, which occasionally operated with astonishing speed. Yet, Mäkelä was mainly responsible for presenting potential scripts and ideas to the board. According to his memoirs, one of his main duties at Fennada was to read and commission scripts and select novels and plays to be adapted.[26]

Mäkelä seems to have remained quite distant from most of his employees, and his role in the company was somewhat indistinct. He himself recollected that he usually visited the set of every production, at least at some point.[27] Daily visits to the studio were not his habit,[28] and if he did spend time at the studio, he kept a low profile, unlike Särkkä. Therefore, it is quite understandable that, especially in the eyes of those professionals who worked for many companies, Mäkelä must have appeared passive and invisible compared with Orko or especially Särkkä. Yet, those who worked close with him usually acknowledged his contribution to Fennada's feature film production and house style. The set designer and cinematographer Ensio Suominen, for example, called him the head dramaturge of the company.[29]

As producer-led as the majors were, feature filmmaking in all three companies was usually carried on independently. The producers, especially Särkkä, kept an eye on the projects, but on the set the director was in charge. Many of the more experienced directors were also involved with the scriptwriting as well as the editing of their films, and they had a say about the casting, the sets and the shooting locations. At least occasionally, directors like Valentin Vaala and Ilmari Unho at Suomi-Filmi, Edvin Laine and Matti Kassila at Suomen Filmiteollisuus, or Roland af Hällström at Fennada could choose the subject matter of their films. As the career of Vaala indicates, however, such creative freedom lasted only as long as their films remained successful.

The ultimate hierarchy of the companies is indicated in the wage scale. According to the existing company papers of Suomi-Filmi, the pay gap between jobs was considerable, albeit endurable compared to Hollywood. In 1936, for example, monthly salaries at the laboratory varied from the assistant's 1,100 FM to the foreman's 4,000 FM.[30] At the same time, the management of the company received 8,000 FM a month plus bonuses.[31] As a point of comparison, it may be noted that, in 1937, the average wage for male industrial workers was 1,620 FM, and for female workers it was 930 FM.[32]

Of the film personnel, directors and cinematographers were among the most highly paid. In 1940, when average wages in Suomi-Filmi's laboratory, office and studio varied between 1,000 and 3,000 FM, the directors Ilmari Unho and Orvo Saarikivi's monthly salary was 4,000 FM, and Valentin Vaala's 5,000 FM. In addition, Unho received an extra bonus of 10,000 FM for each film he directed, and yet another bonus for each script he wrote. For Saarikivi, the film bonus was 12,000 FM, and for Vaala 15,000 FM. Orko's bonus was 5,000 FM for each film he completed as production manager (which means every feature film made at Suomi-Filmi), and 15,000 FM for each film he directed.[33] According to Matti Kassila, Suomen Filmiteollisuus had a similar two-part salary system for directors, consisting of a monthly payment and a bonus for each completed film. In the mid-1950s, however, Kassila and Särkkä agreed on a different system, where Kassila committed to make two films a year with an overall compensation of 600,000 FM for each film. In 1956, he changed over to Fennada with a similar agreement but 800,000 FM per film.[34]

The salaries of cinematographers raised steadily through the late 1930s, especially when Suomi-Filmi started hiring film professionals from France. French film aesthetics were highly valued in Finland at the time, and consulting French cinematographers aimed at bringing 'continental' sophistication to films. Whereas the cinematographer Armas Hirvonen's monthly salary in 1937 was 3,000 FM, Marius Raichi was invited from France with 6,000 FM a month.[35] Next year, another French cinematographer, Charles Bauer, started at Suomi-Filmi with 8,000 FM a month. At the same time, Suomi-Filmi also hired Raimond Grosset from France to supervise the laboratory with a 5,500 FM monthly salary.[36]

The most highly paid employees were almost invariably men, whereas women typically worked in the office, laboratory or wardrobe department

**Figure 4.4** Suomi-Filmi's wardrobe department.

(Figure 4.4), doing jobs that were less well paid and generally non-credited. With the exception of film stars, few women reached publicly visible, let alone influential, positions in film studios. Only four women worked as feature film directors during the studio era: Glory Leppänen, Ansa Ikonen, Kyllikki Forssell and Ritva Arvelo, all of them actors and each of them only once. Some of the most popular and prolific screenwriters were women, though, for instance Kersti Bergroth (pseudonym TET), who together with Valentin Vaala and Lea Joutseno scripted a cycle of screwball-oriented modern comedies for Suomi-Filmi (from *With Serious Intent*, 1943, to *Girl of the Week*, 1946), and Seere Salminen and Elsa Soini, who were responsible for the Family Suominen series (SF 1941–59). However, all of these screenwriters were professional authors who worked for film on a freelance basis.

Judging by Suomi-Filmi's wage scale, a sole exception to the general state of gender imbalance seems to have been Eeva Pullinen, head of the wardrobe department, whose monthly salary of 6,000 FM in 1943 was, while lower than that of the leading directors and cinematographers, still higher than that of most other employees.[37] Although no wage scales from Suomen Filmiteollisuus survive, it can be assumed that Fiinu Autio had a similar position at the rival company. Autio, who was first poached from the National Theatre[38] and who worked for Suomen Filmiteollisuus from the mid-1930s to the early 1960s, was the head of the wardrobe department and sewing section. She was highly respected for her eye for style and her knowledge of how colours were registered in back-and-white.[39] Yet, as strong as her position within the department was, it was only occasionally that Autio got her name into the film credits; usually these were costume films. A much more public figure was Bure Litonius, who as a schoolboy had already begun acquiring a huge collection of uniforms, and whom Suomen Filmiteollisuus often hired as an expert on historical films, starting from *February Manifesto* (1939).[40]

Rises in salary were frequent, not only because of inflation and the steadily mounting cost of living, but also because of the rivalry between studios. In 1936, the board of Suomi-Filmi noted that it was necessary to raise wages because 'new companies' – referring basically to Suomen Filmiteollisuus – tried to attract professionals with higher salaries.[41] Two years later, Suomi-Filmi started preferring long-time contracts with laboratory workers for the same reason.[42] During the 1940s and 1950s, film professionals kept on changing companies, but, according to an unwritten rule, the majors were not supposed to poach staff from one another. This rule, however, was broken from time to time. In his memoirs, Mäkelä reveals one example of this. When Särkkä in 1953 poached Armand Lohikoski, the head of Fennada's short-film department, and made him a director at Suomen Filmiteollisuus, Mäkelä took revenge by hiring Ville Salminen, an established actor-director at the rival company,[43] who, despite his huge success with the musical *Beautiful Vera* (1950) had not been allowed to carry out his own ideas for films. At Fennada, Salminen was able to fulfil at least some of his ambitions, especially with the 'Karelian trilogy', *Säkkijärvi Polka* (1955), *Anu and Mikko* (1955) and *Evacuated* (1956).

Many of the actors, too, were attached to one company with long-term contracts. In the 1930s, the salaries of actors usually remained reasonably modest. Especially young female actors sometimes received low wages even when appearing in starring roles, as is indicated by Helena Kara's 1,500 FM a month and Sirkka Sari's 1,800 FM a month in 1938.[44] The former had already been one of the top-billed actors in *Man's Rib* (1937), while the latter starred in two major films in 1938, *The Women of Niskavuori* and *The Man from Sysmä*, both directed by Valentin Vaala, who had 'discovered' her on one of his trips looking for amateur actors. As a contrast to these emerging female actors, the established male stage actor Paavo Jännes earned 5,000 FM a month, even if he played character parts and not starring roles.[45]

During the war years, the salaries of the leading actors in particular started to rise more steadily than those of other professionals, as the value of stars increased in marketing films; it has been argued that the star system had a late start in Finland compared to many other film-producing countries.[46] In 1941, Helena Kara and Joel Rinne, both top-billing actors, earned 6,000 FM a month, and the character actor Reino Valkama 7,000 FM a month.[47] Two years later, two of the biggest stars of their time, Regina Linnanheimo and Tauno Palo, changed over to Suomi-Filmi from Suomen Filmiteollisuus, the former with 10,000 FM a month and the latter, being in a class of his own, with 25,000 FM a month.[48] Even considering the wartime inflation, these wages were high. This was probably the first time in Finnish studios that stars were valued more highly than directors: Vaala's salary at this time was 9,000 FM a month and Ville Salminen's 7,500 FM a month.[49]

The relatively strong economic position of actors during the 1940s and 1950s was due not only to the star system but also to the fact that actors were better and earlier organised than other filmmaking professions, with the exception of producers. Whereas the Finnish Film Producers Union was founded in 1945, with Särkkä as the chair and Orko as the vice chair, most other professionals organised only after the studio era: the Association of Finnish Film Workers was founded in 1973, and the Association of Finnish Film Directors and the Association of Finnish Cinematographers both in 1983. The most notable effort to organise during the studio years was the founding of the Film People Registered Association in 1944. This, however, was not an actual trade union. The aim of Film People, chaired by the director Ilmari Unho, was to further the general development of the film branch by, for example, approaching the government in order to establish a Finnish film academy. Among the tasks assigned to the academy would have been organising film schooling and establishing a film archive.[50] The Finnish Film Academy was never to be, and the Finnish Film Archive was finally founded in 1957 as a private association, which operated with state funding until 1979, when it was turned into a state office. The activity of Film People had faded by the early 1950s.[51]

As the Film People association was never an actual union, most salaries during the studio era were negotiated directly with the producers without the help of a union.[52] According to the cinematographer Osmo

Harkimo, the unorganised status of film workers hindered not only wage development but also improvement of craftsmanship in general: as film professionals hardly knew their colleagues in rival companies, they had little opportunity to share experience and knowledge.[53] Esko Töyri and Erik Blomberg actually did try to organise a union for cinematographers after World War II, but with no success: after initial enthusiasm, most cinematographers backed out, many of them presumably because their employers objected to their unionising and even threatened them with lay-offs should they participate.[54]

The Finnish Actors' Union, however, was established already in 1913. Originally, it looked after the interests of stage actors, but from early on, it also took into consideration the interests of film actors, as many actors worked for both theatre and film. The long-time chair (1937–74) of the Union, Jalmari Rinne, for example, acted in almost seventy feature films, including the breakthrough lead role in *Superintendent of the Siltala Farm* (SuFi 1935), besides his career in the Finnish National Theatre. The power of the Actors' Union became evident on several occasions. For example, the Union pushed through an agreement that actors, including supporting actors and extras, should be paid by the number of shots they appeared in rather than according to the importance of the role. In the mid-1950s, this agreement was replaced with one based on hourly pay and the size of the role.[55] In the early 1960s, the Actors' Union had a substantial effect on film production by declaring a strike. The Union demanded a 50 per cent rise in actors' fees and a share for actors from television screenings of films. When negotiations failed, members of the Union were not allowed to make new contracts with film companies. As a result, during the two-an-a-half-year strike (1963–5), practically no professional actors appeared in domestic films.[56] While the impact of the strike on the already faltering studio system might sometimes have been exaggerated, its effects on the emerging new cinema were clear: using amateurs, non-acting celebrities, friends and colleagues instead of professional actors fitted perfectly with the new film aesthetic, which distanced itself from studio realism.

## A career in the movies

With the exception of actors, there was no schooling for film professionals before the founding of the Department of Photographic Art at the

Institution of Industrial Arts and Design in 1959. There were two typical ways of making a career in the movies: to learn the profession through apprenticeship or to move into film from the theatre.

Topo Leistelä and Nisse Hirn introduced their 1950 book *Haluatko elokuvanäyttelijäksi* [Do You Want to Act in a Movie?] by stating that:

> the film business welcomes everyone who seriously wants to enter the field. Film is a peculiar branch, since it constantly needs new workers both in front of and behind the camera ... It needs offspring, new maidens, new youngsters, new heroes, heroines, character actors, humourists etc. And directors need new assistants, cinematographers need new pupils, even hairdressers and makeup-artists require help from young people, to whom they can teach their most valuable skills ... The aim of this book is to provide preliminary educational base to those young people who, perhaps in near future, will pick up the courage to approach the chief of staff of a film company and say: 'I'd like to make my way into the film industry. Can you help me with that?'[57]

This was, indeed, the way many film professionals began their careers, some out of interest for film, some because their parents knew someone in a film company, some by pure chance. A prime example of a career started by chance is the cinematographer Esko Töyri. He first entered a film laboratory in 1936 when running into a friend of his, Auvo Mustonen, on a street corner in Helsinki. Mustonen asked him to help carry a heavy editing table up the stairs to Aho & Soldan's laboratory. Upstairs, Heikki Aho, in need of an assistant, asked him to stay. Töyri, who was unsure about his future plans, decided to take up the offer, learned the basics of the job at the laboratory, and later became one of the most distinguished cinematographers of the studio years.[58] Pentti Lintonen, also a cinematographer, is an example of a career started through family connections. With the help of his mother, who worked as an accountant at Suomi-Filmi, he got a job as an usher in the company's flagship theatre, Kino-Palatsi, in 1938, while still in school. During the war years, he entered first into the Suomi-Filmi laboratory, and later had a chance to work his way up in a film crew.[59] Finally, Hannu Leminen, one of those 'young people' who were determined to make a career in the movies, answered a Suomi-Filmi job advertisement and entered the firm in 1937. Studying law but keen on drawing and architecture, he started as a props manager, but was soon promoted to set decorator and studio manager.[60] In 1940, he moved to Suomen Filmiteollisuus, where Särkkä had promised him a chance at directing, and soon became one of the most accomplished directors, working for all the major companies one after another. After leaving the film industry, he had another career in television and became the head of one of the two Finnish television channels in 1965.

These three examples also remind us of the hierarchical nature of the studios. While a young person with no schooling would begin literally at the bottom, someone with an upper secondary school diploma or even a university degree like Hannu Leminen would be on the next level up right from the beginning.

Directors and actors often entered film industry from the theatre. Leminen, Vaala, Aarne Tarkas and Teuvo Tulio were among the relatively few directors who learned the profession without a background in theatre. More common was to start with stage experience, which, according to cinematographers and other film professionals, usually meant having no knowledge of technology and a limited ability to think visually. Edvin Laine, for example, openly acknowledged his dependence on cinematographers, but his ability to work with actors and his willingness to learn film technique was respected by the staff.[61] It was seldom, however, that anyone would be hired as a director straight from the theatre with no experience in film whatsoever. Usually, they first started as actors, like Laine, Ilmari Unho or Wilho Ilmari, or as set designers, like Ossi Elstelä or Ville Salminen.

For actors, there were several ways to enter the movies. Some (usually non-professionals) approached film companies just like Leistelä and Hirn encouraged, either sending in their application letters and photographs or taking part in film star contests such as those announced by *Filmiaitta* magazine in 1924 and 1927. The first of these was organised with Suomi-Filmi and the second, in search for 'the most beautiful Venus-figure',[62] with Komedia-Filmi. Screen tests were promised for the winners of the contests.

Film actors, both starring and supporting ones, were also 'found'. Well-known examples are Helena Kara, who worked as a ticket seller at a film theatre, when Risto Orko spotted her and arranged an audition, and Regina Linnaheimo, who was a schoolmate of Teuvo Tulio and got her first roles in the films of Vaala and Tulio. Vaala was especially known as a star finder. Having no stage background, he preferred mixing professional and non-professional actors, and made an effort to find new actors when shooting on location around the country. Some of Vaala's finds came from Suomi-Filmi's own personnel. Lea Joutseno was a translator of Suomi-Filmi's imported films, and Tapio Nurkka was a studio assistant. Both starred in several of Vaala's 1940s comedies.

Both Suomi-Filmi and Suomen Filmiteollisuus also tried systematic schooling for young screen actors from the late 1930s on, providing teaching in oral expression, gymnastics, plasticity, even in horseback riding and fencing (Figure 4.5).[63] Suomi-Filmi concentrated as much on teaching the actors who were already on the payroll as on finding new ones, but Suomen Filmiteollisuus was more eager to hunt for fresh talent. Studying at the Suomen Filmiteollisuus film school was free, but the students agreed to work for the company exclusively for a certain period of time. Several notable actors graduated from the school, for example Sirkka Sipilä, Toini Vartiainen and Kyllikki Forssell, who was to have a long career not only in movies but also on the stage of the National Theatre, as well as Tapio Rautavaara and Olavi Virta, both of whom became known as top-level popular singers.[64]

Regardless of competitions, film acting schools and 'finds', a remarkable number of actors came from professional theatres. Suomen Filmiteollisuus relied especially on actors from the National Theatre, partly for the sake of prestige and partly for very practical reasons: the National Theatre was located on the same square as the company's head office and just a few blocks from the Liisankatu studios. No doubt, the reliance on actors

**Figure 4.5** Suomen Filmiteollisuus's Film School.

from this large and grandiose theatre also contributed to the company's house style. In contrast to Suomen Filmiteollisuus, Fennada-Filmi had an agreement to use actors from Intimiteatteri in the 1950s, which fitted the more youthful image of Fennada perfectly. Intimiteatteri ('Intimate Theatre') was a small independent group that specialised in modernist drama and featured some of the leading young actors in the country. Many of them, like Lasse Pöysti, Maija Karhi and Jussi Jurkka, were among the main actors at Fennada, and Pöysti also directed eight films for the company. The close connection between Fennada and Intimiteatteri was sealed by the fact that Mauno Mäkelä was a board member at Intimiteatteri for years.[65]

As the major studios were located in Helsinki, stage actors used in films were usually from Helsinki, too, if only for practical reasons: it was next to impossible to film in Helsinki and continue with a stage career somewhere else. Now and then, however, film companies recruited actors from other cities as full-time employees. Edvin Laine, for example, recalls that Särkkä contacted him in 1939 and offered him a monthly salary that was three times as high as what he earned at the Tampere Workers' Theatre.[66]

The growing importance of actors, especially starring ones, for the studios was evident in their contracts. Ansa Ikonen, who rose to stardom in Suomi-Filmi's comedies during the latter half of the 1930s, did not sign a monthly contract with Suomi-Filmi, since she was starting a career at the National Theatre at the same time. Her one-time fee for her first major role in the comedy *Everybody's Love* (1935) was 2,000 FM. The fee rose to 5,000 FM for her next film, the highly successful *Surrogate Wife* (1936), and by the following year, it was already 10,000 FM. Soon, Suomen Filmiteollisuus offered an even more profitable three-film contract that gave her 20,000 FM for each film.[67]

Yet, in spite of their relatively high fees, actors were strictly controlled. Starring actors were expected to represent the studios and their house styles more than any other group of employees. Not only were they supposed to avoid saying anything negative about the film company, on pain of paying damages, but were also expected not to leave the city or the film location without the company's permission. Even off the studio premises, they were supposed to 'act properly', and during the premiere, they were obliged to present themselves 'as Suomi-Filmi sees best'.[68]

By controlling the actors, the studios adjusted the distance between stars and audiences, which obviously differed from that in the big film-producing countries. On the one hand, the stars were homely: anyone could meet Tauno Palo on the streets of Helsinki, in a restaurant, or on tour. In the 1930s and 1940s, film magazines even gave out the home addresses of actors, so that the fans could go and ask for signed photographs. In magazine articles, actors were often depicted in their homes, as 'ordinary' working people, as mothers and fathers or daughters and sons.[69] On the other hand, the notion of the exceptionality of stars started to take shape, which can be seen in the filmgoing memories from the studio era collected in 1975:

> Film stars were looked on as though they were superhuman. If you happened to see a real film star, as I once saw Ansa Ikonen, you kept on telling your friends about it, and it was as though you had been around more than the others, since you had seen a star. You didn't envy film stars, since for ordinary people they were like creatures from a fairy tale.[70]

However, the exceptionality of stars was not always seen in positive light, as is evident in this recollection from the countryside on-location shooting of *Cowherd, Maid and Housewife* (Väinän Filmi 1938): 'The villagers didn't quite like this bunch of actors; the goings-on were a bit sinful, since the ladies and gentlemen had trouble remembering whom they were married to.'[71] As we know from star studies, a dialectic between ordinariness and extraordinariness is essential for film stardom.[72] The tendency of Finnish studios to control the behaviour of their stars stemmed, no doubt, from the size of the film industry: in spite of the increasing glamour attached to the industry, domestic films and their protagonists still seemed very much down-to-earth and neighbourly compared with Hollywood films and their stellar performers. Therefore, the balance sheet remained more on the side of the ordinary than the extraordinary.

## Everyday work at the studio

The temporal organisation of studio filmmaking was always crucially effected by two external factors, the Northern European climate and the fundamental connections with the theatre. While the former determined yearly seasonal routines, the latter dictated the daily schedules of the studios.

Finnish summers are short but summer days are long, whereas winters are long with very little sunlight. This means that summers were usually devoted to on-location shooting and winters for interior shooting and other studio work. Winter scenes were, of course, also needed now and then, and they were typically shot in or near Helsinki. On some occasions, winter locations were constructed in the studio. Even a realistically inclined film like the war epic *The Unknown Soldier* (SF 1955) included some winter shots taken in studio using naphthalene as snow.[73] A few times, as in the filming of *A Summer Night's Waltz* (SuFi 1951), wintery exteriors were built on the studio backlot (Figure 4.6).

It was relatively seldom that a large group of technical crew and actors travelled far from Helsinki during the winter. A notorious exception was Suomi-Filmi's *Green Gold* (1939), exteriors for which were first shot in the winter of 1938 in Kittilä Lapland, about 1,000 kilometres from Helsinki. As the filmed material was damaged, the exteriors had to be reshot the following winter, and as a result, *Green Gold* became the most expensive film Suomi-Filmi had produced. Long shooting trips during winter were also problematic if some members of the crew were involved in theatre work. Therefore, only films with no theatre actors in the lead roles, such as the comedy *Pekka and Pätkä on the Trail of the Abominable Snowman* (SF 1954), could be shot in winter far from Helsinki.

A general rule was thus that on-location shooting took place in summer. If the locations were within reach from Helsinki, then a

**Figure 4.6** Still from *A Summer Night's Waltz* (1951).

cavalcade of cars filled with crew, actors, cameras, lamps, reflectors and filters, sound-recording equipment and an electric generator, as well as catering, would leave early in the morning and head for the location. The actor (and later also director) Åke Lindman recalls such working days at Suomen Filmiteollisuus:

> The Liisankatu studios were swarming with people at 5 a.m., when the shooting crews gathered there at the same time. Actors and extras were made up, the equipment was packed, and at 6 a.m. we got on a bus and drove up to 100 kilometres somewhere... When we got there, we worked from the early morning on for as long as there was light. It was only when the evening sun got so yellow that the light did not match with the images shot earlier during the day that the bus headed back to Helsinki. And the next morning, it started all over again. When the exteriors were ready, they were put on hold, and we began to shoot on-location material for the next film. In this way, exteriors for many films were shot during the summer, and the films were completed in studio in the autumn and winter.[74]

For economy's sake, daily shooting trips were confined to the vicinity of Helsinki whenever possible. However, almost every summer there were also longer trips with dozens of people spending several weeks in whatever place was considered a convenient location for the film in question. Typical locations that were hard to find near Helsinki were wide rivers and rapids for lumberjack films, the plain and flat rural landscapes for films that take place in the western region of Ostrobothnia, or the treeless fells for films set in Lapland. In some cases, when a suitable place was found with a varied landscape and practical accommodation, it would be used over and over again. The best known of these places was the Pyhäniemi Mansion in Hollola, about 100 kilometres from Helsinki. Used first by Suomi-Filmi and then by Suomen Filmiteollisuus in the 1930s and 1940s, the Pyhäniemi Mansion was nicknamed the 'Hollywood of Hollola'.

For the technical crew and especially for the actors, these long shooting trips were often enjoyable experiences, combining work and relaxation with good company in a beautiful milieu.[75] The producers' perspective was more ambiguous. As long as everything went well, a long trip was a more efficient way of covering all on-location shooting for a film than driving back and forth on a daily basis; this is obviously the reason why such trips were planned in the first place. Yet, every now and then, things did not go as smoothly as intended. The main reason for problems was the weather. Even though Northern European summer days are long, the weather is often unpredictable, and sometimes it took days or even weeks to wait for proper sunlight. As the film stock used was slow, sunlight was essential for shooting; a cloudy weather would create grey, flat images. Too much sunlight was also problematic, but that could be controlled to a degree using filters and reflectors. Yet, the most ambitious cinematographers like Esko Töyri wanted to wait for perfect cumulus clouds in order to get the best out of on-location shooting in the countryside.[76]

A notorious case in point is *Beautiful Vera* (SF 1950), a musical comedy that takes place on a turn-of-the-century lake boat. As the boat itself as well as spectacular lake views were essential ingredients of the film, the majority of the scenes were planned to be shot on-location by Lake Saimaa in south-east Finland, and Suomen Filmiteollisuus rented and renovated a boat for the purpose. Dozens of technical crew and cast members travelled to Saimaa in order to shoot the film in a few weeks, some of them actually living on the boat. The weather, however, was exceptionally bad, and it often rained for several days at a stretch. As a result, the project dragged on for weeks and became expensive for the company. As liberating as it usually was to get away from the watchful eye of the producer, the crew eventually became frustrated and some began drinking heavily.[77] According to the cinematographer Osmo Harkimo, by the end of the summer, he only communicated with the director Ville Salminen through the assistant cameraman Pentti Valkeala.[78] *Beautiful Vera* was finally completed, and it even became a huge success, but in some scenes, the quality of the image was below par.

What was common for the on-location and in-studio shooting was that working days were often extremely long, especially at Suomen Filmiteollisuus with its high production volume. The weeks before opening nights were particularly busy. Since Suomen Filmiteollisuus had no flagship cinemas, opening nights had to be booked months in advance, and it was important for the company to abide by the fixed dates, even if it meant working day and night.[79] During the busiest production years of the 1950s, when the company made up to fourteen feature films a year, this meant being in an almost unceasing hurry. With no unions and little regulation, employees did not have much say in the working hours. Afterwards, many former workers recalled having practically lived at the studio before opening nights.[80]

Even standard shooting days at the studio were usually long, since daily routines had to be adjusted to the schedules of those actors who were working at a theatre. Even though all major companies had contract actors who worked exclusively on films, in most productions a proportion of the actors had permanent engagements with a theatre. Those who worked both for stage and film included both starring actors like Tauno Palo and Ansa Ikonen and distinguished character actors like Uuno Laakso and Aku Korhonen. The standard day at a theatre consisted of a rehearsal between 11 a.m. and 3 p.m. and a performance at night. This meant that the filming with theatre actors started very early in the morning, continued in the afternoon and often again late at night, after the theatre performance.[81]

Since the theatre was the main employer of these actors, film companies usually had little room for bargaining. On the contrary, the actors had to be careful to be on time at the theatre and never to show up with their film costume or make-up on. Tauno Palo recalls that the National Theatre in particular had a negative attitude towards the film industry, and that he and Ansa Ikonen even tried to keep their film work a secret, which of course proved to be impossible because of their huge success.[82] In the late 1930s, several theatres joined forces to have better control over actors' side jobs in film and radio. Even though previous contracts had, in fact, already forbidden actors from performing elsewhere during the theatre season without permission from the theatre, a new and even more unambiguous contract model was now drawn up. Film companies were also expected to insure actors against accidents that might happen during filming.[83] Strict as these restrictions were, theatres seldom downright forbade actors from performing in films, as long as it had no effect on their work on stage, possibly because they were afraid of losing the actors entirely to film companies with their alluring salaries.

Judging by their subsequent recollections, there was considerable variation in the actors' attitude towards film work. Some, like Hannes Häyrynen and Matti Oravisto, quite openly despised film acting and seem to have done it only for the money.[84] Others, like Tauno Palo, appreciated the opportunity to work for film companies and cherished the devotion of the fans and admirers, while still admitting that they 'belonged to the theatre'.[85] Yet others, like Ansa Ikonen, found genuine delight in working in film and considered it not a minor sidestep but rather as a rewarding line of work that ran parallel to their theatre career.[86]

Whatever their attitude with regard to their career and creativity, few actors totally denied the attraction of the film studios. Even with all the fights with the producers, the dreadful working hours and the contempt expressed by the theatre world, there was still something fascinating about film. Part of that fascination undoubtedly had to do with the glamour and nationwide fame that film brought them; even the best-known theatre actors were only ever seen by relatively small and mainly local audiences, whereas film stars were known by all. Another part of the fascination was probably in the atmosphere of the studios. Despite the obvious hierarchy in the division of labour, many employees, not only those at the top of the pile, have emphasised the familial working conditions at the studios, especially during the on-location shooting trips.[87]

## Notes

1. 'Uusia, innostuneita työntekijöitä', *Elokuva-Aitta* 23/1940: 340.
2. 'T.J. Särkkä 50-vuotias', *Elokuvalukemisto* 10/1940: 7.
3. Suomen Filmikuvaamo's payroll list No. 9, 1921. Suomi-Filmi Collection, Helsinki: National Audiovisual Archive.
4. Suomi Filmi's payroll list No. 12, 1924. Suomi-Filmi Collection, Helsinki: National Audiovisual Archive.
5. 'Pikku paloja Suomi-Filmistä', *Suomi-Filmin Uutisaitta* 3/1935: 3.
6. An appendix to Suomi-Filmi's board meeting 9 May 1941. Suomi-Filmi Collection, Helsinki: National Audiovisual Archive.
7. Uusitalo 1994: 280.
8. Ibid.: 304, 319.
9. '10 vuotta SF-elokuvia', *SF-Uutiset* 1/1944: 12.
10. 'SF:n toiminnan lopettaminen', *Uusi Suomi*, 15 December 1965.
11. Kalevi Koukkunen, email to the author 25 May 2021. Koukkunen's esimation is based on his extensive interviews with Mauno Mäkelä in 1983.
12. On the Hollywood central producer system, see Bordwell, Staiger and Thompson 1985: 134–7; on the comparison between Finnish and American producer systems, see Nieminen 2004: 69–73.
13. Hupaniittu 2019a: 20–31.
14. Nieminen 2004: 72–3.
15. Wuolijoki wrote her plays under the pseudonym of Juhani Tervapää, but soon after the premiere of *The Women of Niskavuori* (1936), her identity seems to have become an open secret.
16. Uusitalo 1999: 92.
17. Von Bagh 1991a: 17.
18. Uusitalo 1975, 57–8.
19. Uusitalo 1988, 187.
20. Uusitalo 1975: 195.
21. Von Bagh 1991b.
22. Von Bagh and Riikonen 1990: 25
23. Töyri 1983: 241.
24. Ibid.: 74.

25. Uusitalo 1992: 33.
26. Mäkelä 1996.
27. Ibid.: 116.
28. Elo 1996: 36.
29. Von Bagh 1992a: 39.
30. Suomi-Filmi's board meeting 20 October 1936. Suomi-Filmi Collection, Helsinki: National Audiovisual Archive.
31. Suomi-Filmi's board meeting 12 November 1936. Suomi-Filmi Collection, Helsinki: National Audiovisual Archive.
32. This estimation is based on the figures given in *Suomen tilastollinen vuosikirja* 1938: 294.
33. Suomi-Filmi's board meeting 15 August 1940. Suomi-Filmi Collection, Helsinki: National Audiovisual Archive.
34. Matti Kassila, an interview by Kalevi Koukkunen, Kimmo Laine and Juha Seitajärvi, 5 February 2013. Considering inflation and the mounting cost of living, Kassila's salary at Suomen Filmiteollisuus is relatively comparable with what Vaala earned at Suomi-Filmi in 1943.
35. Suomi-Filmi's board meeting 21 January 1937. Suomi-Filmi Collection, Helsinki: National Audiovisual Archive.
36. Suomi-Filmi's board meeting 28 June 1938. Suomi-Filmi Collection, Helsinki: National Audiovisual Archive.
37. Suomi-Filmi's board meeting 24 February 1943. Suomi-Filmi Collection, Helsinki: National Audiovisual Archive.
38. Firinä: 'Vihreiltä laitumilta palatessa', *Teatterimaailma* 6–7/1938: 111.
39. Santakari 2019b: 139, 145.
40. KAR: 'Suomen sotaisten muistojen vaalija', *Seura* 16/1939, 6–7.
41. Suomi-Filmi's board meeting 20 October 1936. Suomi-Filmi Collection, Helsinki: National Audiovisual Archive.
42. Suomi-Filmi's board meeting 15 February 1938. Suomi-Filmi Collection, Helsinki: National Audiovisual Archive.
43. Mäkelä 1996: 140–1.
44. Suomi-Filmi's board meeting 15 February 1938. Suomi-Filmi Collection, Helsinki: National Audiovisual Archive.
45. Suomi-Filmi's board meeting 28 June 1938. Suomi-Filmi Collection, Helsinki: National Audiovisual Archive.
46. Nieminen 2004: 168–9.
47. Suomi-Filmi's board meetings 14 March and 9 May 1941. Suomi-Filmi Collection, Helsinki: National Audiovisual Archive.
48. Suomi-Filmi's board meeting 14 July 1943. Suomi-Filmi Collection, Helsinki: National Audiovisual Archive.
49. Ibid.
50. 'Suunnitelma suomalaisen elokuvan tukemiseksi', *Suomen Kinolehti* 10–12/1944: 192.
51. Uusitalo 1965: 145.
52. Von Bagh 1991b.
53. Töyri 1983: 71.

54. Ibid.: 51, 167, 265.
55. Kassila 2004: 216–17.
56. Lounela 2004: 292–3.
57. Toni 1950: 7–8.
58. Töyri 1983: 243–4.
59. Ibid.: 157–62.
60. Ibid.: 144–6.
61. Ibid.: 265, 275.
62. 'Vartalon kauneuskilpailu', *Filmiaitta* 16–17/1927: 269.
63. 'Filmitähdet koulunpenkillä', *Suomi-Filmin Uutisaitta* 8–9/1940: 4–5; 'SF perustaa filmikoulun', *SF-Uutiset* 1/1938: 5–7.
64. Pennanen 2019: 119–30.
65. Mäkelä 1996: 135–6.
66. Laine 1973: 180.
67. Contracts between Suomi-Filmi and Ansa Ikonen 28 June 1935; 16 January 1936; 15 May 1936. Suomi-Filmi Collection, Helsinki: National Audiovisual Archive. A contract between Suomen Filmiteollisuus and Ansa Ikonen 8 September 1936. Suomen Filmiteollisuus Collection, Helsinki: National Audiovisual Archive.
68. A contract between Suomi-Filmi and Ansa Ikonen 16 January 1936. Suomi-Filmi Collection, Helsinki: National Audiovisual Archive.
69. See, for example, Film-fan: 'Ansa Ikonen ja hänen pikku Katriinansa ovat hyviä ystäviä', *Elokuva-Aitta* 15–16/1942: 280–1.
70. Questionnaire survey 22 (1975), K22/379. Helsinki: Finnish Heritage Agency.
71. Questionnaire survey 22 (1975), K22/688. Helsinki: Finnish Heritage Agency.
72. Dyer 1979: 49–50.
73. Santakari 2019a: 116.
74. Lindman 1992: 94.
75. See Seitajärvi 2019: 94.
76. Von Bagh 1993b.
77. Von Bagh 1991b.
78. Töyri 1983: 72.
79. Von Bagh 1991b.
80. Ibid.
81. Lindman 1992: 94.
82. Palo 1969: 102.
83. Koskimies 1972: 380–2.
84. Von Bagh 1999b.
85. Palo 1969: 112.
86. Ikonen 1980: 99.
87. Von Bagh 1991b; Elo 1996: 29; Kalemaa 2008: 21.

## Chapter 5

# Genres, cycles and series

While the output of Finnish film industry was so limited that it hardly makes sense to speak of genuinely domestic genres, indigenous interpretations of such transnational genres as crime films, musicals, screwball comedies or melodramas were common. In general, however, I would suggest that Finnish studio cinema did not rely heavily on fixed genres, but rather invested in more limited and short-lived groupings of films that can be characterised as cycles, sequels and series. This chapter explores the strategies employed by Finnish film studios to plan their output, be it in the long run (production levels or genres), the short run (sequels) or somewhere in between (cycles or series). Special attention is paid to the lumberjack film, which is arguably the only domestic film genre, the cycles of historical dramas, problem films and Schlager films, and three long-lasting series: Family Suominen (1941–59), Pekka Puupää (1953–60) and Inspector Palmu (1960–9).

## Classifying films

One of the frequently discussed topics in Finnish film journals during the studio years was film criticism itself. Who was qualified to write reviews? Should domestic films be approached according to the same principles as international films? What were the general criteria of a good film?

The first question divided reviewers, other journalists and filmmakers sharply. While reviewers obviously defended their profession – explaining the undeniably varied quality of reviews by the lack of schooling – high-brow journalists often attacked the reviewers openly. A telling nickname for a newspaper review was a 'cognac critique', referring to the practice of the studios giving lavishly serviced press screenings: the implication was that the film producers provided the reviewers with delicious foods and drinks in order to get favourable reviews. Filmmakers, too, seemed to have a less than a flattering opinion of reviewers, albeit for different reasons. The nickname 'errand boy critique' implied that the filmmakers and producers assumed that film reviewing was held in such low esteem in newspapers that a review could be written by anyone who was available. This insinuation was even captured in a film. The comedy *Am I in a Harem?* (SF 1938) features a self-reflexive scene in an editorial office in which an errand boy is sent to a cinema. A conversation ensues between a newspaperman and the errand boy:

> Newspaperman: Listen, Kalle, they've remade the 'Harem' [the first adaptation of the play *Am I in a Harem?* was made in 1932]. Go and see it, and write a review for tomorrow's paper.
> Errand boy: Can I take my gal with me?
> Newspaperman: Sure, here you have free tickets for two.

The status of domestic films among the film offerings varied considerably during the studio years. During the 1920s and 1930s, domestic films were generally handled with kid gloves, as if building a strong national cinema was a common project shared by critics as well as by filmmakers and the cultural authorities. During, and increasingly after, World War II, as the aesthetic ideals of, for example, Italian neorealism gained ground among critics, the privileged status of domestic production started to falter. Domestic national cinema became a problem to be solved rather than a goal to achieve, as it had been previously.

As for the general criteria for a good film, a typical way to evaluate a film, especially during the first period of the studio era, was to weigh it as a representative of its kind. Just what was meant by 'its kind' was seldom specified, but usually it was a question of rather broad categories, as is implied by this article from 1938:

> It should not be too hard to draw up a few categories according to the elements of, say, drama, humour and farce, and then place the film one is reviewing into one of these categories and award it 'one to ten points'. It is quite astonishing that the necessity of even such a basic classification has not been considered; instead, a Finnish film has been merely a Finnish film, a unitary and undivided concept. This being the case, are we to think that reviewing has fulfilled its responsible duty?[1]

Classifying films into two or three broad categories was, indeed, common. Suomen Filmiteollisuus used the categories of drama and comedy in a complementary manner to justify its production decisions. Month after month, the company pondered on the boundaries of 'light' and 'serious' art, not denying the existence of these categories, but questioning their exclusiveness. A serious drama could and should entertain on the one hand, it was claimed, and humour could be both sublime and topical, on the other, and offer 'something that is essential for the Finnish character'.[2] In the autumn of 1939, after the outbreak of World War II and shortly before the release of the military comedy *Serenade with a War Trumpet*, Särkkä wrote in an editorial in *SF-Uutiset*:

> The Finnish people have always loved their army. Never have they loved it as they do now. The reception of SF's previous military film, *The Regiment's Trouble-Boy* [1938], was an immediate reflection of the affection our nation has for its soldiers. Premiering at the moment this magazine comes out, *Serenade with a War Trumpet* is even more 'a picture for today'. It, too, is lively, high-spirited, frisky and funny – it, too, will sow the seeds of good humour among the people.[3]

Interestingly enough, the same basic division between drama (or melodrama) and comedy (or farce) – melodrama and farce being used in a pejorative sense – was often adopted by the next generation of critics commenting on studio cinema in the 1960s and 1970s. 'Production of old Finnish Cinema was characterised by an ironclad duality,' wrote Markku Koski in 1977: 'what was made was either serious or light, either farce or melodrama' – nothing in between, as in post-studio modernism. According to Koski, dramas were meant to polish both the medium's and the producer's image, whereas with comedies the producer intended to make money.[4] This is obviously not entirely untrue; in fact, Särkkä's claim that comedies had serious aspirations too might be seen to back this idea – why else make excuses for producing entertainment? On the other hand, not all serious dramas were made for prestige reasons only. Quite the contrary: historical dramas like *February Manifesto* (SF 1939) and *Activists* (SuFi 1939), in particular, were among the most successful films of their time.

The ideological backdrop for the contemporary views on 'the kinds' of films expressed by the producers differed naturally from that of the critics writing from the critical perspective of the 1970s. Whereas for the former, all films, be they dramas or comedies, were 'flesh out of their own flesh' for domestic audiences,[5] for the latter they represented, regardless of the mode, an illusory reality embellished by bourgeois hegemony, a version of the world without contradiction.[6] Nonetheless, what was common to both views was a tendency to emphasise standardisation and downplay differences between films, to reduce all studio films to comedies and (melo)dramas that, in the last resort, all served the same purpose, whether it was labelled as reinforcing national unity or bolstering bourgeois views of the world.

Yet, despite such views, not all studio films were the same, either from contemporary or subsequent perspectives. Insomuch as the film industry emphasised unity of both its products and its audiences, it did so mainly for the sake of nationalist rhetorics. In practice, films were differentiated in many ways and for many purposes, in order to organise production and attract different audiences. As for subsequent views, from the 1980s on, critics and scholars have been much more willing to adopt a genre perspective on the studio era than during the immediate post-studio decades. Book-length studies have been conducted on, for example, Finnish children's films,[7] melodramas,[8] military comedies,[9] women's films,[10] Schlager films,[11] road movies[12] and biopics[13].

The aim of this chapter is to discuss product standardisation and differentiation from both contemporary and subsequent points of view. Of the mechanisms of classification discussed here, production levels and cycles were primarily the film industry's own ways for organising production, whereas the perspective of genre, in the Finnish context, was more often adopted by later critics than by the industry. The fourth category, series, was the one that connected the perspectives of producers, viewers and critics more than any other did.

Generally, these different forms of film classification are based on varying parameters. First, is the classification historical or theoretical,[14] that is, did it exist at the time when the film was produced, or was it constructed retrospectively? A textbook example of a historical genre is film noir, categorised and labelled as such by European critics only years after the emergence of the films themselves in Hollywood in the early 1940s. Only decades later still did film historians extend the concept of film noir to cover pessimistic, low-key crime films made in Japan, Europe – including Finland – and elsewhere during the 1940s and 1950s.[15]

Second, who or what is behind the classification? Some genres and other categories lead back to other media (lumberjack film that can be traced to the popular stage and literature), while some find their form in the practices of film production itself (the social problem film), and others still are constructed by critics (the rillumarei film).[16]

Third, is the classification based on national or transnational practices? Regardless of the enormous national significance of *The Unknown Soldier* (SF 1955), it was still a war film that shared genre conventions with many war films coming from other film-producing countries. *At the Rovaniemi Fair* (SF 1951), on the contrary, related very little to low-brow comedies made elsewhere and made sense mainly in relation to other Finnish rillumarei films and rillumarei culture.

Fourth, is the classification descriptive or prescriptive? A filmmaker's, as well as a critic's, attitude towards classification can be either neutral and flexible or restrictive and normative.[17] When Särkkä got hold of Reino Helismaa's script *Caught and Held Fast* about two silly inventors, he decided to change their names to Pekka and Pätkä, add a subtitle *The New Adventures of Pekka and Pätkä*, and mould the script to fit the ongoing series of Pekka Puupää comedies. In 1955, the series was still new and flexible enough to fit in a relatively different script. However, when the director of the series, Armand Lohikoski, offered his own script 'Pekka and Pätkä in the Maelstrom of Politics' a few years later, Särkkä turned it down, thus signalling that the template for the series had grown normative and unable to contain a political satire.

Fifth, is the classification exclusive or inclusive?[18] As we shall see, rillumarei is sometimes discussed as a limited corpus of only five or six films, and sometimes as a broad category that covers most low-brow comedies made between the late 1940s and early 1960s. There is, of course, a general difference in scale involved here: while genres and cycles in Hollywood, or even in a big European country like Great Britain, Italy or France, might consist of dozens or hundreds of films, in a small nation like Finland the volume of film production is always relatively low. Therefore, an exclusive classification would easily lead to very small corpuses.

## As, Bs and Cs

The concept of production level is used here to refer to the way film companies organised their overall production, with production costs and cultural status as decisive factors. At the one end of the scale were elaborate prestige films with high production values; at the other end were quickly made farces.

Even if the division into A and B productions was never as systematic as it was in Hollywood (as the double bill system never took root in

Finland), it is evident that, from the 1930s on, the majors made a distinction between prestige films and other kinds of films. The fact that Suomen Filmiteollisuus attempted to downplay this distinction at first, as discussed above, proves the point. One of the few existing documents that articulate this classification clearly – dividing films into not two but three categories – is an unsigned proposal from 1949 for new production practices at Suomi-Filmi:

> The classification would mostly be based on the technical quality and the cost of the film: the 'major films' of A-level, the 'ordinary' art films of B-level, the 'undemanding' popular films of C-level ... The only prerequisite for level C is that the film is produced as cheaply and quickly (which, of course, is the same thing!) as possible and that neither artistic achievement nor prestige status is pursued; rather, the initial aim is to rely on certain limited sales and, as a result, immediate profits. Such movies could be used as a means to try out new directors and give them a chance to improve their skills, as well as to perform other kinds of experiments.[19]

This document is formulated as a proposal, but actually it can be seen as an attempt to systematise a practice that had been in use since the late 1930s both in the major and the minor studios; for obvious financial reasons, though, the minors usually specialised in B- or C-level films. Thus, on the production level, feature film output during the studio years can be roughly divided into three categories:

1. Prestige films (major films or A-level films, as in the document quoted above)
2. Social problem films (ordinary art films or B-level films)
3. Popular films (undemanding films or C-level films).

At the core of prestige productions were historical films like *February Manifesto* (SF 1939), *The Activists* (SuFi 1939) or *The Dance Over the Graves* (SF 1950), literary adaptations like *The Village Shoemakers* (SuFi 1923 and 1957; SF 1938), *Seven Brothers* (SF 1939) or *Children of the Wilderness* (Fennada 1954), and, especially during the 1920s, 'ethnographic' depictions of folk life like *Anna-Liisa* (SuFi 1922) or *The Logroller's Bride* (SuFi 1923 and 1937).

Like Hollywood's A-productions, Finnish prestige films were the companies' flagships. Not only were they the most expensive and elaborately crafted films, but they were also the most efficiently marketed ones (Figure 5.1). While other films were marketed as embodiments of a

**Figure 5.1** *Activists* (1939): a rail built for an elaborate diagonal tracking shot.

genre, cycle or series, a prestige film would rather be treated as a unique achievement, as one of a kind. With reference to national cinema, prestige films were promoted as the most national of all the films. In a typically emotive, yet cleverly effective rhetoric, Suomen Filmiteollisuus declared that *February Manifesto* starred 'the Finnish People',[20] thus indicating that it was not only about the people but also of the people and by the people. The marketing campaign implied that watching *February Manifesto* was almost a national duty. Schoolteachers, for example, were encouraged to ensure that all their pupils had a chance to see the film.[21]

Among the aims of prestige films was to enhance the cultural status of both the producer and the film medium. This would not only win over the educated middle class and the cultural elite, but also please the authorities in the hope of favourable tax decisions or even state subsidies. Yet, gaining prestige was far from being the only motive for making A-level films. High production values guaranteed elaborate settings and spectacular scenes for historical and ethnographic films, and the high-brow novels and plays adapted for screen usually contained romance (*Silja – Fallen Asleep When Young*, Adams-Filmi 1937, Veikko Itkonen 1956) or humour (*The Village Shoemakers*). Often, prestige films were among the most successful films. *February Manifesto*, for example, was seen by more than 700,000 viewers,[22] about twice as many as an average domestic film in the 1930s. The popular success of prestige films was often boosted by reports of grand opening nights, attended by not only film people but also the cultural and political elite. President Kyösti Kallio's presence at the premiere of *Activists* in April 1939 was widely reported in the press,[23] as well as in the short film *Kevätkatsaus* (1939) produced by Suomi-Filmi itself.

The willingness to address as large audiences as possible is the probable explanation for the rather small role played by religion in prestige films, even if Finnish nationalism in general was characterised by religious undertones. During the 1918 Civil War and the interwar decades, the Church had clearly sided with the bourgeois 'white' Finland and acted as its moral mouthpiece. In cultural debates, the church intellectuals had adopted a critical stance towards aesthetic modernism, psychoanalysis, vitalism and other trends favoured by the liberal intelligentsia. Even cinema as a medium aroused suspicion in the minds of some religious debaters. It is no wonder, then, that religious themes were largely avoided in films, as the position of religion among such integral parts of the potential film audience as the working class and the liberal intellectuals was ambiguous. The main exceptions to this are films about marginalised revivalist groups (*As Dream and Shadow*, SF 1937; *The Logroller's Bride*) and a few wartime films like *The Transfigured Heart* (SuFi 1943), about the inner conflict of a priest who has an obligation to serve at the front while feeling responsible for his parish, too.

The caution with which the film companies treated religious themes did not mean that they categorically avoided contentious issues. On the contrary, the B-level films in particular, almost by definition, capitalised on contradiction. Suomen Filmiteollisuus announced in 1938 that it had broadened its repertoire considerably during the previous year, indicating that the categories 'light' and 'serious' were not enough to describe the whole output of the company. The third group of films was characterised in terms of psychology, social awareness, ethicalness and artistry. In other words, this group consisted of films that were to be described as 'problem films' or 'social problem films'. Of all the studio films, problem films were the ones that most keenly tackled the topical issues of the day. Therefore, problem films emerged in cycles, arising frequently throughout the studio years, from the psychological turn Suomen Filmiteollisuus announced in the late 1930s, through the post-war 'multi-problem' films, to the youth problem films of the late studio era.

The basic inner contradiction of problem films was that on the flipside of the topicality and artistry was sensationalism. In the eyes of the contemporary film reviewers, there was often a thin line between artistic inclination and social awareness on the one hand, and sensationalist marketability on the other. In a typical attack on mainstream problem films, young critics Jörn Donner and Martti Savo claimed in 1953 that Finnish problem films did not rise from social reality. The problems highlighted in these films, as well as the 'arty' image of the films, were primarily a means to deceive film reviewers and the censorship office, that is, to ensure favourable reviews and a tax reduction. In reality, argued Donner and Savo, the social relevance of the films was shallow and based on the producers' ambition to make a profit. The model for depicting, for example, contemporary crime was not adopted from social analysis, but rather from Hollywood films, which, for their part, based their depiction of crime on genre conventions, not on reality.[24] Thus, Finnish crime films were twice removed from real contemporary problems.

The term used in the anonymous Suomi-Filmi document for B-level films, 'ordinary art films', is interesting. 'Ordinary' probably connotes two things. First, these films were ordinary, since they dealt with topical issues and everyday life, however inadequate their aspiration towards realism might have seemed in the eyes of young critics. And second, they were ordinary in the sense that they were not prestige films, which, by definition, were special and exceptional, not ordinary. On the other hand, these films were considered 'art', since, while prestige films represented the cutting edge in filmmaking, one was more likely to find stylistic experiments and innovations, or the 'French style', in problem films. Thus, the phrase 'ordinary art film' connotes an oxymoron by referring to something that was ordinary and extraordinary at the same time.

The most typical C-level films were comedies and farces with the lowest production values and the lowest cultural status. According to the Suomi-Filmi document, subjects for these undemanding popular films could easily be found in romantic and comic novels of the 'weekly magazine kind'.[25] In addition to such novels, the popular stage was a fruitful source for, for example, military comedies, starting with *The Regiment's Trouble-Boy* (SF 1938) that owed at least part of its huge success to the original play (1933), performed in dozens of theatres from the 1930s to the 1960s.

It has to be noted, though, that not all comedies were counted as C-level quickies. Suomi-Filmi, especially, produced comedies with high production values across the decades. Sophisticated, well-made comedies with top stars and lavish sets, often directed by Valentin Vaala, were actually among the trademarks of the company. Vaala's comedies like *Surrogate Wife* (SuFi 1936), *The Bride Springs a Surprise* (SuFi 1941), *Gabriel, Come Back* (SuFi 1951) or *The Apple Falls* (SuFi 1952) gained not only large audiences but also favourable reviews. They were generally praised for their craftsmanship, and in some occasions (*Hulda from Juurakko*, SuFi 1937)[26] also for their social relevance.

Moreover, not all C-level films were comedies. Minor and independent companies sometimes produced adventure films (*The King of Karmankolo*, Suomen Kuvatuote 1937) or melodramas (*The Secret of the Summer Night*, Fenno-Filmi 1945) with low production values. The latter was, quite typically, greeted by reviewers as a poorly made, daydream-like adaptation of a 'Friday-magazine story'.[27] Another indicator of the low prestige value of the C-film was provided by the State Film Censorship Board, which defined not only the ratings but also the taxation of the films. Whereas prestige films were (depending on the period) usually either tax-free or lightly taxed, C-level films were the ones that were in the danger of being punished with the 'penalty tax', whatever the genre. Therefore, however low the production costs might have been, C-level films were not necessarily an easy way to make profits.

## Genres

In relation to the cinema of a small nation, genre obviously means something quite different from what it might in Hollywood or a big European production country. Even if the film industry had wanted to invest in nationally exclusive genres (which is doubtful), a yearly output of ten to thirty films left little room for fully fledged domestic genres. As far as the notion of genre is meaningful in the context of Finnish cinema, this is mainly in relation to trans- or international, and in some cases intermedial, genres.

Yet, as regards Finnish film historiography, there has been a great amount of interest in genres. Veijo Hietala, one of the advocates of the notion of domestic genres, has paid special attention to two groups of films, lumberjack films and vagabond films.[28] These could, admittedly, be counted as the closest Finnish cinema got to nationally distinctive genres. Lumberjack films were made from the early 1920s all through the studio years. Taking the form of either melodrama or comedy, they are male-centred narratives about a group of men cutting wood and floating logs down the river to saw mills (although the destination of the logs is seldom an issue in these films). Typically, lumberjack films focus on romances between these men and the women they encounter while rolling down the river, and on conflicts between the men and the local communities, often prejudiced against the seemingly rootless loggers. Within this framework, lumberjack films raised topical issues of modernity concerning, for example, whether the rapids should run free and left untouched, or whether they should be harnessed to generate electric power. Interestingly, and perhaps illustrating the ambiguity of the problem, the films provided diverse solutions to this. While films like *We're Coming Back* (SF 1953) and *Oh, Do You Remember...?* (SuFi 1954) clearly imply that building a power plant is a positive development for the riverside community, *Two Old Lumberjacks* (SF 1954), written by Reino Helismaa, the same screenwriter who wrote *We're Coming Back* a year earlier, takes the opposite stance. The protagonist, a stressed-out forest industrialist, returns to the lumber camp of his youth only to realise that what this film represents as a traditional way of life in the woods, driving logs, is worth saving. As a result, he cancels his plans to harness the river.

One is not likely to find generic equivalents to the lumberjack film in other film cultures, apart from occasional individual films; Luis Trenker's *Der verlorene Sohn* (Germany, 1934) with a lumberjack protagonist going to America during the Great Depression might be a case in point. Therefore it is paradoxical that the cinematic prototype of the genre is considered to be Mauritz Stiller's *The Song of the Scarlet Flower*, made in Sweden in 1919. Successful as this film was around the world as one of the key works of the 'golden age' of Swedish cinema, it did not launch a genre in Sweden. In Finland, however, it was influential to the point that, as argued by Jaakko Seppälä, it inspired a logrolling scene to be added to *Anna-Liisa* (1922), which was based on a famous play with no such scene.[29] From there on, logrolling was seen in many films.

At the time, *The Song of the Scarlet Flower* was often considered almost as a domestic film in Finland. Not only was Stiller born in Helsinki, but the film was adapted from a Finnish novel (1905) by Johannes Linnankoski. Along with Teuvo Pakkala's play *The Log Drivers* (1899, filmed in 1928, 1937 and 1951) and Väinö Kataja's novel *The Logroller's Bride* (1914, filmed in 1923 and 1937), Linnankoski's novel introduced most of the themes and narrative conventions of the lumberjack genre. These include the tension between the traditional agrarian community and the lumberjacks, who floated down the river and represented modern paid work and freedom from tradition, as well as the use of the free-flowing river as a symbol of unbound sexuality. Lumberjack films invested in such themes, with the added value of the spectacular logrolling scenes. *The Song of the Scarlet Flower* itself became one of the most popular sources for film adaptations in Nordic countries, with three versions in Sweden (1919, 1934 and 1956) and two in Finland (1938 and 1971).[30]

The intermedial background for vagabond films is not as straightforward as that of lumberjack films. The immediate inspiration is considered to be the song 'Vagabond's Waltz' by J. Alfred Tanner, based on a Swedish tune. It provided a starting point for a script commissioned by Särkkä and written by the author Mika Waltari in 1941. The script combined vagabond romance, embodied by Tanner's song, with various other ingredients such as Romani and country house romance, known from nineteenth century fiction, and became a hugely successful package: with 1.2 million attendances, *The Vagabond's Waltz* (SF 1941) remained the biggest box-office hit in Finland until 1955, when *The Unknown Soldier* (SF) broke all previous records. *The Vagabond's Waltz* is a story of a nineteenth-century nobleman named Arnold who, having wounded a Russian officer in a duel, is forced to leave his home and become an unknown vagabond wondering from one adventure and from one romance to another. Finally, he falls in love with Countess Helena, wins her love and, with his Romani allies, steals her away from her unwanted wedding before revealing his real identity.

The phenomenal success of *The Vagabond's Waltz* has traditionally been explained as escapism and nostalgia, as an invitation to a romantic, exciting and relatively harmonious world contrasting with the dreary reality of the war years. True, Suomen Filmiteollisuus invested everything that it had in the film: as many as forty-two lavish sets were designed for the film, which was very unusual (only the historical dramas of the late 1930s like *February Manifesto* and *Activists* came close to that), and it featured the most popular star couple in Finland, Ansa Ikonen as Helena and Tauno Palo as Arnold, both at the peak of their careers (Figure 5.2). On the other hand, despite the historical setting, the film tangled with contemporary issues, at least indirectly. For example, like in many other historical films of the period, Russians are represented in a dubious light. The Russian officer whom Arnold confronts in a duel appears to be inferior to Arnold and initially tries to cheat. Even if actual commenting on the ongoing war

**Figure 5.2** Still from *The Vagabond's Waltz* (1941).

with the Soviet Union was restricted by the Censorship Board and was relatively rare in fictional films, innuendos like this were commonplace. Another topical issue indirectly touched upon in *The Vagabond's Waltz* was that of social mobility. Even though we know all the time that Arnold is a baron, the film toys with the possibility that a countess would elope with a penniless vagabond and that a baron would ally himself with travelling Romani people. Such testing of established social relations was in fact as common in lumberjack films as in the later vagabond films. Both *The Song of the Scarlet Flower* and *The Log Drivers* already introduce a central character who presents himself as a common penniless lumberjack and wins the heart of the daughter of a wealthy farmer, before revealing that he himself is actually an heir to the prosperous farm. As these turn-of-the-century examples remind us, testing social boundaries was, on the one hand, a long-term theme that had to do with the restructuring of social and class relations in modernity and, on the other hand, also highly topical, since the ongoing war brought new pressures for national unity, solidarity and equality in a country that had suffered a terrible civil war just over two decades earlier (1918).

The genre status of the vagabond film is less clear than that of the lumberjack film. Not only is there no noteworthy literary or theatrical tradition to back up the films, but the actual number of vagabond films remained low through the studio years. In spite of its phenomenal success, *The Vagabond's Waltz* did not inspire competing studios to try their luck with vagabond stories until the 1950s, with *The Vagabond's Girl* (SuFi 1952), *Vagabond King* (Fennada 1953) and *The Vagabond's Mazurka* (Fennada 1958). Somewhat surprisingly, even Suomen Filmiteollisuus itself did not return to vagabond films after its successful start, but rather invested in country house romance in films like *Beautiful Regina of Kaivopuisto* (1941, starring Tauno Palo) and *Catherine and the Count of Munkkiniemi* (1943), with no vagabond themes. This indicates that *The Vagabond's Waltz* was originally not associated with a vagabond genre, and to the extent that it launched such a genre, this was only years later. The subsequent notion that the vagabond film was one of the major genres in Finnish studio cinema is therefore based on the iconic position *The Vagabond's Waltz* gained in Finnish film history, rather than on the actual number of vagabond films. In film historical memory, *The Vagabond's Waltz* came to represent much more than itself.

Whatever their actual genre status, lumberjack films and vagabond films are among the relatively rare groups of films that are often considered as genuine domestic film genres; this is demonstrated in standard reviews accompanying the regular television screenings of these films. Military comedy, too, might be considered domestic in origin by current reviewers. However, in the view of contemporary critics from the 1930s to the 1950s, it was quite clear that Finnish military comedy was a hybrid of various national and transnational elements. It combined ingredients from classic literature, for example from the comic parts of Johan Ludvig Runeberg's war epic *Fänrik Ståls sägner/The Tales of Ensign Stål* (1848/1860), from army-related comical plays that had been popular in Finland on both the professional and amateur stage from the 1910s on, and from the dozens of film comedies imported from Germany, France, United States and, especially, Sweden. The transnationality of this seemingly national genre is indicated by the fact that popular stories could be remade in various countries, the case in point being the Finnish comedy *The Little Bride of the Garrison* (Karhu-Filmi 1943), based on the Swedish film *65, 66 and I* (1936), based on a Danish stage play of the same name (1935) by Axel Frische. The shared origin did not mean that there were no local or topical differences between the versions, though. Especially during the war years,

Finnish military comedies were expected to be more solemn and patriotic in mood than their counterparts in the politically neutral Sweden.[31]

In general, genres were not the primary way of classifying films during the studio era. While critics were, at least occasionally, inclined to pinpoint either domestic genres or local variations of international genres, the film industry itself was seldom eager to promote genres as such. As Rick Altman argues in his distinguished revisionist account of film genres, even Hollywood, which is usually considered the stronghold of genre filmmaking, was often reluctant to classify films into clearly defined genres. Especially big-budget A-movies tended to combine diverse elements like adventure, romance and comedy rather than focus on one generic element only, thus addressing as many audience segments as possible. In this ongoing process, genres were in constant movement, changing and hybridising all the time, intentionally blurred in their boundaries.[32]

Something similar can be said of the Finnish film studios. Genres were utilised in promoting films, by hints and allusions in posters and taglines for example, but they were seldom mentioned explicitly. In addition to such allusions, film advertisements were dominated by stars, sometimes by directors, or, in the case of adaptations of popular or prestigious literary works, by authors. A case in point is the musical. While retrospective accounts tend to agree that a number of musicals were made during the studio years (Jorma Kakko argues that, in terms of narrative, most post-war comedies made by Suomen Filmiteollisuus could be counted as musicals[33]), the term was seldom used by the film studios. Of the two early 1940s examples most often referred to as musicals in film histories, *Poretta, or the Emperor's New Points* (SuFi 1941) was called a 'jubilee with music' by Suomi-Filmi and a 'revue' by several critics. *SF Parade* (SF 1940) was not marketed as belonging to a particular genre either, but rather as a star vehicle for Tauno Palo and Ansa Ikonen; both were known as singing as well as dramatic stars. The tagline of the poster states: 'Music, singing, dancing, joy and youth "over and under the roofs of Helsinki"! Something new in Finnish cinema.' Expectations concerning genre were thus channelled indirectly, not by referring to the genre itself, but rather to a well-known and highly valued individual film, René Clair's groundbreaking city-musical *Under the Roofs of Paris* (France 1930).

This strategy of not assigning a film to a genre extended well into the post-war years. In narrative terms, *We Songsters* (SF 1951), for example, is as much a backstage musical as *Poretta* or *SF Parade*, but concrete references to the musical genre were still absent. The poster of the film prioritises two elements. The first one is Henry Theel, a popular singer who starred as a singing actor in four feature films in the late 1940s and early 1950s. The second one is the Punainen Mylly ('Moulin Rouge'), a popular and controversial revue theatre that operated between 1946 and 1965. Even Punainen Mylly is not directly referred to in the advertisements, although the theatre is featured in the film itself; this is perhaps due to the fact that the theatre was in constant friction with the censorship authorities because of political and moral issues. Once again, the connection is created by allusions rather than references: by an image and the name of the director-actor Ossi Elstelä, who was the manager of the theatre, and an image of a scantily clad dancer, a distinctive feature of both Punainen Mylly and its Parisian prototype, the original Moulin Rouge.

Parallel to what Altman argues about Hollywood cinema, Finnish critics were often more disposed than the producers and distributors to classify films into genres. Even in the case of such narratively standardised groups of films as military comedies, the producers usually preferred free and descriptive characterisations to genre labels. *The Regiment's Trouble-Boy* was a 'piece of Finnish military life, coloured with sparkling humour', while its follow-up, *Serenade with a War Trumpet*, was a 'spirited movie about the defenders of Finland'. In the post-war years, emphasis shifted from the patriotic to the light-hearted, but still with no genre label. *Serenading Lieutenant* (SF 1949) offered, according to the producer, 'charming music, fabulously funny mishaps, singing, romance, humour'. Critics, however, had no trouble grouping all of these films as military comedies.[34]

To sum up, the Finnish film industry readily played with the audience's genre expectations by hinting at varying elements from different genres, be they cinematic or intermedial, domestic or transnational. Yet, individual films were rarely marketed as belonging to a particular genre, and genre was seldom a decisive factor in planning future productions. More important from the point of view of the producers were other means of regulating standardisation and differentiation: cycles and series.

## Cycles

In retrospect, the operational logic of the studio-era film companies might seem systematic and consistent. Certainly, the goal of the producers was to make well-reasoned long-term plans and stick to them. The everyday reality of filmmaking, however, was quite different. The core decades of studio filmmaking were made up of constant changes, ruptures and challenges: the internal and external crises arising from infighting within the companies, the periods of economic recession, World War II and its aftermath, the coming of television, rapid urbanisation and demographic transformation, and so on. Events and processes like these were a constant threat to the kind of stable and smooth development of filmmaking the film industry would undoubtedly have preferred. Therefore, disregarding the costliness and relative slowness of filmmaking, and notwithstanding the fact that certain individual film projects were a long time in the making, production decisions were often made quickly, based on ad hoc presumptions. This means that filmmaking was characterised most of all by the logic of cycles. Whatever their long-term plans, the producers were quick in reacting to:

1. their own successes – whenever an individual film proved successful, the possibility of a follow-up (same author, same characters, same thematic, etc.) was considered;
2. the successes of other Finnish production companies – producers were never shy about stealing, borrowing or adopting ideas from their competitors;
3. the successes of imported films – production companies were always as quick to respond to transnational as to domestic influences;
4. intermedial successes – the production companies always kept an eye on successful novels, plays, comic strips, songs and so on as possible sources for new kinds of films;
5. extra-cinematic changes – shifts in the cultural, social and political atmosphere impacted considerably on production decisions, sometimes with surprising rapidity.

Rick Altman defines film cycles as processes in which a production company combines elements from existing genres in a new way and keeps on testing these novel recipes, until they become relatively established – if they ever do. When a cycle begins to stabilise, it might develop into a genre, and it is at this point that other companies often begin to show interest and consider investing in the new-born genre.[35] Altman's analysis of the cycling process has been slightly challenged by, for example, Amanda Ann Klein, who, referring to numerous examples from both the studio and the post-studio eras, claims that Hollywood companies have always been anxious to sniff the air and react immediately to the successes of their competitors. Unlike Altman, Klein argues that a typical cycle does not stay under one company's control for long, but rather spreads throughout the industry. In this view, a cycle is more than just a vague phase before the establishment of a genre. It may be a quick and a passing fad, but it is also the standard mode of operation in Hollywood, and undoubtedly also in any other environment of film production that is built on the principles of rivalry and rapid profit-making. Cycles may develop into genres, but sometimes they just come and go, and this is all that is expected of them.[36]

Once again, too, the scale of the film cycle in Finnish cinema was very different from that in Hollywood. A typical Finnish film cycle consisted of a handful rather than dozens of films. Yet, the logic of cycles was quite similar: competition between studios was as essential to it as it was in Hollywood, according to Klein's analysis. This logic was, in fact, so well known at the time that it could be made fun of. In 1941, Suomen Filmiteollisuus noted with irony in *SF-Uutiset*, referring to characters from Finland's national epic, *Kalevala*: 'If one company makes a film about Väinämöinen, the other makes a film about Joukahainen.'[37] Matti Kassila tells an anecdote that affirms this practice from his early career as a film director. In 1950, Särkkä handed him a script he had adapted three years earlier of Artturi Leinonen's novel *It Happened in Ostrobothnia* (1920), a story that takes place among nineteenth-century farmers in the Ostrobothnia region. Kassila tried to resist but, as a novice director, he had no choice but to submit to the producer's demands. Only afterwards did he realise that the main reason for this production was that Suomi-Filmi had started shooting its own historical Ostrobothnia film, *Ten Men from Härmä* (1950), scripted by the same author. Särkkä was simply not willing to play second fiddle, even if Suomi-Filmi's production was released four months earlier than his, and proved to be more successful.[38]

Typical Finnish cycles, covering different phases of the studio era, include historical films of the late 1930s, problem films of the post-war era, rillumarei films of the early 1950s and the Schlager films from the last years of the studio era.

The short cycle of 1930s historical films started with the highly successful *A Yager's Bride* (Sufi 1938), based on a popular World War I adventure drama that contained many catchy songs. It was followed by *The Stolen Death* (directed by Nyrki Tapiovaara and produced by Erik

Blomberg 1938), an independent, stylishly innovative drama that takes place among the resistance movement in 1904, during the so-called first Russification period. In 1939, Suomen Filmiteollisuus produced *February Manifesto*, Suomi-Filmi *Activists*, and Jäger-Filmi *The Great Wrath*. The first is a story of Finnish resistance between 1899, when Czar Nicholas II issued a manifesto that radically decreased the autonomous status of Finland, and 1918, when Finland had gained independence and suffered a civil war. Like its source of inspiration, Frank Lloyd's *Cavalcade* (USA 1933), it follows the fate of two families, one from the upper class and the other from the working class. *Activists* is a patriotic adventure film, also about Finnish resistance, but it concentrates on the relations between Finns and Russians covering a shorter period of time just before and during the March Revolution in 1917. *The Great Wrath* goes further back in history, to the time of the Great Northern War in the early eighteenth century, when Russia occupied most of Finland, which, at the time, was part of the Swedish Empire.

As different as these historical films are from each other as regards mode, style and content, all of them are heavily involved with Finnish–Russian relations. The cycle of historical films was thus inspired not only by the success of *A Yager's Bride*, and by the critical acclaim received by historical epics like Jean Renoir's *La Marseillaise* (1938), but also by the political situation of the late 1930s. As political tensions increased both within Europe in general, and between Finland and the Soviet Union in particular, film producers responded by exploring the latter in historical terms. Even if these films were literally about pre-revolutionary Russia, it is obvious that their relevance for contemporary viewers was in the manner they mirrored Finnish–Soviet relations. Suomen Filmiteollisuus was, in fact, quite explicit in this regard, declaring in *SF-Uutiset*:

> The central idea of *February Manifesto* is that all layers of Finnish society – that is: Finns as a nation – have to recognise their most dangerous external threat: Russia. A vivid consciousness of this danger, and acting against the oppressor in all segments of the population, were the most powerful factors in the struggle for independence in Finland.[39]

Wavering between past and present tenses in this quote is hardly a mistake; Särkkä, who was personally responsible for many of the anonymous writings in *SF-Uutiset*, was an excellent writer, meticulous in his choice of words. While specifically writing about the struggle for independence of the first two decades of the century, Särkkä at the same time fed the sentiment of Russophobia that prevailed especially among the political Right.

The cycle-like nature of these films is highlighted by the fact that no fewer than three of these films were originally planned to have a similar prologue that would have covered the early stages of Finnish anti-Russian activism. In the end, *February Manifesto* was the only one that included such a montage sequence. The makers of *The Stolen Death* might have changed their plans regarding the prologue because, as politically leftist and liberal intellectuals, they were actually trying to avoid anti-Russian and anti-Soviet sentiments. In the case of *Activists*, the most probable explanation for the last-minute exclusion of the prologue is that *February Manifesto* opened just two months earlier, and comparison between the two films was unavoidable. Building a cycle requires an amount of similarity, but this would have been too much.

The cycle of historical films was quick and intense: in a precise sense, it was over by the end of 1939. Even if these prestige films were among the most laborious projects initiated at the time, the producers reacted surprisingly swiftly to the demand for such films; this was, of course, possible only because of the unforeseen boom in the film industry generally. Conversely, during the war years, investing in such huge productions would have been more difficult due to the lack of material resources. In terms of political content and explicit anti-Russian sentiments, the war years brought a new cautiousness, perhaps paradoxically, as we shall see in Chapter 7. This does not mean, however, that historical films stopped being produced once and for all. The emphasis merely changed from explicitly political themes to biopics of cultural figures (*The King of Poets and the Bird of Passage*, SF 1940, about the poet Johan Ludvig Runeberg; *Ballad*, SF 1944, about the composer Fredrik Pacius) or costume dramas (*The Wagabond Waltz, Beautiful Regina of Kaivopuisto, Catherine and the Count of Munkkiniemi, White Roses*, SF 1943, *The Green Chamber of Linnais*, SuFi 1945). Since all of these films take place in the nineteenth century, when Finland was a grand duchy under the Russian czar, most of them touch on the theme of Finnish–Russian relations in some way or another. However, as we have seen when discussing *The Vagabond's Waltz*, this was done in a more subtle and allusive way than in the political-oriented historical films.

The post-war problem film was a transnational phenomenon, combining realist aesthetics and topical (often also somewhat sensational) social problems with an ominous and melodramatic mode. Often, an element of crime was involved, and in many respects the problem film morphed into what was later to be known as film noir, first with regard to Hollywood, and later, increasingly also to the rest of the filmmaking world.[40]

Problem films had first emerged much earlier than during the post-war years: the first considerable cycle of Finnish problem films was produced in the late 1930s. In 1938, a commentator under the pseudonym Niko suggested in *Elokuva-Aitta* that Finnish cinema should follow the example of French filmmakers and 'step closer to living and topical themes'. There was no lack of themes worthy of handling in film; as examples he mentioned the language problem (tensions between Finnish-speaking and Swedish-speaking Finns), the flood of new students and other problems faced by youth, the rapid demographic movement from country to city, 'mental unemployment' and the assumed immaturity of Finnish culture. What the writer demanded was not general pondering on the question of good and evil, but rather more precise perspectives on contemporary issues.[41] In other words, there should be more realism and less melodrama.

As if in answer to Niko's critique (and possibly answering quite literally), Suomen Filmiteollisuus soon after outlined its goals for the 1938–9 season:

> The eight films SF will release this year result from a determined choice. It is remarkable that seven of these belong to the 'serious' side of films ... Considering that *Are They Guilty?* is a modern psychological art film; that *A Stranger Came into the House* and *The Village Shoemakers* represent classical depictions of folk life; that *Forward – Toward Life* is a social-oriented drama of ideas; that *God's Doom* is an ethically artistic depiction of the soul; that *February Manifesto* is an epic national drama; and that *Scorned* is an artistic action drama touching on the language problem and the Finlandisation of economic life, it is easy to see that SF has expanded its sphere of operation considerably in just one year.[42]

Even if not all of these films could easily count as a problem film, the use of such terms as 'modern', 'psychological' or 'social-oriented' suggests a general turn towards greater realism and a desire to deal with topical issues. This proved to be a short-lived phenomenon, though, at least for Suomen Filmiteollisuus. A year later, in the spring of 1939, Särkkä declared: 'Away with overly literary repertoire!', referring to films that dealt with delicate matters and got good reviews but low attendances.[43] Särkkä did not specify the films he considered 'overly literary', but presumably among these were at least *Are They Guilty?*, *A Stranger Came into the House* and *Scorned*, each with an attendance of only around 300,000, against the 700,000 of both *February Manifesto* and *The Regiment's Trouble-Boy*.[44] Clearly disappointed, Särkkä stated that it had become apparent that a film should not teach or comment on anything, and that delicate subjects should be left to literature.[45]

A return to delicate matters emerged at the end of the war. According to Sakari Toiviainen, the path for the re-emergence of problem films was heralded by *Anja, Come Back Home!* (SF 1944), a remake of Erik 'Hampe' Faustman's Swedish film *Sonja* (1943). In this film, the depiction of everyday life in a working-class milieu was melded with a relatively conventional 'fallen woman' melodrama in a novel way.[46] As Anu Koivunen's study on Finnish women's films of the 1940s demonstrates, prostitution and other issues relating to the assumedly problematic female body became burning matters of public debate during the post-war years.[47] Therefore the in itself conventional theme of the fallen woman achieved a flavour of topicality in such films as *Love's Sacrifice* (Jäger-Filmi 1945), *The Decoy* (Fenno-Filmi 1946) and *Cross of Love* (Teuvo Tulio 1946).

Among other themes in post-war problem films that combined melodramatic sensationalism with topicality were illegitimate children (*The Sixth Command*, SF 1947; *Ruined Youth*, Adams-Filmi 1947), drug and alcohol abuse (*Little Matti Out in the Wide World*, SF 1947; *The Singing Heart*, SF 1948), the problems of homecoming soldiers (*Olli Pulls a Surprise*, SF 1945; *Youth in a Fog*, SF 1946), and venereal (*The Tracks of Sin*, SF 1946) and other diseases (epilepsy in *The Barren Tree*, SF 1947). Critics, in fact, named the whole post-war cycle of problem films as 'syphilis films'. This label was catchy but somewhat exaggerated, since, in the end, only a handful of the problem films dealt with venereal diseases.[48]

The post-war problem film was a highly hybrid form. While melodrama and sensationalism were usually an essential part of it, elements from the family film (*Olli Pulls a Surprise*), the children's film (*Little Matti Out in the Wide World*), the crime film (*In the Shadow of the Prison Bars*, SF 1945) or even the musical (*The Singing Heart*), for example, might also be woven into it. Furthermore, a typical problem film was actually a multi-problem film, combining a set of issues into a complicated and difficult-to-solve web. Thus, the young men returning home from the front in *Olli Pulls a Surprise* and *Youth in a Fog* have to face not only the difficulties of going back to school, but also unemployment, venereal diseases, alcoholism, and the lure of black marketeering and crime. It is, perhaps, logical that the film Toiviainen sees as culminating the cycle, *Song of the City Outskirts*

**Figure 5.3** Still from *Song of the City Outskirts* (1948).

(SF 1948), is a virtual catalogue of the problems typical for the cycle – from juvenile delinquency and alcoholism to poverty and prostitution – all centred around an imaginary, studio-realistic 'Sin Alley' (Figure 5.3).[49]

Of all Finnish film cycles, the rillumarei phenomenon of the early 1950s comes closest to a cycle dominated by just one company, Suomen Filmiteollisuus. The background of this cycle was thoroughly intermedial. In the spring of 1951, the composer Toivo Kärki persuaded Särkkä to visit a show at a nearby people's hall, starring Esa Pakarinen, Reino Helismaa and Jorma Ikävalko, all of whom had years of experience in singing, playing and performing comic acts, first as war-front entertainers and then as semi-professional performers touring the country. According to an often told story, Särkkä invited all three for a screen test right on the spot, and soon signed all of them to star in *At the Rovaniemi Fair*, scripted by Helismaa from his own play. The film premiered in October, merely half a year after their first encounter.[50]

*At the Rovaniemi Fair* became an instant success, backed on the one hand by the trio's down-to-earth popularity as performers, tested in front of audiences for years, and on the other hand by Helismaa's writing skills as a lyricist, an author of popular plays, revues and radio shows, and an incomparable improviser. The film tells a story of three gold washers in Lapland, honest but equipped with a common sense that helps them to outsmart a bunch of pretentious crooks. *Rovaniemen markkinoilla* includes more than twenty songs by Kärki and Helismaa, some of which are only brief themes integrated into the narrative, while others are fully developed, usually performed by the main characters either on stage or on a train with the other passengers as an audience. Many of the songs were also soon recorded, and the title track, sung by Kauko Käyhkö, became the best-selling record of 1951.

The success of *At the Rovaniemi Fair* was quickly capitalised on by Suomen Filmiteollisuus: the follow-up, *Mr Coolman from the Wild West*, premiered in April 1952, and the next one, *The Girl from Muhos*, based on a popular song by Kärki and Helismaa, in October 1952. According to some later critics like Peter von Bagh, the cycle included only two or three films besides these first ones.[51] Some others have seen the boundaries of rillumarei as more flexible than that: a remarkable proportion of the comedies produced by Suomen Filmiteollisuus during the 1950s and early 1960s, and definitely of the thirty films scripted by Helismaa, share essential ingredients with the rillumarei films.[52]

Part of the difficulty in defining the corpus of rillumarei films lies in the fact that what makes rillumarei a cycle in the first place is somewhat less clear than in the case of the other cycles discussed here. There is little in common between even the few films von Bagh considers to compose the core of the rillumarei: most, but not all, feature Esa Pakarinen; most, but not all, are scripted by Reino Helismaa; the narratives vary from a folksy railway comedy set in northern Finland (*The Girl from Muhos*) to a harem comedy set in North Africa (*Adventure in Morocco*, SF 1953). It seems obvious that Suomen Filmiteollisuus did not set out to plan the films as a unified cycle. Särkkä merely built upon what seemed to sell, as quickly as possible. Helismaa was an extremely swift writer who, anecdotally, could provide a film script overnight, if needed. Accordingly, the scripts were often sketchy. A Pekka Puupää script by Helismaa might include something like: 'Shots 15–35: funny gags, the director will know.'[53]

Rillumarei films were, in fact, first recognised as a unified group by contemporary critics, who picked the nonsensical phrase 'rillumarei' from the chorus of the title song of *At the Rovaniemi Fair*, and started to use it as a derogatory nickname for all of Suomen Filmiteollisuus's lowbrow comedies. Särkkä, having adopted a highly populist attitude and always willing to range himself against the critics, finally verified the existence of

**Figure 5.4** Severi Suhonen gets acquainted with high culture in *Hei, Trala-lala-lalaa* (1954).

the cycle by producing a film called *Hei, rillumarei!* (*Hei, Trala-lala-lalaa*) in 1954. In this film, the protagonist, Severi Suhonen (Esa Pakarinen reappearing in his familiar gold washer role from *At the Romaniemi Fair*), takes a train to Helsinki in order to get acquainted with high culture. In the end of the film, he inevitably takes a train back north, only to run into his friends from the previous film, also heading northward. Having visited a ludicrous classical concert (Figure 5.4) and an absurdist play called *We Are All Insane*, and having met with a pompous art critic, it is easy for him to convince his friends, along with audience of the film, that his prejudice against the hypocritical and elitist high culture was well justified.

However intrinsically rillumarei films were associated with Suomen Filmiteollisuus, the competitors still tried to follow suit. Suomi-Filmi, which usually specialised in urban sophisticated comedies, tried its luck with a folk comedy, *Oh, Do You Remember...?* (1954). It met with only modest success, even though Suomi-Filmi hired Jorma Nortimo, the director of *At the Rovaniemi Fair*, to direct the film. Fennada's lumberjack comedy *Snow White and the Seven Loggers* (1953), directed by Ville Salminen, who was also associated with the rillumarei films at Suomen Filmiteollisuus, had rillumarei-like qualities, too. Fennada's Mauno Mäkelä later confessed, to his regret, that the Fennada comedy *The Haunted Inn* (1954) was a very conscious attempt to cash in on Suomen Filmiteollisuus's concept.[54] The critic Eugen Terttula, who originally adopted the term 'rillumarei film', had to admit in his survey article: 'It may sound unbelievable, but apparently not just anyone can cobble together a trashy film that would be successful. Judging by the experience so far, the keys seem to be solely in the hands of Reino Helismaa and T. J. Särkkä.'[55]

The last notable cycle of the studio era was the Schlager film, which has been seen as a response by the film production companies to the challenge posed by television, the music industry, travel, dance and other amusements.[56] However, the emergence of Schlager films was not based only on intermedial competition. Part of the survival strategy of the film companies was to ally themselves with the music industry: many of the Schlager films were collaborations between a film production company and a record company, featuring only artists from the latter's stable.[57] This merger was clearly visible also in popular film magazines like *Elokuva-Aitta*, which included ever more material on popular singers, before being finally replaced by actual music magazines in the 1960s.

The Schlager film cycle is usually considered to consist of seven or eight films made between 1959 and 1966.[58] They always include a maximum number of (mainly backstage but sometimes also integrated) musical numbers. These are woven together by a more or less loose story, often filled with metafictive elements. A typical example is *Hit Parade* (Fennada 1959), which begins with the president of a record company (played by Hannes Häyrinen, the real director of the film) meeting with film producer Mauno Mäkelä (the real producer of the film) and suggesting an idea for a music film (Figure 5.5). What follows is a medley of musical numbers, some of them merely performed one after the other

**Figure 5.5** *Hit Parade* (1959): producer Mauno Mäkelä and director Hannes Häyrinen with their backs to the camera, cinematographer Esko Töyri at the extreme left of the image.

by varying artists, and some integrated into the narrative. The narrative centres around two young singers (Pirkko Mannola and Lasse Liemola, both real popular singers) trying to get a record deal and becoming romantically involved with each other.

While the Schlager film, with its countless intertextual and intermedial references to contemporary Finnish entertainment, was in many ways a domestic phenomenon, it also alluded to international trends in music, film and television. Among the variety of musical numbers were domestic Schlagers by established singers in the style that had been popular since the 1930s, Finnish versions of European popular songs of the day, especially from Italy and Germany, and domestic or domesticated rock songs ('Long Tall Sally' in *A Song Hit Parade*, Filmi-Tria 1960). In terms of genre, the most important source of influence was probably the German Schlager film, a thoroughly urban and socially optimistic mode of film that 'celebrated a modern leisure society'.[59] While American rock 'n' roll films were, arguably, not as explicitly influential as German Schlager films, the emergence of the new youth music could not be totally ignored by the film companies either. The first screenings of *Rock around the Clock* (USA 1956) in the autumn of 1956 caused small riots in Helsinki and some other cities in Finland, and record companies started to search for their own rock singers. Film companies followed suit, and soon singers like 'Rock-Jerry', who at the age of sixteen won the first Finnish rock music competition, were cast as singers in the Schlager films.

Regarding television, of all cinematic genres and cycles of the studio era, the Schlager film was arguably the one that most obviously paved way for television formats. One of the earliest and most persistent forms of television entertainment was the revue that alternated musical numbers with a loose narrative frame and comic sketches, much like the Schlager film.

Even if the number of actual Schlager films was limited, the Schlager film can also be seen as a hybrid format that infiltrated into other forms of Finnish film in the late 1950s and early 1960s. Diegetically performed songs, as well as dances, could be found in countless other films, too, especially in comedies. *A Girl and Her Hat* (SF 1961), for example, includes many songs and stars Pirkko Mannola, a singing actor of several Schlager films. The emphasis in this episodic story about a young woman wondering around and encountering a songwriter, a circus troupe and other people is just a little bit more focused on narrative and less on music numbers than in Schlager films per se. Even a straight comedy like *Wild*

*Generation* (Fennada 1957), a re-adaptation of Mika Waltari's 1930s play about the generation cap in a well-to-do family, includes an ostensibly improvised rock number.

## Series

The logic of film cycling was often close to that of serialisation. Besides being part of the same cycle, *At the Rovaniemi Fair* and *Hei, Trala-lala-lalaa* also featured the same central characters, thus constituting what could have been the beginning of a series. In a sense, there was, indeed, a series, however loose it was both temporarily and thematically. Two more films appeared over the decades featuring Esa Pakarinen's central character, Severi Suhonen: *Helter-Skelter* (Veikko Itkonen 1961), a Helismaa-scripted revue film with a few songs and comedic scenes by Pakarinen/Suhonen; and *It's Up to Us* (Fennada 1973), Matti Kassila's relatively unsuccessful attempt to revive the rillumarei tradition twenty years after. Furthermore, the serial-like character of Severi Suhonen was strengthened by the intermedial fact that Pakarinen kept on performing as Suhonen in his live acts across the decades.

Generally, there was a thin line between different kinds of recycling and reiterating themes, subjects and characters. The logic of capitalising on tried-and-tested themes was basically the same in adaptations, cycles, genres, remakes, sequels and series. When does a cycle turn into a genre? How many sequels does it take to make a series?[60]

The general dependence of Finnish cinema on recycling subjects in general and serialisation in particular is indicated in Kari Uusitalo's short history of Finnish film series. Uusitalo lists more than forty different series, starting from the 1910s and ending in the 2010s.[61] About half of the series included in the book date from the studio era, and most of the remainder from the post-studio years. Although some of the items on the list are series only in a limited sense of the term, like the two adaptations of Väinö Linna's novel trilogy, *Here, beneath the North Star* (1959–62), both released in two parts (Fennada 1968, 1970; Artista-Filmi, 2009, 2010), the overall importance of serialisation cannot be denied.

While Finnish cycles, with the relative exception of the rillumarei films, usually emerged when producers quickly responded to the success of their competitors, a series was typically one company's way of rationalising its output. All the major companies produced several distinctive series over the studio years; for independents, this was obviously more challenging, since creating a series required continuity and stability of production. In the post-studio era, too, series has been the trade mark of (and at the same time, of course, a means to success for) the most prosperous and long-lasting companies. Indeed, the all-time longest-running film series was the chain of twenty Uuno Turhapuro comedies made between 1973 and 2004, created, produced and partly scripted by Pertti 'Spede' Pasanen. Centring on the work-shy, grotesque and verbally acrobatic trickster figure of Uuno, these films were phenomenally successful, even at the time when cinemagoing was generally in decline: five out of the ten biggest box-office hits of the last fifty years have been Uuno films.[62]

Although a series was usually the property of one studio, it does not mean that others had no interest in getting in on the act. On the contrary, several 'takeovers' of film series took place during the studio years. Retrospectively, the most notorious of these concerns the Inspector Palmu detective stories, based on Mika Waltari's novels and directed by Matti Kassila. The first film, *Inspector Palmu's Error*, was produced by Suomen Filmiteollisuus in 1960. Särkkä had purchased the rights for Waltari's novel years earlier and finally managed to get Kassila excited by allowing him to do a period piece and set the film in the 1930s. Creating the 1930s atmosphere involved not only set design and costumes, but also reinstalling into the studio ceiling the heavy arc lights that had been out of use for years.[63]

With its unique mixture of detective fiction, comedy and Gothic horror (Figure 5.6), *Inspector Palmu's Error* received excellent reviews, was a box-office success and was voted as the best domestic film of the year by the readers of *Elokuva-Aitta*. While it is not quite clear whether Särkkä would have wanted to produce a sequel for the film, the fact is that Fennada's Mäkelä had bought rights for the other Palmu novel Waltari had published two decades earlier. According to his memoirs, Kassila was not happy about this takeover which he assumed was done behind both Särkkä's and his own back. Yet, since the principal actors playing the police officers, Joel Rinne, Matti Ranin and Leo Jokela, had apparently already accepted Mäkelä's offer, Kassila once again moved over to Fennada to direct *Gas Inspector Palmu!* (1961), as well as two more sequels, *The Stars Will Tell, Inspector Palmu* (1962) and *Vodka, Mr Palmu* (1969).[64] The former was based on Waltari's draft, which he developed into a novel at the same time as Kassila and Kaarlo Nuorvala elaborated it into a film script,

**Figure 5.6** Still from *Inspector Palmu's Error* (1960).

and the latter was written directly for a film, with Waltari's permission to use the characters.

The takeover of the Palmu films reveals one crucial characteristic of Finnish film series: most of them were originally not planned as such. As with cycles, the producers usually reacted to sudden successes by trying out a sequel, whenever it seemed lucrative. If the sequel was successful enough, too, what started as a single film could develop into a series. An extreme example of this logic is the series of three films based loosely on the life of the songwriter J. Alfred Tanner. The first one was *The Orphan's Waltz* (SF 1949), a biopic that covered Tanner's life to his deathbed. The ending is a definitive proof that Suomen Filmiteollisuus had no intention of making a sequel, but the unsuspected success of the film drove the company to act on an ad hoc basis and plan two more films, in 1951 and 1952. Obviously, they did not go on from where *The Orphan's Waltz* had ended, but rather centred on ever more fictitious episodes of Tanner's early life and invested especially in his popular songs.

Still, there were at least partial exceptions to the general rule that film series were not planned beforehand. Even though no extant company papers prove this, it seems plausible to assume that two of Suomen Filmiteollisuus's longest and most characteristic series were started with at least a possibility of sequels in mind. The first of these centred on an upper-middleclass family called Suominen. In accordance with the tradition of family films, the Suominen films cover the everyday life, mishaps, joys and misfortunes of both the parents and the children of the family. As the series evolved, it focused more and more on Olli, the somewhat reckless but kind-hearted son on the family, played by the talented Lasse Pöysti who was chosen for the part from 250 auditionees. In this respect, the series has parallels with MGM's Hardy Family series (1937–58), which started as a family story but later centred on the son Andy, played by Mickey Rooney. Indeed, while searching for young actors to play the parts of Olli and his sister Pipsa, Suomen Filmiteollisuus enquired: 'Where are the Finnish Shirley Temple and Mickey Rooney?'[65]

The making of the first film, *The Suominen Family* (1941), was suggested to Särkkä by the authors Seere Salminen and Elsa Soini, who wrote the first version of the script, which was then turned into a shooting script by Särkkä. It was presumably easy for Särkkä to accept the offer, since the subject had already proven its popularity: *The Suominen Family* had been enormously successful as a radio serial scripted by Salminen and Soini, from 1938. The radio serial was also an adaptation, or, in fact, an adaptation of an adaptation. It was based on the Swedish radio serial *Familjen Björck* (1936–43), which bas based on a Danish serial, *Familjen Hansen* (1929–49). The continuing saga of a middle-class family was thus a genuinely trans-Nordic phenomenon, proven to resonate with audiences throughout Scandinavia. Considering the popularity and the serial-like nature of both the radio serial and the Hardy Family films, it is likely that Särkkä had sequels in mind right from the beginning. Suomen Filmiteollisuus finally produced five Family Suominen films between 1941 and 1945, ending with the death of Yrjö Tuominen, the actor who played the father. One more film was made in 1959, possibly inspired by the information that the long-lasting radio serial was nearing its end.[66]

Investing in the rillumarei tide, Suomen Filmiteollisuus launched the longest-lasting series of the studio era, the Pekka Puupää (Pete Blockhead) series, with thirteen films made between 1953 and 1960. Scripted at first by Reino Helismaa and starring Esa Pakarinen, the series featured the Puupää family, the simple, lazy but relatively kind and honest Pekka and his battle-axe wife Justiina, and Pekka's eccentric best friend, Pätkä, who lives variably in a tree house, under a boat or, literally, in Pekka's closet. As opposed to the Suominens, Pekka and Justiina live in a small apartment in Kallio, a working-class district of Helsinki, and Pekka is constantly looking for odd jobs. Being significantly non-political and work-shy, Pekka and Pätkä are working-class characters only in a limited sense. Yet, in a rillumarei vein, there is a constant populist sting in these films, directed at bankers, bureaucrats and social climbers dwelling in the bourgeois neighbourhoods.

As with most series, the Puupää films, too, had an intermedial origin. The characters were based on Ola Fogelberg's comic strip that had started in 1925 in a workers' co-operative magazine, at first combining education, advertising and humour but gradually developing into a more conventional humour strip. Fogelberg died before the first film adaptation, but his daughter continued drawing and writing the strip until 1976. From the early 1940s on, the Puupää strips were also published as yearly books, reaching the peak of their sales in the early 1950s. As a proof of the comic strip's and the character's popularity, Pakarinen recorded a song 'Pekka Puupää' by Kärki and Helismaa, before the first film adaptation. Given the intermedial success of Puupää, it seems obvious that Särkkä had a series of films in mind in this case, too. In fact, according to an often-told anecdote, the company lawyer of Suomen Filmiteollisuus fooled Fogelberg's widow into selling rights not just for one film but for potential sequels, too.[67]

Generally, although there was much in common between series and cycles, there were considerable differences, too. Both cycles and series began as tests of potentially sellable subjects that typically had an intermedial or transnational background, or both. If the test proved successful, a sequel was considered, and this, in turn, could lead into a series or a cycle of films. However, while a series usually stayed within one company (with a few remarkable exceptions), a typical cycle began to grow when the competitors responded to a sudden success of one company.

The most important difference between cycles and series concerns the long-term logic of the production companies' operations. Whereas cycles came and went, sometimes quite quickly, series often represented continuity within one company's output. Such series as the Family Suominen films and the Puupää films at Suomen Filmiteollisuus, or the urban and internationally oriented 'Dead Man' adventure films at Suomi-Filmi (1942–4),[68] were at the core of their production company's output: the house styles and the values of the companies were most clearly manifested in series such as these. A series might have begun by testing and experimenting with novel ingredients, but, as the series took off, differentiation was displaced by standardisation. Each following entry in the series was supposed to rely more on what was familiar and less on broaching new territories.

## Notes

1. 'Arvostelijan vastuu', *Suomi-Filmin Uutisaitta* 3/1939: 12.
2. Sulka: 'Lukijalle', *SF-Uutiset* 4/1937: 3.
3. Sulka: 'Lukijalle', *SF-Uutiset* 9/1939: 3.
4. Koski 1977: 21.
5. 'Suomalaisen filmin oikeutus', *SF-Uutiset* 3/1937: 11.
6. Toiviainen 1975: 27–30.
7. Sihvonen 1987.
8. Toiviainen 1992.
9. Laine 1994.
10. Koivunen 1995.
11. Kärjä 2005.
12. Römpötti 2012.
13. Lehtisalo 2011.
14. See Todorov 1980: 13–14.
15. See Pettey and Palmer 2014, especially the chapter on Nordic Noir by Andrew Nestingen (Nestingen 2014).
16. See Altman 1999: 72–82.
17. Ibid.: 1–12.
18. See Altman 1987: 12–15.
19. An unsigned memo 12 January 1949. Suomi-Filmi Collection, Helsinki: National Audiovisual Archive.
20. Film advertisement for 'Helmikuun manifesti', *Helsingin Sanomat* 19 March 1939.
21. 'Helmikuun manifesti', *Opettajain Lehti* 12/1939: 333.
22. T. J. Särkkä's memo on the profitability of domestic film production 31 May 1945. Suomen Filmiteollisuus Collection, Helsinki: National Audiovisual Archive.
23. 'Työ on tehty – ja nyt kelpaakin jo hymyillä', *Suomi-Filmin Uutisaitta* 4/1939: 15.
24. Donner and Savo 1953: 16–19.
25. An unsigned memo 12 January 1949. Suomi-Filmi Collection, Helsinki: National Audiovisual Archive.
26. Based on a play by Hella Wuolijoki, *Hulda from Juurakko* tells a story of a poor young countrywoman who through her determination receives a university degree in the city. The play was adapted in Hollywood as *The Farmer's Daughter* (H. C. Potter, RKO 1947).
27. See Uusitalo et al. 1993: 384.
28. Hietala 1992: 10–14.
29. Seppälä 2017.
30. See Soila 1994.
31. See Laine 2012.
32. Altman 1999.

33. Kakko 2019: 205–8.
34. Laine 1994: 147.
35. Altman 1999: 115–21.
36. Klein 2011: 79–80.
37. 'Pikku paloja elokuvamaailmasta', *SF-Uutiset* 6/1941: 14.
38. Kassila and Jutila 2014: 75–6.
39. 'Pikku paloja elokuvamaailmasta', *SF-Uutiset* 3/1939: 14.
40. On film noir in Nordic countries, often combining noirish aesthetics with social criticism, see Nestingen 2014.
41. Niko: 'Probleema kotimaisessa elokuvassa', *Elokuva-Aitta* 7/1938: 155.
42. 'Aivan uskomattoman työmäärän suoritti SF viime kesänä', *SF-Uutiset* 4/1938: 5.
43. 'Ensi syyskauden ohjelmistoa', *SF-Uutiset* 5/1939: 4.
44. T. J. Särkkä's memo on the profitability of domestic film production 31 May 1945. Suomen Filmiteollisuus Collection, Helsinki: National Audiovisual Archive.
45. 'Ensi syyskauden ohjelmistoa', *SF-Uutiset* 5/1939: 4.
46. Toiviainen 1993: 644.
47. Koivunen 1995: 107–45.
48. Hakosalo 2008: 118.
49. Toiviainen 1993: 646–8.
50. Pennanen and Mutkala 1994: 123–6.
51. Von Bagh 1992b: 397.
52. Kakko 2019: 205–8.
53. Jokinen 1989: 70.
54. Mäkelä 1996: 138.
55. Terttula 1955: 67.
56. Kärjä 2005: 122–3.
57. Gronow 2002: 282–7.
58. Ibid.: 282; Kärjä 2005: 123.
59. Ascheid 2012.
60. On the relation between film series and other kinds of film recycling, see Leitch 2010.
61. Uusitalo 2011.
62. On the Uuno Turhapuro series, see Hietala et al. 1992.
63. Uusitalo et al. 1991: 461–2.
64. Kassila 2004: 263–305.
65. *Helsingin Sanomat* 12 June 1940.
66. Uusitalo et al. 1991: 375.
67. Jokinen 1989: 69.
68. The 'Dead Man' series was actually cut short and consisted of only two films by Suomi-Filmi. Suomen Filmiteollisuus took over the character and tried out one film in 1952, but with little success.

# Chapter 6

# House styles

From the early 1930s on, when the relative dominance of Suomi-Filmi gave way to first two (Suomi-Filmi and Suomen Filmiteollisuus) and then three (Fennada) major production companies, an idiosyncratic house style became a necessary precondition for the success of a studio. Certainly, Suomi-Filmi had already determinedly constructed a company image in the 1920s, but with little competition there was not much need to differentiate its films from those of the rivals. More important was to stand out as a domestic company and create a distinctive style for domestic productions. This aspiration continued through the studio years and was shared with other Finnish production companies; after all, even in the most productive times, the domestic output remained only a small fraction of the whole supply of films. Yet, with other equally strong domestic rivals, the distinction strategy became a double strategy: on the one hand, it was a common interest of all domestic films to stand out as recognisably Finnish films with identifiable national characteristics; on the other hand, all studios attempted to do this in their own distinctive way and stand out not only among the foreign but also among the domestic competitors.

The differentiation process is already evident in the names of the production companies. In August 1940, the editorial of Suomi-Filmi's journal *Uutisaitta* warned against the potential overproduction of domestic films should the importation of foreign productions become difficult because of the ongoing war:

> If such false market conditions lead to the release of substandard films, there is a danger of the concept of the domestic film as such being condemned. Despite repeated efforts, the public has not yet learned to tell company logos apart. They are still randomly mixed up with one another, and are usually credited to Suomi-Filmi. This is because almost all domestic film producers have chosen names that resemble Suomi-Filmi as much as possible.[1]

There is obvious bitterness in these words towards Suomi-Filmi's main competitor, Suomen Filmiteollisuus. Indeed, when Erkki Karu, after his forced departure from Suomi-Filmi, launched his new company in 1933, he deliberately chose a name that resembled that of his old company. Suomen Filmiteollisuus (Finnish Film Industry) echoed Suomi-Filmi (Finland-Film), while it also alluded to the major Swedish production company Svensk Filmindustri (Swedish Film Industry). What increased Suomi-Filmi's bitterness even more was that Karu registered the abbreviation SF for his new company, even though Suomi-Filmi had unofficially used the same initials for years. In the first issue of *SF-Uutiset* in 1935, Suomen Filmiteollisuus spelled this out:

> SF is the abbreviation for *Suomen Filmiteollisuus Ltd*. This abbreviation was *officially* certified on 2 December 1933, on the same day that the constitution of the company was ratified ... Suomen Filmiteollisuus was given an *exclusive right* to use this trademark in all of its photographic and cinematic products, in printed publications as well as in signs.[2]

Suomi-Filmi's irritation about the company name was primarily but not exclusively directed at Suomen Filmiteollisuus. Indeed, many other companies also appealed to national sentiments in their names. Valentin Vaala and Teuvo Tulio's Fennica was one of them, and another was Suomen Kuvatuote (Finnish Image Product), which produced only one feature film, *The King of Karmankolo* (1938). Later on, the name of the third major company, Fennada-Filmi, connoted Finnishness, too, as did that of its precursor, Fenno-Filmi (Finnish Film). In fact, Suomi-Filmi's irritation would be justifiable even decades later: at the time of writing, old domestic films from the studio era are still, regardless of the actual production company, often referred to as 'suomi-filmis' in television reviews and public debate.

While it seems plausible that some independent companies, indeed, tried to cash in on Suomi-Filmi's fame, and that Suomen Filmiteollisuus at first wanted to confuse the company images, in the long run most studios emphasised the ways their films differed from those of their rivals. The aim of this chapter is to examine the dialectic of standardisation and differentiation inherent in developing the studios' house styles. What methods did the studios use to mark their films out as specific and distinctive, while at the same time borrowing and stealing from and being influenced by the other studios, as we saw in the previous chapter?

Neither the term 'house style' nor any equivalent of it was in use during the Finnish studio years. However, both the studios themselves and contemporary critics often spoke of the distinctiveness of the films made by a given studio, albeit in vague and varying phrases. It can thus be said that the notion of house style existed, even though the term did not. In film historical studies, the concept has referred to the various ways in which generic material finds a matching tone, sometimes with an emphasis on the star–genre combinations specific to a studio, and sometimes on visual style per se.[3] In the previous chapter, I have already argued that, in Finland, studio-specificity manifested itself in certain cycles and series, like the rillumarei and Pekka Puupää films of Suomen Filmiteollisuus and the urban international adventures of Suomi-Filmi. In this chapter, the concept of house style is considered, first, from the more general content-related perspective of subject matter, second, from the point of view of visual style, and third, in terms of audience differentiation.

## Subject matter

In a sense, a distinct house style became a relevant issue only in the mid-1930s, as Suomen Filmiteollisuus became a credible opponent for Suomi-Filmi. Certainly, Suomi-Filmi was already seeking consistency and distinctiveness during the Erkki Karu era in the 1920s and early 1930s, but with little domestic competition this was not particularly demanding. Jaakko Seppälä has described the early output of Suomi-Filmi in terms of 'essentialist cinema'. Wanting to create films that intended to represent the essence of the nation and evoke emotions of belonging and togetherness in the newly independent country, Suomi-Filmi invested in the domestic traditions of landscape painting, photography, literature and theatre. The most notable and prestigious films were adaptations of either established nineteenth-century literature, like *Anna-Liisa* (1922, based on a play by Minna Canth, 1895) and *The Village Shoemakers* (1923, based on a play by Aleksis Kivi, 1864) or contemporary popular carriers of tradition, like *The Logroller's Bride* (1923, based on a novel by Väinö Kataja, 1914). These films centred on peasant life and invested in ethnographic accuracy in the spirit of the nineteenth-century Fennoman movement, while being, perhaps paradoxically, strongly influenced by such Swedish 'golden age' films as Mauritz Stiller's *The Song of the Scarlet Flower* (1919) and *Johan* (1921).[4] On the other hand, the nationally charged novels and plays adapted by Suomi-Filmi were not only hallowed classics but also, as Tytti Soila has noted, 'well-known popular rural melodramas they had played during their tours around the country'.[5]

As popular and distinguished as these essentialist films were, they represented only a part of Suomi-Filmi's repertoire during the Karu era. Such films as *When Father Has Toothache* (1923), *Summery Fairy Tale* (1925) and *The Supreme Victory* (1929) pursued cosmopolitan tendencies by adapting international genres such as, respectively, the urban slapstick comedy, the high-society comedy and the spy film. Moreover, the few competitors Suomi-Filmi had during this era also tended to invest in similar, internationally oriented films with contemporary themes, termed by Seppälä as 'epochal films'.[6] Prime examples are *On the Highway of Life* (Komedia-Filmi 1927) and *The Wide Road* (Fennica 1931).

Suomi-Filmi's stance towards the two production tendencies, essentialist and epochal films, was ambiguous. On the one hand, it turned to epochal impulses itself, increasingly towards the end of the 1920s. In 1929, it promoted *The Supreme Victory* in words that alluded to the problematic tension between the two kinds of films:

> A 'friend' of domestic cinema has complained that we have not yet reached the level of drawing-room films; instead, we still brood over domestic subject matters ... based on local country life with the – admittedly beautiful – nature of our land as background. However, a drawing-room film seems to be on its way now, featuring a countess, a baron and other sights to see, hotel life, driving around in sports cars, as well as other kinds of fuss, love – and political intrigue.[7]

On the other hand, Suomi-Filmi cherished its essentialist studio image all through the Karu years. This ambiguous attitude was at its clearest in Suomi-Filmi's anti-internationalist attacks on Komedia-Filmi and Ufanamet during the 'trust war' of the late 1920s, as we saw in Chapter 3.

Many contemporary critics acknowledged the two-sidedness of Suomi-Filmi's output. Some encouraged the company to stick to tradition: 'If Finnish film avoids the depiction of rural life, as has been demanded, this would be disastrous for Finnish film production in general and comedy in particular.'[8] Some, like the author Erkki Kivijärvi (admittedly partial as the screenwriter and leading actor of *Summery Fairy Tale*), differed over the centrality of rural films. He complained about what he thought of as the Swedish-influenced excess of 'maidens in national costume, midsummer dances, milk pails, village brawls and rapid shootings'.[9]

An interesting mediating view was offered by the future film director Roland af Hällström, who refused to see rural films only in terms of tradition:

What, then, would be the rejectable direction? The depiction of the peasant, it is said – the same bloke whom Mika Waltari has chased away from literature. What the criticisers ignore is that, so far, the content of Finnish films has not centred on peasant life, but rather on modern folk life, which is quite a different thing. And the emphasis is not on the word 'folk' but on the word 'modern'.[10]

Af Hällström's view ties the 1920s cinema with contemporary Finnish literature. Such authors as the 1939 Nobel laureate F. E. Sillanpää have been described as 'rural modernists', who, even when setting their narratives in the rural environment, used modernist literary devices like self-reflexive narration and literary montage, displayed interest in psychoanalysis and vitalism, and introduced modernity-oriented themes and issues such as what it means to be an individual in modern society.[11] Af Hällström, in fact, states that Karu's adventure film about spirit smuggling, *The Fisherman of Storm Island* (1924), was 'more modern than our literature has come up with so far' (Figure 6.1).[12]

Curiously, af Hällström's perspective had changed by 1936, when he published *Filmi – aikamme kuva*, the first book-length study of film history and aesthetics in Finnish. Af Hällström made use of material

**Figure 6.1** *The Fisherman of Storm Island* (1924): modern adventure film. All exterior scenes were filmed with two cameras to be on the safe side.

he had previously written for newspapers and magazines, but here and there his word choice was different. Instead of representing cutting-edge modernity, *The Fisherman of Storm Island* was now merely 'a well-designed attempt to introduce the theme of folk life during prohibition to film'.[13] In 1929, af Hällström had described Karu's characteristics as a film director with words like simplicity, clarity and self-confidence.[14] In 1936, these were joined by folkishness and carefulness. Such qualities, according to af Hällström, found best expression in films about the peasants and fishermen, the same kinds of films that a few years earlier had represented modernity for him. Karu's little weakness, continued af Hällström, was having a penchant for the cultural circles of Helsinki, culminating in *Summery Fairy Tale*, a drawing-room comedy filled with ill-conceived 'literary' and 'aesthetic' aspirations.[15] The changes af Hällström made to his writings are small but telling. Karu, and with him Suomi-Filmi during his leadership, had turned from epochalist to essentialist.

Af Hällström's willingness to disregard and downplay the epochal efforts of Finnish cinema in general and Suomi-Filmi in particular has been echoed by countless commentators ever since. The existence of Finnish city films and drawing-room films was, of course, recognised, but typical commentators of the 1930s and 1940s found the essence of domestic cinema to lie in rural topics and peasant films. Drawing-room films especially were seen as an imported and poorly imitated product that had little resonance in Finnish culture.[16] As Anu Koivunen has remarked, drawing-room films and modern social comedies were also readily associated with women's genres, which further lowered their cultural status in the eyes of contemporary (mainly male) critics.[17]

The notion of the centrality of rural films prevailed through the remainder of the studio years. It was confirmed by, for example, Jörn Donner in his influential 1961 text 'Finnish Cinema Year Zero'.[18] Whereas Donner recognised the existence of urban films, even if he was of the opinion that the quality of rural films was more important than the undeniable quantity of city films, the next generations of critics distorted the relation between rural films and city films in a curious way. They ended up with a view that Finnish cinema 'found' urban culture only with the 1960s New Wave and that, until then, the agrarian way of life had dominated:

> The atmosphere of Finnish cinema up to the 1960s was determined mainly by an agrarian outlook on life, according to which the city was

a sinful place, since man has his roots in the countryside, in a life lived close to nature and in harmony with it. It is this worldview, mixed with Christian and agrarian maxims, which one meets continually in old Finnish films, which are very popular these days on television. Up to the end of World War II, industrialisation developed quite slowly in Finland, so it is mainly during the last thirty years that a major change in social structure has taken place ... Thus the history of traditional Finnish cinema can be read against the leitmotiv of country life and ideals, with urban life only a minor theme.[19]

This view of the centrality of rural films and the anti-urban tendency of the studio era has become so predominant that historians and sociologists have tended to use old films as self-explanatory evidence of the assumedly delayed breakthrough of the urban mentality in Finland. Drawing unproblematised parallels between sociological data and films, scholars argue that the urban mentality existed only marginally before the 1960s and that a proof for this can be found in films that 'created and reproduced stereotypical conceptions of the city as a nest of haste, bustle and sin'.[20]

Where does this unbalanced picture of studio-era cinema stem from? In part, it is a question of the dynamics between generations. Just as the 1930s generation distanced itself from the silent film era, the 1960s generation sought a radical break from the ideals and values of the past, assumedly presented by cultural products such as films. There was also a concrete material basis for the notion of a total break in film history. Whereas Donner, having started as a critic already in the early 1950s, was familiar with studio-era production, the next generation had limited access to old films, mainly through occasional television screenings of a handful of films. Some of the central filmmakers who started in the 1960s, like the director Risto Jarva and the cinematographer Lasse Naukkarinen, verified this generational gap by stating that they were not 'very closely connected with the main course of the Finnish film tradition, which broke up in the beginning of the 1960s'.[21]

Although the conception of the assumedly problematic country–city duality of studio-era films was consolidated by the post-studio generations, its roots can be traced back to studio differentiation itself. When Risto Orko in 1933 took over the production section of Suomi-Filmi, the company quite clearly focused on epochalist rather than essentialist films. The first films directed by Orko were city comedies like *Me and the Cabinet Minister* (1934), manor house comedies with mainly upper-class characters like *Superintendent of the Siltala Farm* (1935) or modern adventure films like *VMV6* (1936). Hiring Valentin Vaala as the second director in 1935 must have seemed like a logical step, since Vaala was identified with modern, urban subjects.

In subsequent interviews, Orko has emphasised his personal preferences as the main motive behind the urban image of the new Suomi-Filmi.[22] Yet, the mechanics of differentiation cannot be overlooked either. It seems obvious that Suomi-Filmi sought to distance itself from both the old Suomi-Filmi of the Karu era and from Suomen Filmiteollisuus, the new company Karu established after leaving Suomi-Filmi. In this process, the company image of the old Suomi-Filmi was typically reduced to associations with the rural and traditional, not only by Orko but also by Suomen Filmiteollisuus, which pictured itself as the carrier of the tradition. When Karu died in 1936, the author Artturi Järviluoma wrote in an obituary in the company journal *SF-Uutiset*:

> Erkki Karu was first and foremost a Finn, he loved Finnish nature and people. Each of his films had to be backed by Finland's smiling mother's face, and the way he portrayed the Finnish people was affective. He never approved of seeing country folks as fools or dopes to be laughed at, as used to be a habit in old genteel plays and still is in many films.[23]

While the tone of Järviluoma's writing is, of course, solemn, as was typical for obituaries, it also paved the way for Särkkä's editorials of the coming years. An exalted, nationally charged style was used as a means to not only promote the company's new films but also comment on film politics and, every now and then, taunt rivals. In Jarviluoma's writing, the critical sting concerned laughing at country folks and was quite clearly directed at Suomi-Filmi's *Superintendent of the Siltala Farm* and *Everybody's Love* (1935), both of which featured rural people mainly as comical side characters.

As a result of this process involving self-definition and mutual distinction making, the company images of Suomi-Filmi and Suomen Filmiteollisuus became established in dualistic terms in the 1930s. While both companies made city films and country films of various sorts over the years, these images stuck with them all through the studio era. Suomen Filmiteollisuus carried on with the overtly national and rural, or essentialist tradition, associated with the prestige films made by Suomi-Filmi during the Karu era. Suomen Filmiteollisuus favoured the countryside, farmland or small towns as settings, and the typical characters were farmers, craftsmen or vagabonds. Even when the films take place in a city, as in the Family Suominen or Pekka Puupää series, the atmosphere is that of a small town, emphasising family ties, friendship, mundanity and community. Both series take place in Helsinki, the former in the bourgeois or middle-class district and the latter in the working-class district. The Kallio district of the Puupää films is not unambiguously idyllic. Pekka and Pätkä often meet with rude and swindling characters, willing to take advantage of Pekka's assumed simplicity, but they still live in a place where people know their neighbours. The Töölö district of the Family Suominen films, for its part, is a safe and familiar place, where children can play ball or ride a bike on their own, or even go skiing. Although in the later films of the series like *Olli Falls in Love* (1944) and *Olli Pulls a Surprise* (1945), urban dangers like smoking and drinking loom, the problems are solved in a traditional manner with fatherly guidance.

With such hybrid forms, Suomen Filmiteollisuus quite clearly wanted to dispel the duality between country and city. The characters of both the Puupää films and the Family Suominen films were recognisably urban, but at the same time they played by traditional rules and morals. In addition, Suomen Filmiteollisuus produced countless in-between films of another kind over the years. Often, the action takes place in a small, typically nameless or imaginary town, as in Matti Kassila's comedy *Hilma's Name Day* (1954), which begins with a voice-over narrator stating: 'As you can see, we are now in a small town – the name is of no importance . . .'. The film features an ensemble of characters including a judge, a pharmacist, a post office worker and a storekeeper. While these are all modern occupations, the small-town atmosphere where everyone knows one another separates *Hilma's Name Day* from actual city films.

Suomi-Filmi's new image under Orko's leadership as a modern, urban and internationally oriented studio lasted all through the studio era, even if the company produced a variety of historical and rural films over the years. Valentin Vaala, who remained loyal to Suomi-Filmi until his retirement in the 1970s, embodied this studio image as a director. An admirer of Ernst Lubitsch and Frank Capra, Vaala co-scripted (often with female authors) and directed a cycle of modern comedies with independent and strong-minded female protagonists and swift, screwball-oriented dialogue. While the films based on novels or plays by the popular author Hilja Valtonen (e.g. *Surrogate Wife*, 1936, and *Safety Valve*, 1942) take place in remarkably modern small-town milieus, the comedies co-scripted by Vaala, the leading actor Lea Joutseno and the author Kersti Bergroth (e.g. *The Bride Springs a Surprise*, 1941, and

*Dynamite Girl*, 1944) typically involve upper-class or upper-middle-class characters who live in the wealthy parts of Helsinki and spend time in the trendy cafés and restaurants of the city centre. More willing to invest in original scripts than its main competitor, Suomi-Filmi announced a competition for potential screenwriters in 1940, with a specific intent to find subject matter for comedies and adventure films.[24] The winning script was *The Dead Man Falls in Love* by the popular author Simo Penttilä, an adventure comedy that featured a mysterious, The Saint/Simon Templar-like character on the borderline between law and crime. Filmed by Ilmari Unho in 1942, *The Dead Man Falls in Love* once again highlighted upper class environment occupied by international spies and *femmes fatales*, launching yet another internationally oriented cycle of films by Suomi-Filmi.

After the war years, modern sophisticated comedies no longer formed the bulk of Suomi-Filmi's output, not even of Vaala's oeuvre, as such male-oriented genres as the crime film, lumberjack film, military farce or war film took over. Nevertheless, Suomi-Filmi held on to its urban and international characteristics until the end of the studio era. Orko was always strict to differentiate his company's films from those of Suomen Filmiteollisuus. When asked about the assumed crisis in Finnish cinema in 1952, he answered:

> If ditties and jingles form the basis of both the music and the literary content of a film, and if the majority of films are of this sort, then something is wrong ... The fact that an unacceptable amount of biopics of Sandras and Sannis have been made during the last few years is of no merit to domestic cinema.[25]

Orko's comment is openly directed towards Suomen Filmiteollisuus, which from the early 1950s on increased its production volume precisely with quickly made films based on popular songs rather than carefully developed film scripts. The best known of these were *Beautiful Vera* (1950) and *At the Rovaniemi Fair* (1951), and at the time of the interview, more were on the way, including *Ferryboat Romance* (1952), whose protagonist is nicknamed 'Sanni of the logging site'.

When Fennada established its position as the third major in the early 1950s, finding a niche was not necessarily easy in the somewhat dualistic field of film production shaped by the competition between Suomi-Filmi and Suomen Filmiteollisuus. Fennada tried its luck with rural dramas (*And Helena Plays on*, 1951, and its two sequels, 1954 and

1957), lumberjack films (*The Log Drivers*, 1951) and prestige literary adaptations (e.g. *Children of the Wilderness*, 1954), thus entering the zone occupied by the two older companies. The most important means of differentiation adopted by Fennada were, arguably, seeking a more youthful approach than the other majors, and orienting towards American rather than European cinema. The youthfulness is apparent, for example, in Fennada's military comedies that came out frequently almost every summer as a programme filler all through the 1950s. Both Suomi-Filmi and Suomen Filmiteollisuus, as well as some minors, had produced military comedies ever since the huge success of *The Regiment's Trouble-Boy* (SF 1938), and as much variation as there already was, from wartime patriotism to the light-hearted military musicals of the post-war years, Fennada brought a new angle to the genre. Fennada's protagonists were typically recruits from the city, be they wealthy playboys (*The Millionaire Recruit*, 1953), aspiring authors (*Conscript Hero*, 1955) or streetwise pranksters (*The Soldier Boy's Sweethearts*, 1958). Elements of new urban culture like motorcycle gangs and rock music entered the barracks, and even such old narrative elements as crossdressing got a more ambiguous and daring twist than before (*The Girl in the Barracks*, 1956). American influences, often associated with youthfulness in contrast to 'old' Europe, were evident in the many noir-oriented films by Fennada, be they adventure comedies (*Tough Guy*, 1954) or actual noir thrillers (*We're All Guilty*, 1954, and *Something in People*, 1956).

## Visual style

The differences in subject matters also entailed differences in visual style. Especially in the 1930s and 1940s, the modern and urban settings of Suomi-Filmi's films often brought about a certain experimentation and stylisation (Figure 6.2), in contrast to the blunt style of Suomen Filmiteollisuus. A typical example of the experimental side of Suomi-Filmi is *And Below Was a Fiery Lake* (1937), shot by the Swedish cinematographer Albert Rudling. It displays sharp contrasts between light and shadow, expressionistic use of cast shadows, extreme low angles, Dutch tilts, deep staging and other striking techniques.

Such cinematic expression was often referred to as the 'French style' or 'French cinematography' in Finnish film aesthetic debates of the

**Figure 6.2** Playing with urban neon lights in Valentin Vaala's *The Substitute Husband* (1936).

time. As a general concept, it suggested an impressionistically defined atmosphere of sophistication:

> The question is – what is meant by French style? It involves light imaginativeness, ironic charm, bittersweet melancholy, sophisticated satire, fury and tenderness, light-hearted elegance, sense of justice, desire for freedom, praise for gallantry, as well as certain humanity in emotion, passion and the fundamentals of being. These fine qualities are to be found in several French films – and these are precisely the films that have stuck to our minds.[26]

The admiration of French aesthetics was evident in Suomi-Filmi's employment politics. The French cinematographers Marius Raichi and Charles Bauer were employed in 1937 and 1938, respectively, and the laboratory head Raimond Grosset in 1938. Some of the Finnish employees, like the studio manager Hannu Leminen and the cinematographer Felix Forsman, made educational trips to French film studios. A few years later, as impressed as he was by French cinematography, Forsman expressed an ambiguous attitude towards it, implying that it had become mannered. Accordingly, Forsman described this style in a much more concrete way than most critics did, as a selection of specific cinematic devices:

> The French school of style is – or rather was – a so-called effect style of cinematography: lights and shadow, but lights as little as possible and shadow as much as possible; high and low angles, diagonal and distorted angles, imagery that is often quite incomprehensible and that bypasses

the eye and tries to speak straight to one's instinct. When it was taken too far, it became a test for virtuosity and a fashion, and in time, it will be considered a fruitful experimental phase in the history of lighting. The American 'clear' style will rule once again: in the dim and even in the dark, one has to *see*, one has to see everything to the detail. One has to be able to create an atmosphere without being incomprehensible or leaving things open to speculation. Yet, one has to use lighting sparingly. The fewer the lighting sources, the purer the light and the objects and surfaces that are lighted.[27]

The ambiguity in Forsman's attitude is, arguably, partly explained by the fact that, at the moment of the interview in 1940, he had changed over from Suomi-Filmi to Suomen Filmiteollisuus; the interview was, in fact, published in the company's journal, *SF-Uutiset*. However, Forsman directed his criticism not only towards Suomi-Filmi but also towards the films by two independent directors, Nyrki Tapiovaara and Teuvo Tulio. Tapiovaara's *Stolen Death* (1938) and *Mr Lahtinen Takes French Leave* (1939) were the most experimental Finnish feature films of the 1930s and probably of the whole studio era. Influenced not only by the French poetic realism of the 1930s but also by the avant-garde movements of the 1920s, Tapiovaara frequently favoured potentially defamiliarising techniques like extreme high angles and shots framed by objects in the foreground (Figure 3.2). Such techniques, while astonishing and functioning as an experimental attraction, also make familiar settings seem almost unrecognisable.[28] Certain montage sequences and superimpositions do the same. An illustrative example is the beginning of the wedding sequence in *Mr Lahtinen*. First, we see a row of church bells swinging sideways; then, a quick dissolve to a row of top hats, shot from the same angle and swinging in the same rhythm as the bells; then a cut back to the bells, and so on, until there is a dissolve to a collar of a priest. This is followed by a montage sequence with quick shots of hands, feet, heads from behind, and so on, with no recognisable faces. This sequence serves several purposes simultaneously. Drawing parallels between church bells and top hats is, first, a defamiliarising effect, since by this comparison both objects are detached from their usual contexts and given a new meaning. Second, it is also an Eisensteinian intellectual montage,[29] creating a third meaning by relating two seemingly incomparable elements. This generates not only a denotative meaning, wedding, but also a series of ironic connotations, as Church and wealth, religion and secularity, are juxtaposed.

Teuvo Tulio, with whom Forsman had worked on two films after departing from Suomi-Filmi, developed an over-the-top melodramatic style that was influenced by German Expressionism, French poetic realism and Czech cinema, especially the films of Gustav Machatý, whose *Ecstasy* (1933) had been a great critical success in Finland. At the same time, Tulio's style was highly distinctive and remained relatively unchanged through the studio years. Unlike his former filmmaking partner, Valentin Vaala, who became the master of continuity editing, Tulio focused on separate images and compositions at the expense of continuity and spatial logic. Tulio's visual characteristics in such films as *Song of the Scarlet Flower* (1938), *The Way You Wanted Me* (1944) and *The Cross of Love* (1946) can be seen, on the one hand, in the lyrical and pictorial shots of idyllic countryside and nature and, on the other hand, in carefully framed close-ups of faces detached from their background. The lighting of especially close-ups is stylised and strikingly non-naturalistic, and the acting is, alternately, either melodramatically excessive in facial and bodily expressions, or passive and stationary in the prolonged close-ups (Figure 6.3). Tulio's use of repetitive elements in visuals and music is also excessive.[30]

Compared to the striking 'French style' of some of Suomi-Filmi's and especially Tulio's and Tapiovaara's films, the typical expression in the films of Suomen Filmiteollisuus was blunt and pragmatic with visibility and seamless narrative as guiding principles. High-key lighting was preferred to low key, and as is witnessed by those who worked at Suomen

**Figure 6.3** Close-up of Regina Linnanheimo in *The Cross of Love* (1946).

Filmiteollisuus, the arc lights in the studios were extremely bright and hot. According to the cinematographer Unto Kumpulainen, who started as a camera assistant in Suomen Filmiteollisuus in the 1930s, 'if [Eino] Kari used a lot of light, [Theodor] Luts used it excessively'.[31] Whereas in the 'French style' there was a certain self-sufficiency and expressiveness in the camera angles, movements and compositions, in a typical Suomen Filmiteollisuus film, the main focus was always on the characters. Reframing motivated most camera movements, since the central function of the camera was to follow the actor. A characteristic device in the films of Suomen Filmiteollisuus, an early precursor of a zoom lens called a 'transfocator', was also usually used in a character-centred manner, to emphasise the character's reactions with a quick zoom-in to a close-up of a face.

It is probably no coincidence that Särkkä often relied on the talents of well-known stage directors like Wilho Ilmari, Jorma Nortimo or Edvin Laine, none of whom had had notable experience in the cinema before starting to direct films. These directors usually focused on guiding the actors, while the cinematographers decided on camera angles, lighting, movements and lenses. This practice started in Suomen Filmiteollisuus from the moment Särkkä took over. Eleven of his first films were co-directed with Yrjö Norta as a technical expert. Such a division of duties no doubt contributed to the character-oriented expression in the films of Suomen Filmiteollisuus.

Moreover, while almost all production companies relied on stage actors, Suomi-Filmi was more eager than its main rival to 'find' new actors with little or no experience in the theatre. Särkkä, for his part, gladly turned to well-known stage actors, preferably from the Finnish National Theatre. The difference in the acting styles between Suomi-Filmi and Suomen Filmiteollisuus was evident. Whereas Suomi-Filmi preferred a relatively subtle and restrained acting style, acting at Suomen Filmiteollisuus in general and in Särkkä's films in particular was often considered ponderous and emotional. Decades later, Felix Forsman analysed Särkkä's conception of film acting as an indication of his inexperience in film aesthetics:

> The director, who sits beside the camera, does not see the image the way the camera does, whether it is a close-up, a medium shot or a long shot. Thus, the director works like on a stage: like it was a long shot all along. This is why the facial expressions of the actors are overblown, as if they were performed for the third row in a theatre.[32]

It was only in the 1950s, with the growing production volume and the increasing investment in popular cycles and series like the rillumarei and Puupää films, that Suomen Filmiteollisuus began to resort to non-professional actors, including the singers and entertainers Esa Pakarinen, Reino Helismaa and Henry Theel, or the singer and beauty queen Pirkko Mannola. However, a tendency towards theatricality and pomposity remained a trademark of Suomern Filmiteollisuus even after that, although young directors like Matti Kassila brought new dimensions both to the acting styles and to cinematic expression in general.

Just as with subject matters, there was no readily available niche for visual style when Fennada entered the field in 1950. Perhaps the most easily recognisable characteristic of the Fennada style is the 'Rembrandt lighting', evident in both melodramas like *Beautiful Inkeri and the Railwayman* (1950) and noir thrillers like *We're All Guilty* and *Something in People* (1956). The antithesis to the abundant use of light by Eino Kari and Theodor Luts at Suomen Filmiteollisuus, this technique was mastered by the cinematographers Esko Nevalainen and Esko Töyri, who had already reduced the use of lights when working for Fenno-Filmi on such melodramas as *The Decoy* (1946) and *The Northern Express* (1947) (Figure 6.4). Töyri, who served as a mentor to many younger cinematographers, became known for his motto: 'One lamp in the right place.'[33]

**Figure 6.4** Noir lighting in *Northern Express* (1947).

## Audience differentiation

The major producers kept on repeating throughout the studio era that since Finnish films were primarily targeted at domestic audiences, and since the population in Finland was only about 3.5 or 4 million, there was no possibility of making films for specialised audiences. Mauno Mäkelä articulated this in 1952 in these words:

> The attendance of each and every film is like a Gallup survey that states the cold facts to the filmmakers. If one does not consider the indications, one might end up in a situation of ending a career. Making films is so expensive and so full of risks that one flop can bring an end to an enterprise ... This means that, in our situation, it is impossible to make a film for a target audience. Therefore, a youth film, for example, is out of the question.[34]

In a round-table discussion between film producers in 1956, it is stated that an audience of 100,000 or 200,000 might be enough to break even for a 'waistcoat pocket office', a package production, where the producer rents a studio and the equipment and hires the staff for only one film. However, for the permanent production companies with a studio and a regular staff, this was not nearly enough.[35] Accordingly, in the late 1930s, Särkkä had announced being disappointed in the attendances of certain 'overly literary' films[36] like *Are They Guilty?* (1938) or *Scorned* (1939) which received positive reviews but only about 300,000 viewers.

The general attitude of the major producers was thus that, in order to be profitable, Finnish films had to address as large an audience as possible. This was the rhetoric used in professional contexts, for instance in a trade journal like *Kinolehti* or when addressing authorities about taxation or other financial issues. When speaking to the public, the necessity was made into a virtue. Särkkä especially mastered the patriotic rhetoric of addressing the nation as a whole. According to Särkkä, Finnish films in general, and obviously the films of Suomen Filmiteollisuus in particular, were for Finnish spectators 'flesh out of their own flesh'.[37] In accordance with this logic, the ultimate legitimation of domestic cinema followed from the populist reasoning that the popularity of Finnish films was possible only because they had the backing of 'the people'. In the late 1930s, at the time of the premiere of *February Manifesto* (1939), 'the people' in Särkkä's rhetoric referred to all social classes:

> It is often remarked on these pages that, in modern society, cinema more than any other art form 'belongs to the whole people'. The film

audience is made of practically all population groups, since the success of cinema cannot be explained in any other way. The working man and the schoolteacher, the farmer and the bank manager, the housemaid and the professional woman, all sit side by side at the cinema, as a grand democracy of the auditorium, waiting to see the imaginary world that is mediated to the screen with the technical means of film art.[38]

While it is undoubtedly true that, especially with large-scale prestige productions such as *February Manifesto* or *Activists* (1939), the producers really attempted to reach the widest possible audience, this was not the case with every film. Already in the 1930s, it seems evident that Suomi-Filmi's specialties were women's films of various kinds, both drama and especially comedy. In her study on 1940s Finnish cinema, Anu Koivunen points out that, even if neither Suomi-Filmi nor other production companies ever actually used the term 'women's film', Suomi-Filmi's modern comedies, as well as the maternal melodramas and fallen woman films of the 1940s, addressed predominantly female audiences, featured female protagonists and female-oriented themes, and were usually based on novels or scripts by female authors.[39] As a contrast, Suomen Filmiteollisuus readily emphasised that it was a company owned and run by men and that it produced films for 'manly men'.[40] Generally, however, neither of the companies wanted to take the risk of losing potential audiences by explicitly gendered segmentation. Suomen Filmiteollisuus also entered the field of women's films itself during the war years with highly successful costume dramas like *The Vagabond's Waltz* (1941) and *Catherine and the Count of Munkkiniemi* (1943). Yet, throughout the studio decades, it maintained a certain male-centred orientation, which manifested itself variously in rillumarei films, lumberjack films or Puupää films.

According to a similar logic, even if Mauno Mäkelä complained about the impossibility of audience differentiation, the youth-oriented comedies and urban noir thrillers of Fennada implied targeting certain audiences. According to Mäkelä:

> The viewers will not watch a domestic film just because it is in Finnish, as they used to do. They have already learned to watch and understand foreign films. Both language skills and the will to learn have increased, and the viewers are already so used to reading subtitles that this causes no problem. Only the countryside devotes itself to domestic films anymore, and there they are the lifeblood to many cinemas.[41]

A survey from 1957 clearly backed up Mäkelä's view: domestic films were now preferred by elderly people living outside of cities and towns, whereas young and urban audiences favoured especially American and French films.[42] While recognising and admitting this state of affairs, Mäkelä at the same time attempted to take advantage of it by investing in youthful and American-influenced films and thus beating imported films at their own game. Yet, as we have seen, Fennada kept on making other kinds of films, too, including rural dramas, lumberjack films, vagabond films and adaptations of prestige novels, presumably with different audiences in mind.

All in all, the major companies seem to have adopted a double strategy in their audience address, arising from the logic of studio differentiation. On the one hand, they spoke of their willingness and ability to address the Finns as a unified nation, as well as of the impossibility of audience differentiation in a small country. On the other hand, they specialised in certain kinds of films with no intention of reaching every audience segment with each particular film. It is obvious that neither the populist rillumarei films of Suomen Filmiteollisuus, the gritty noirs of Fennada nor the glamorous upper-class comedies of Suomi-Filmi were geared to meet all tastes. As long as the average film received the 300,000 or 400,000 attendances that were needed to make a reasonable profit, and the occasional prestige film exceeded these figures, that was enough to keep the business going.

## Notes

1. 'Kotimaista vai ulkomaista', *Suomi-Filmin Uutisaitta* 2–3/1940.
2. 'SF – Mikä se on ja mitä se on?', *SF-Uutiset* 1/1935: 9. Italics in the original.
3. Cagle 2014: 47–53.
4. Seppälä 2017.
5. Soila 1998: 36.
6. Seppälä 2017.
7. 'Korkein voitto', *Elokuva* 4/1929: 7.
8. V. K–nen: 'Eikö suomalainen yleisö välitä huvinäytelmäfilmeistä?', *Filmiaitta* 17/1929: 23.
9. Erkki Kivijärvi: 'Suomalainen elokuva', *Helsingin Sanomat* 21 June 1932.
10. Roland af Hällström: 'Jätkä suomalaisessa elokuvassa', *Elokuva* 9–10/1929: 16. The author and later screenwriter Mika Waltari was, in the late 1920s, part of the literary group Tulenkantajat ('Torch Bearers'), which sought for urban and cosmopolitan approach under the slogan 'Open the windows to Europe!'
11. Karkama 1994: 175–91.
12. Roland af Hällström: 'Jätkä suomalaisessa elokuvassa', *Elokuva* 9–10/1929: 16.
13. Af Hällström 1936: 230.
14. Roland af Hällström: 'Suomen kolme filmiohjaajaa', *Aamulehti* 6 January 1929.

15. Af Hällström 1936: 228–30.
16. Halonen 1945: 118.
17. Koivunen 1995: 221–2.
18. Donner 1961: 44.
19. Malmberg 1975: 9.
20. Kolbe 1999: 156–70. For a critique of this view, see Laine and Laine 2008.
21. Hillier 1972: 36, 42.
22. Von Bagh 1993a; Mäkinen 1999.
23. Artturi Järviluoma: 'Erkki Karu In memoriam', *SF-Uutiset* 1/1936: 14–15.
24. Uusitalo 1994: 180.
25. 'Kotimaisen elokuvan arvostelu on aiheellista, myöntävät tuottajat', *Vapaa Sana* 2 February 1952.
26. Picciolino: 'Ranskalainen tyyli', *Elokuva-Aitta* 9/1943: 202.
27. 'Elokuvan luo kamera', *SF-Uutiset* 7/1940: 6–7. Italics in the original.
28. See Laine 2019: 553–5.
29. See Aumont 1987: 159–70.
30. See Bacon, Laine and Seppälä 2019: 156–95.
31. Töyri 1983: 133–6.
32. Von Bagh and Riikonen 1991: 25.
33. Töyri 1983: 135–6.
34. 'Kotimaisen elokuvan arvostelu on aiheellista, myöntävät tuottajat', *Vapaa Sana* 2 February 1952.
35. Maire Haahti: 'Elokuvatuottajat ja suomalainen elokuva', *Kinolehti* 5/1956: 8.
36. 'Ensi syyskauden ohjelmistoa', *SF-Uutiset* 5/1939: 4.
37. 'Suomalaisen filmin oikeutus', *SF-Uutiset* 3/1937: 11.
38. Sulka: 'Lukijalle', *SF-Uutiset*, 2/1939: 3.
39. Koivunen 1995: 45–51.
40. See Laine 1999: 227.
41. 'Kotimaisen elokuvan arvostelu on aiheellista, myöntävät tuottajat', *Vapaa Sana* 2 February 1952.
42. Janne Hakulinen: 'Kuinka käydään elokuvissa ja mitä elokuvia katsotaan?', *Kinolehti* 2/1957: 6–7.

# Chapter 7
# Film politics and censorship

In April 1943, at a moment when the ongoing World War II and the Finnish–Soviet Continuation War were having a massive effect on both filmmaking and the film trade, Ensio Hiitonen wrote an article for the social democratic newspaper *Kansan Lehti* called 'Film as an Economic, Political and Cultural Factor'. Hiitonen, a representative of the Finnish Film Chamber and one of the crucial actors in Finnish film politics during and after World War II, surveyed the relationship between state and cinema, outlining four more or less interconnected perspectives. First, film was a business, an economic factor that from the state point of view had meant that it was primarily a target for taxation. Second, by favouring domestic production over imported films the state had a possibility of implementing national cultural politics. A radical means of regulating the proportion of domestic films to imported ones was to impose import restrictions. Third, film was a powerful weapon for various forms of propaganda. This, of course, was especially evident at the time the article was written. And fourth, film was an object of censorship, not only during the exceptional circumstances of the war years, but also during peacetime.[1]

This chapter will discuss the relations of the state authorities and cinema from the four perspectives raised in Hiitonen's newspaper article: film as the object of taxation, film as an object of censorship, film as propaganda, and film as a means of doing national and international politics. Some of these perspectives concern the film studios directly, and some indirectly, either as active agents or as objects of the state's politics, or both. Yet, each of these factors crucially affected the preconditions and circumstances the studios operated in.

## Film and taxation

A common complaint among film critics and professionals during the studio years was that, from the state's perspective, film was seen primarily as a source of income and only secondarily as a cultural factor. Typical is the director Ilmari Unho's bitter criticism from 1945:

> As film has achieved a growingly significant position as a cultural factor, as true folk art, as a force shaping the views and ideals of – especially young – people, and as it has, at the same time, developed into a substantial national economic factor, the relation between film and the state has become ever more crucial. It is quite natural that the state has had to adopt a stance towards cinema. What is unnatural is that the stance is exclusively negative. Film is to the state merely an object of taxation and censorship, nothing else.[2]

Unho wrote his article at a moment when cinema indeed laboured under a heavy tax burden: the tax rate had been raised twice during the war years. This meant that even if attendances were high, it was increasingly difficult to break even with domestic productions, not only because of the taxes, but also because of increasing inflation and the shortage of raw film stock and other materials.

Film screenings had been taxed in Finland right from beginning. First, the exhibitioner had to pay a certain fixed amount for each screening, in a same way as the organisers of circus or variety shows paid for each performance. During the World War I, in 1915, when the state was searching for additional sources of income, a new form of taxation was adopted: now the exhibitioner had to pay a certain percentage of the ticket income to the state. In the beginning, this new form of 'amusement tax' was applied equally to all sorts of public events, be they sports, culture or entertainment. With the 1921 'stamp tax' reform, however, public events were differentiated from each other on the basis of their estimated quality. The tax for circus, panoramas, wax shows and other forms of low entertainment was 50 per cent, for cinemas 30 per cent, and for opera, concerts and legitimate theatre it was 10 per cent. Five years later, the latter, established art forms were freed of the stamp tax altogether.[3]

In her study on the history of cultural politics of Finnish cinema, Mervi Pantti sees the 1921 tax reform as the beginning of the use of taxation as a means for cultural distinction. While the primary purpose of the tax was to collect money for the state, it also became a tool for differentiating art from entertainment and, in time, domestic productions from imported ones.[4] Therefore, it crucially affected film cultural discussions during the studio years. As cinema was in legal terms determined to be among the low arts that should be 'punished' by heavy taxation, speaking and writing about cinema was inevitably defensive. 'Does anyone think', asked Unho in his above-mentioned article, 'that it is more effective to refine the artistic taste and support the moral and social backbone of our people by subsidising literature, theatre or music than by raising the standards of Finnish art films?'[5]

The 1921 tax reform marked the beginning not only of differentiating between art forms but also of differentiating between various kinds of films. While the general tax for film screenings was 30 per cent, for screenings of 'scientific and art films' it was 20 per cent. The classification was carried out by the State Film Censorship Board. In 1926, scientific and educational films were freed of taxes altogether, and the tax rate of art films was lowered to 15 per cent.[6] What is of interest regarding domestic film production is that, while in terms of the law, domestic and imported films were treated in the same way, in practice, virtually all Finnish feature films during the 1920s were classified as art films. Another interesting interpretation of the law was that *Our Boys* (1929), Suomi-Filmi's fictive and partly comical account of army recruits, was freed from the tax and thus treated as an educational film.

Differentiating domestic productions from imported films was finally drawn up in the stamp tax reform of 1930. Finnish films were now freed from taxes altogether. This can be seen as the first stage of state support for film production, even if this still took the form of the indirect privileging of domestic films over others rather than actually subsiding such films. Yet, it was an important step both symbolically and concretely. It was a signal for film producers, albeit still a relatively weak one, that the state valued films, at least as a branch of industry, if not so much as art. And in a very concrete way, it helped film production to survive the difficulties caused by the Great Depression and the coming of sound.

An additional concession concerned the production of short films. After a systematic lobbying by the Film Theatre Owners Union (from 1940 on, the Finnish Film Chamber), a new tax reduction system took effect in 1933. Taking its model from Germany, this system allowed a 5 per cent tax reduction for any screening that started with a domestic short film; at the moment the law was enacted, this, of course, meant screenings of imported feature films, since Finnish ones were freed from taxes. According to the prescribed criteria, a deductible short film should be at least 200 metres (about seven minutes) long and should be a scientific, educational or art film, or a film about domestic trade and industry.[7]

There were some obvious shortcomings and loopholes in the system: old films from the silent era were resubmitted for examination in order to pass as a deductible short film; feature documentaries were re-edited over and over again to create 'new' short films; and out-and-out advertising films were disguised as films about trade and industry. Yet, the short-film tax reduction system that was in force from 1933 to 1964 proved to have lasting effects. Right from the beginning, it gave a remarkable boost to the film industry, still struggling with the Depression. It succeeded in helping the exhibition branch of the industry, which, of course, was one of the original purposes of the system. It crucially prompted short-film production. While the yearly number of short films before the law was around twenty, in 1933 it was more than ten times that. Short films were produced by both specialised companies like Aho & Soldan and by diversified major companies like Suomi-Filmi, which remained among the central short-film companies through the studio years. The tax reduction system also gave an opportunity to produce a wide variety of non-commercial films, such as the Bauhaus-influenced street scenes, travelogues or industrial films by Aho & Soldan, or the academically accurate ethnographic films by Kansatieteellinen Filmi. Finally, short-film production proved to be a significant school for feature filmmakers: many directors, cinematographers and editors learned the profession first by making newsreels and other short films.

Against the background of the 1930s concessions, the World War II–era decision to start taxing domestic films again obviously seemed like a backlash, even if it was based on war-related economic reasons only. Starting from 1941, the tax rate for art films was 10 per cent and for others it was 15 per cent, and two years later, the rates were raised to 25 and 35 per cent, respectively. Yet, the rates for imported films were even higher, having risen to 50 per cent for any other than art films.[8]

After the war years, the tax rate started gradually to lower again, albeit with an interesting additional reform. Starting from 1946, films were categorised into three groups instead of the previous two. The first one included, as before, art films (25 per cent), the second one 'entertainment films' (30 per cent) and the third one 'substandard films' (35 per cent). The third tax category was soon nicknamed the 'penalty tax'. This three-tier system lasted with some variation until 1958, when, in the middle of a deepening profitability crisis, Finnish domestic films were freed from taxes again, with the exception of the substandard films. Even the penalty tax, however, was much lower than before at only 10 per cent.[9]

The penalty tax remained disputed through the studio years, especially since the criteria for what was considered 'substandard' appeared arbitrary.

Sometimes it seemed to refer to the technical quality of the film and sometimes to the content or the assumed morals of the film. The role of the State Film Censorship Board thus became important not only in making the actual censorship decisions but also in putting the tax rating into practice. As a consequence, the tax rating system had an amount of guiding effect, and the Censorship Board wielded considerable guiding power. At times, the system clearly favoured the major companies at the expense of the minors and independents. During World War II, practically all films by the majors were classified as art films attracting the lower rate, regardless of their genre, whereas several comedies and melodramas by minor companies were 'punished' with a higher rate. A case in point is *The Little Bride of the Garrison* (1943), a military comedy by Karhu-Filmi, discussed in Chapter 3. From the late 1940s on, the penalty tax often fell upon Suomen Filmiteollisuus with its increasing output of low-cost and lowbrow farces. Typically, in his reply to the Appeal Board of Film Classification, T. J. Särkkä would respond in populist terms:

> By making *Mr Coolman from the Wild West* [1952] we have aimed at a harmless and enjoyable comedy, an entertainment film that is well made for its kind and that will provide counterbalance to the everyday worries and troubles of ordinary people. The story of the film is highly positive: the simple and decent people end up doing well – if after a series of mishaps – whereas those who try to prosper dishonestly will get what they deserve. In terms of morals and ethics, there is nothing in the film that would call for the highest tax rate.[10]

As in many other cases, the appeal for *Mr Coolman from the Wild West* was unsuccessful. Särkkä further appealed to the Supreme Court, which was the final appeal court, but still with no success. At this period, in fact, the output of Suomen Filmiteollisuus was so abundant and the average cost of the comedies so low that Särkkä's readiness to appeal against every penalty tax decision might have been partly symbolic; it was hardly realistic to expect that the Appeal Board would overturn decisions made by the Censorship Board, especially in the cases of the controversial rillumarei films such as *Mr Coolman from the Wild West*. Yet, in some instances, the tax ratings affected filmmaking decisions directly. When the penalty tax was imposed on the comedy *My Beloved Thief* (1957), Suomen Filmiteollisuus reacted differently from the usual rillumarei cases. Unlike the rillumarei films, *My Beloved Thief* was a highbrow kind of a 'serious' comedy, scripted by Walentin Chorell, one of Särkkä's favourite authors. Rather than just writing an appeal letter, Särkkä now added a new ending to the film and asked for a re-examination. In the original version, the female protagonist, a kleptomaniac pickpocket, goes unpunished, but in the new ending, she gives herself up and voluntarily serves a prison sentence. This time, Särkkä's efforts paid off, and the film received a lower tax rate.[11]

After domestic films regained tax exemption in 1958, the penalty tax appeared to be targeted at independent productions again, with the exception of Suomen Filmiteollisuus's sensationalist youth film *The Gang* (1963). The first penalty tax cases involved two of the central modernist filmmakers, Maunu Kurkvaara and Eino Ruutsalo, both visual artists who turned to independent filmmaking. Kurkvaara's *Car Girls* (1960) was a social problem film about young female hitchhikers. It had undeniably deliberate sensationalist elements, but, as many contemporary critics remarked, no more than some of the films by the major companies at the time. Furthermore, although a low-budget production, *Car Girls* was generally praised for its cinematographic quality, which means that the penalty tax could not have been based on the technical grounds.[12] As a result, even the reviewer of the conservative *Uusi Suomi* wrote that 'imposing a penalty tax on this film seems like an unreasonable suppression of enterprise; the various cycles of Schlager films, for example, in their business-like calculatingness would have better deserved to be punished.'[13]

The case of Ruutsalo's *Moment's in the Night* (1961) was even more controversial. While some critics regarded this experimental and largely non-narrative feature film as clumsy and amateurish,[14] others hailed it as the most innovative work since Nyrki Tapiovaara's films of the 1930s.[15] Yet, whatever the critic's stance towards the merits of the film, the penalty tax decision was generally considered utterly unfair. This time, an appeal to the Supreme Court was successful, but as the process took half a year, it did not do much to help the distribution of this uncommercial film.[16] As a symbolic gesture, however, the Supreme Court's decision was better than nothing: at least it gave a signal that the state representatives were not against new forms of film culture.

## Film censorship

From the beginning of the studio era until the outbreak of World War II, film censorship in Finland was, in principle, voluntary in nature. The background for this lay in the Grand Duchy era, when censorship caused constant problems for cinema owners. At first, Russian imperial regulations concerning printed material were applied to films, too, which meant that local authorities oversaw all film screenings, either by preliminary examination or by simply interrupting the screening in midstream. After a public debate between 1907 and 1910 about the low morality of films and especially the bad influence they had on children, film censorship was finally centralised in the Grand Duchy of Finland in 1911. Practical attempts to set up an organised central examination system failed, however, and during the 1910s, films were still often inspected by the local police.[17]

From the perspective of the theatre owners, the situation remained unsatisfactory in its arbitrariness, and therefore, as ambiguous as their attitude towards preliminary examination was in principle, they were active in promoting a truly organised central system. An additional motive behind the theatre owners' activity was that during the years after Finland gained independence in 1917, there was public debate over municipalising or nationalising the film industry. By taking a proactive role in solving the assumed moral problems in the films, the theatre owners ensured that they were able to keep control of their business.[18]

As a result, Finnish film censorship ended up being, in the terms of the censorship historian Jari Sedergren, 'semi-official'. From 1921 on, the examination of films was centralised in the State Film Censorship Board, which, in spite of its name, was funded by the film industry. Once a film passed examination by the Board, it could be screened anywhere in the country. The Board could, and often did, make conditional decisions: a film could pass if inappropriate parts were cut. The semi-official status of the Board meant that, even if pre-examination of films was, in principle, voluntary, practically all films exhibited in cinemas were examined. Not only did this prevent potential problems that might emerge after a film had already premiered, but since the Censorship Board was also responsible for the mandatory tax rating, all films had to be pre-examined anyway.[19] Film censorship maintained its semi-official status until the outbreak of the Finnish–Soviet Winter War, when it became obligatory as part of general war censorship in early December 1939. After World War II, in 1946, film censorship finally became officially obligatory, even in peacetime. This change was not dramatic, though, as the standard practice of film examination remained similar to what it had been before the war years. The most important change was that in contradictory cases, it now became possible to appeal to the Supreme Court.[20]

The earliest examination guidelines were short and imprecise. Among the things not to be shown were murders, robberies and other outrageous scenes, images that could be considered politically, morally or religiously offensive, as well as images that might have a brutalising or juridically confusing effect. It was up to the board to interpret what these instructions might mean in practice.[21]

In 1934, under pressure from several civic organisations and conservative politicians, a committee was set up by the Ministry of Education to draft more precise instructions for film censorship. A year later, a detailed list of 'don'ts and be carefuls' was introduced. The detailed instructions can be divided into four thematic areas. The first (section 4) concerned religion and aimed at regulating the ways God, religion, religious people and ceremonies were portrayed.[22] Seldom relevant with respect to domestic films, the religious regulations were applied to, for example, the Hollywood film *The Green Pastures* (1936), which featured biblical stories played out by an African American cast. The play the film was based on had already created a great stir among the political right during the early 1930s, when the far-right Patriotic People's Movement demanded a ban on the play. The State Film Censorship Board finally banned the film version, apparently basing its decision on the same issue that was at the core of the theatre controversy: portraying God as a black character.[23]

The second area of instructions (sections 5 and 6) restricted portrayals of violence and crime. In general, films should not encourage copy-cat crimes, nor should criminal plots or criminal characters be a predominant element of the film. The detailed instructions listed among the forbidden or avoidable subjects, for example, meticulous depictions of murder, suicide, execution, robbery, kidnapping and smuggling, prolonged scenes of violence and cruelty, and brutal and lengthy scenes of drug or alcohol abuse.[24] These restrictions, too, were applied more likely to imported than to domestic films. Among the well-known and much-debated cases of films banned on the grounds of crime depiction were some of the most prominent American noir films, like *The Big Sleep* (1946), *The Killers* (1946) and *White Heat* (1949).[25]

Sections 7–10 concerned sexuality and morality. In general, films should not offend the sanctity of marriage or home, nor should they lead spectators to think that despicable sexual relations were acceptable or common, let alone desirable. The full list of unacceptable issues was quite detailed. Among the things that were forbidden or to be avoided were passionate kisses and positions, obscene insinuations, words and gestures, indecent nudity (even in silhouette) or dances, sexual aberration, white slavery and labour pain. Many of the restrictions were expressed conditionally: venereal diseases, disreputable places or moral deterioration of a young person should not be shown, except as warning examples. Furthermore, erotic scenes could be included, if they were an essential part of an otherwise acceptable plot and if the intention was not to excite the spectators. Even nudity could be acceptable, if it was not 'indecent' and if the purpose was not to excite.[26] It was concessions like these that gave room for a certain ambiguity in relation to the moral restrictions, and many of the notable censorship cases of the studio years were about negotiating this ambiguity.

One of the most heated censorship debates was around Suomi-Filmi's *The Women of Niskavuori*, directed by Valentin Vaala in 1938. The film was based on a play by the left-wing author Hella Wuolijoki, who used a (male) pseudonym, Juhani Tervapää, in order to avoid political prejudice. The play premiered in 1936 with success and critical praise and was soon performed on stages around the country. However, when the identity of the playwright was revealed, the attitude of especially the extreme right became highly critical.[27] By the time the film version premiered, the identity of the author was no longer a secret to anyone. In fact, Wuolijoki had already been publicly celebrated a few months earlier, at the premiere of *Hulda from Juurakko* (1937), the first one of Suomi-Filmi's adaptations of her plays written under the same pseudonym.[28]

*The Women of Niskavuori* was the first in a series of five plays, all of which have been adapted to film, recounting the story of a wealthy Niskavuori farm from the 1880s to the 1940s. The first play, as well as its cinematic adaptation, takes place in the contemporary time and focuses on the farmer Aarne Niskavuori, who is unhappy in his marriage and falls in love with the new idealistic teacher Ilona. Finally, having caused a scandal in the small village community, the two leave for the city.

The censorship controversy over *The Women of Niskavuori* started after a relatively routine decision. The Board ordered a 12-metre cut from a scene in which Aarne and Ilona are shown talking while lying fully clothed on a bed (Figure 7.1). While such short cuts were not uncommon, Suomi-Filmi reacted in an unusual way: it refused to make the cut, after which the film faced a total ban.[29] Suomi-Filmi's appeal to the Appeal Board of Film Classification did not change the decision, but the vote was close, and two of the members of the Appeal Board expressed their opinion that, even if *The Women of Niskavuori*

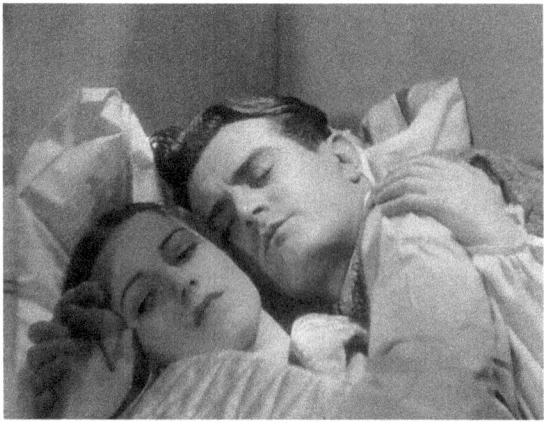

**Figure 7.1** Still from *The Women of Niskavuori* (1938).

was daring, it was nonetheless a morally consistent and artistically high-quality film.[30]

After the Appeal Board's decision, Suomi-Filmi finally agreed to make the cut, but the matter had already created quite a public stir. Many reviewers, in fact, saw the debate as free advertising for Suomi-Filmi, especially as the company publicly announced that it would cut only the release prints and not the negative, in order to be able to export the film in its entire state. According to the company, censorship officials had achieved a Pyrrhic victory.[31]

Indeed, public opinion was quite clearly on Suomi-Filmi's side. Reviewers throughout the political field considered the cut unnecessary, albeit for differing reasons. In social democratic and independent newspapers, *The Women of Niskavuori* was regarded as a first-class film that did not deserve the 'arbitrary' editing ordered by the Board.[32] On the political right, the film was often seen as problematic, but in such a way that no single cut would improve. The reviewer of the conservative *Uusi Suomi* wrote: 'I presume one does not have to be especially narrow-minded to intuitively oppose the way this . . . play presents free and secret love as proud and triumphant over social commitment and family morals.'[33]

Yet, even the conservative and extreme right reviewers had to admit the artistic value of the film. Therefore, *The Women of Niskavuori* was a highly ambiguous censorship case. Regarding it as a controversial borderline film, the Censorship Board presumably had to react somehow and so required a short and relatively standard cut. By refusing to make the cut, Suomi-Filmi turned the case from standard to unusual, forcing reviewers to take sides in a way that both highlighted the artistic value of the film and displayed the loopholes in the detailed examination instructions that had proven to be problematic in the eyes of producers and distributers.

As a censorship case, *The Women of Niskavuori* was also a reminder that moral issues were inseparable from politics. The debate can be seen as part of a larger controversy over art and morality during the interwar years, often referred to as a 'cultural crisis'.[34] Concerning such issues as tradition versus modernity, nationalism versus internationalism and idealism versus materialism, the debate was essentially politicised, as can be sensed in the words of a reviewer in the far-right newspaper *Ajan Suunta*, commenting on the unpunished adultery in *The Women of Niskavuori*: 'There are eternal laws that must not be undermined in the name of human freedom and happiness. If something like this happens, that is Bolshevism.'[35]

Post-war censorship cases concerning sexuality and morality differed from the politicised debate around *The Women of Niskavuori*. Typically, censorship problems centred on (mainly female) nudity. Due undoubtedly to cultural traditions, sauna and swimming scenes were to a degree treated as exceptions to the general rule that no nudity should be shown. Film producers exploited this relative permissiveness repeatedly, testing the willingness of the Censorship Board to interpret such scenes as 'not indecent'. In some cases, cuts were required. For example, 10 metres were cut from a sauna scene between two women in *The Decoy* (Fenno-Filmi 1946), and several scenes, including one in which the female protagonist swims in the nude, were shortened in *Prelude to Ecstasy* (SF 1961). Uncut versions of both films were exported to several countries with some success. 'Daring' scenes like these became a central selling point in exporting Finnish films during the post-war era, especially after the breakthrough of 'Nordic eroticism' in the early 1950s with Arne Mattsson's *One Summer of Happiness* (1951) and other Swedish films.[36]

Finally, section 11 of the detailed censorship instructions concerned overtly political issues with respect to both internal and foreign policy. A disrespectful attitude towards Finnish history, institutions, laws, well-known persons, national sentiments or the national flag was prohibited. Both domestic and foreign political propaganda were also to be avoided, and neither matters of national defence nor the people's will to defend their country were to be degraded. Furthermore, other nations should not be purposefully offended. In October 1939, after the outbreak of World War II, section 11 further specified that films 'liable to impair relations with foreign states or jeopardise the neutrality of the country' were to be banned.[37]

Political censorship was applied to imported films both before, during and after the war years, depending on the prevailing political reality. This means, for example, that, whereas very few Soviet films were seen in Finland during the 1930s, several hundred were screened during the post-war studio years. Very few of them encountered problems with censorship, and those that did usually caused negotiations with Soviet representatives, who were highly influential in Cold War–era Finland.[38]

As for domestic films, political censorship was applied especially during and immediately after the war years. A case in point is *The Great Wrath* (Jäger-Filmi 1939), a story about the resistance of a small Eastern Finnish village against invading Russian Cossacks during the Great Northern War (1700–21). Finland was at the time a part of the Swedish Empire, which, as a result of the war, ceased to be a major European power. *The Great Wrath* was a prime example of the potential risks encountered by a politically oriented historical film, even if the political ambitions were disguised as a historical allegory. When the film was first reviewed by the Censorship Board in the end of September 1939, several parts that were considered to offend the Soviet Union were ordered to be cut, including, for example, a dialogue line that names Moscow 'our arch enemy'. Also, a scene where Cossacks ride into a church in the middle of a sermon was to be shortened.[39]

In early October, due to the ongoing Finnish–Soviet negotiations, *The Great Wrath* was banned altogether, before it had premiered, undoubtedly because it was 'liable to impair the relations with foreign states'. The situation changed again in the end of November, when the Winter War broke out between Finland and Soviet Union. Now, the ban was overruled, and the film could premiere in December with no age restrictions; the original rating had been R-16. After the Winter War, *The Great Wrath* was banned again, only to be re-released when a new war, the Continuation War, broke between Finland and Soviet Union in the summer of 1941. Finally, there was a third ban when Finland and Soviet Union concluded a peace agreement in 1944.[40]

Along with *The Great Wrath*, several other historical films that contained anti-Russian sentiments were also banned in 1944. These included the most prestigious pre-war films by the major studios, *February Manifesto* (SF 1939) and *Activists* (SuFi 1939). Still other films, like the adventure film *Horse Swindler* (SF 1943), which depicts

Finnish independence fighters in 1916 and 1917, just before the Russian Revolution, and *The Girl Goes Out into the World* (SF 1943), about the women's military organisation Lotta Svärd, were voluntarily withdrawn from distribution by the producers themselves. Whether historical or contemporary films, they all contained such negative representations of Russians or Soviets that they would likely have caused problems if screened in post-war Finland.

## Film as propaganda

As we have seen, from the filmmakers' and producers' perspective, the state was usually interested in film only in negative terms. The editorial of *Elokuva* magazine summarised this clearly in 1929:

> One can hardly speak of the relation of the state to cinema; at the most, one should speak of its attitude towards it, and this attitude is basically negative. For the state, film seems to be an object of taxation, or, alternatively, film represents something evil that the Censorship Board has to keep a constant eye on in order to protect the good citizens.[41]

Arguing for lower taxation and other benefits for domestic films, the editor reminded his readers of the potential propaganda value of films, both abroad and in Finland. As an example of the former, he mentioned *Finlandia* (1922), Suomi-Filmi's feature documentary presenting the nature, culture and industry of Finland, targeted specifically at foreign markets. An example of a film that had positive value for the state in the domestic markets was Suomi-Filmi's *Our Boys* (1929), a fictional account of army recruits that was earlier in this chapter mentioned as a rare example of films exempted from the tax at the time. Suomi-Filmi's application to the Censorship Board was accompanied by a letter from two high-ranking army officers speaking for the film:

> By depicting the circumstances in army in a truthful way . . . the film is likely to give a realistic impression of the army life and work. This was the initial purpose, and that is why the army has contributed to the making of the film. Therefore, and especially since the film promotes to strengthen the will to defend one's country . . . it would be appropriate to exempt the film from taxes.[42]

As we have seen, domestic film production was soon given a privileged position regarding taxation, albeit, arguably, for economic rather than artistic or ideological reasons. During World War II, however, the situation was different as the state took a somewhat more active stance regarding film. The main focus was on documentary films, and as part of the Propaganda Division of the Headquarters (during the Winter War) and the State Information Bureau (during the Continuation War), a weekly *Newsreel of the Finnish Defence Forces* was released throughout the war years. Many of the top cinematographers were enlisted to shoot material for the newsreels, and directors like Hannu Leminen, Valentin Vaala and Orvo Saarikivi compiled and edited the films.[43]

Yet, even if many filmmakers were involved in actual war efforts, whether serving at the front, making documentaries or performing with the entertainment corps, it seemed to be in the interest of the state that the production of feature films continued, too. While the Censorship Board actively kept an eye on potential political excesses – with the help of military experts when necessary – making feature films remained basically independent through the war years. With regard to feature films, the state was thus more active in what is sometimes called 'negative propaganda', in regulating what was not to be shown, than in 'positive propaganda', attempting overtly to influence people's thoughts and actions.

It is, perhaps, telling that the fictional feature films that faced a total ban after the war were made before and not during the war. There seems to have been mutual understanding between the film producers and state officials that making openly propagandistic, war-related films celebrating the superiority of Finns over the Soviets would have been unwise, if only for the fact that feature film production would have been much too slow to react to the rapidly changing situations. The most obvious exceptions to this were the small number of military comedies like *That's How It Is, Boys* (SF 1942) and *Yes and Right Away* (SuFi 1943) that featured crude stereotypes of Russians (Figure 7.2) or contained degrading dialogue and songs. The former film was later voluntarily shortened by the production company itself and the latter, also voluntarily, withdrawn from distribution.

Instead of war propaganda, what state officials expected was light entertainment; Risto Orko later revealed that the army headquarters had asked Suomi-Filmi to make comedies.[44] 'Maintenance of morale' was the term often used in relation to wartime entertainment, referring to an urge to sustain routines and accustomed habits on the home front. This was openly articulated by the screenwriter Olavi Linnus in the trade journal *Suomen Kinolehti* in 1941: 'The present-day total war attempts to

**Figure 7.2** Stereotype of a Soviet soldier, with a portrait of Stalin in the background in *Yes and Right Away* (1943).

grab hold of all areas of life. It has therefore become all the more crucial that the usual way of life is maintained for all it is worth. Cinema plays a substantial part in this effort.'[45] The role of cinema was especially important, since access to most other forms of entertainment was limited, due either to lack of material or to prohibition, as in the case of dancing. Film attendances were higher than ever before or after the war, and in addition to regular cinemas and home-front roadshows, films were also screened for soldiers in outdoor or makeshift theatres. Therefore, it is understandable that during the long period of position warfare from the late 1941 to the spring of 1944, filmmakers and actors often got extra leave in order to be able to keep feature film production going.

## Film and international politics

Unlike in major European countries like Great Britain, France or Germany,[46] no actual film quotas were put into operation in Finland. Considering that domestic production was, at best, relatively modest in quantity, there was a continuous need for foreign films, and from the perspective of theatre owners, import restrictions would have made little sense. However, as we have seen, individual films were banned by the Censorship Board, and the importation of, for example, Soviet and German films varied according to the political atmosphere. The higher taxation imposed on imported films in comparison to domestic films was, furthermore, sometimes considered a 'luxury tax'.[47] Yet, no general restrictions were involved in these instances.

During World War II, however, there were attempts to restrict or even prohibit the importation of Hollywood films. In 1939, the central organisation of the film industry, the Society of Finnish Cinema, joined the International Film Chamber, changing its name to the Finnish Film Chamber at the same time.[48] In addition to its proclaimed ambition to enhance the position of European cinema, the German-led International Film Chamber clearly aimed at expanding German cultural influence and consolidating German control over the European film economy. These goals became increasingly obvious when the International Film Chamber was reorganised in a Berlin meeting in 1941.[49]

The Finnish Film Chamber was one of the organisations from seventeen European countries present in Berlin. Interestingly, from the point of view of the Finnish delegation, the Berlin meeting took place in July 1941, only a few weeks after the launch of Operation Barbarossa, the German invasion of the Soviet Union, and of the Finnish–Soviet Continuation War. This means that, at the time of the meeting, Finland and Germany were practically allies, even if the Finnish government readily insisted that Finland was waging a 'separate defensive war' on its own.[50]

Finland's representative in the Berlin meeting was Yrjö Rannikko, Secretary of the Finnish Film Chamber and the Editor of the trade journal *Suomen Kinolehti*. Together with Matti Schreck, the CEO of Suomi-Filmi and the Chair of the Finnish Film Chamber, he became the most eager advocate of the international parent organisation in Finland. In spring 1942, Rannikko and Schreck attempted to persuade the Finnish Film Chamber to join the central initiative of the Germans, to refrain from screening American films. Unable to convince the majority of the need for a boycott, the German-minded fraction of the Film Chamber resigned to form a new organisation, the Film Union of Finland. Among the companies that joined the Film Union were some of the biggest distributors like Adams-Filmi, as well as the majority of the production companies, including Suomi-Filmi and Suomen Filmiteollisuus. The American offices of Fox, MGM, Paramount and Warner Bros. naturally remained in the Finnish Film Chamber, as did several other import companies and independent production companies like Jäger-Filmi, Karhu-Filmi and Väinän Filmi.

A total boycott of American films thus never came into force. In fact, even if the number of American premieres decreased considerably after 1939, it nevertheless exceeded those of German or any other films through the war years.[51] Nonetheless, the polemic between the organisations remained bitter. Rannikko continued as the editor of *Suomen Kinolehti*, which became the official organ for the Film Union, whereas Finnish Film Chamber adopted the Theatre Owners' journal *Elokuvateatteri* as their mouthpiece, with Ensio Hiitonen as the editor. The debate centred in these journals, since the State Information Bureau forbade all discussion on the subject in newspapers, and neither professionals nor the audience were allowed to express general opinions about American cinema publicly. The reason for this ban was twofold: on the one hand, the debate implied an unwanted political rupture within the home front, and on the other hand, the state officials were, with good reason, anticipating a negative reaction from the US Embassy.[52]

From the point of view of the production companies, the debate concerned as much the availability of raw film stock as the screening of American films. At the beginning of the Continuation War, raw film was available only from Germany, and the producers willingly emphasised that for this reason cooperation with Germany was necessary.[53] In the autumn of 1944, soon after the peace agreement between Finland and Soviet Union, Rannikko attempted to explain the rationale behind the dispute solely in terms of raw film:

> The supply of raw film stock from Germany would already have ended two years ago because of the 'film dispute', had there not been a new organisation which guaranteed that the cinemas presenting domestic films made with German raw film did not make contracts about showing American films. If German pressure had not coerced us into this, shortage of raw film stock would have caused unemployment among our film professionals, as it does at the moment. There would never have been a film dispute had there been enough raw film on the market.[54]

It is true that raw film stock became a tool in international politics. Having realised the importance of raw film, the American Embassy contacted the Finnish Foreign Office and after unofficial negotiations promised to supply a reasonable amount of raw film stock, if the Finnish government would support the Finnish Film Chamber in its efforts to oppose the ban on American films. While the government remained officially silent, with the general purpose of keeping a low profile in the dispute, it did inform both the Finnish Film Chamber and the US Embassy that it had no intention of restricting the importation and exhibition of American films. As an exchange, the Americans did import some raw film stock, starting in 1943, though the amount remained modest at first.[55]

As central as the issue of raw film stock was for the film dispute, and as eager as Rannikko was afterwards to explain the events solely in relation to material necessity, for some of those involved there was more to it than that. A Suomi-Filmi board meeting from May 1942 suggests an active attitude in the matter:

> The Chair [Schreck] gave an account of the conflict raised in the Finnish Film Chamber's meeting on 28 May 1942, as a result of which Suomi-Filmi and those working for the company had resigned ... Furthermore, it was considered to be in the interests of the company to favour the operations of the International Film Chamber, and it was decided that the company should vigorously support the activities of the new Finnish Film Union.[56]

As the reporter of *Elokuvateatteri* argued, the Film Union's demand to ban all American films was an overreaction, since the International Film Chamber's initial demand was to forbid only the screening of 'incitement films', which would have been possible by merely following the standard censorship procedures.[57] Furthermore, the views expressed especially by Rannikko and Schreck indicated a strong political and ideological involvement. In the autumn of 1942, Schreck wrote in an article entitled 'Film and the Modern Times':

> European cinema, still modest at that time [during and after World War I], was, with the exception of the Nordic countries, almost entirely in Jewish hands, too. The National Socialist [Nazi] movement has provided new conditions for the extensive production of a national cinema, and other leading European countries, Italy in particular, have followed Germany's path. Knowing the antagonism between New Europe and Judaism, it is not surprising that the Jewish film industry used all means available to debase the actions, achievements and leading men of the Axis Powers.[58]

Rhetoric like this, invoking anti-Semitic sentiments and exploiting Nazi-associated expressions like 'Lebensraum', proved to be incriminating evidence after the war. There was also evidence that the relations between the Finnish Film Chamber and the German Film Chamber was not limited to practical issues. In November 1942, Rannikko led a delegation of Finnish film people to Germany. The delegation included the actors Lea Joutseno, Helena Kara, Regina Linnanheimo, Irma

Seikkula and Leif Wager and the directors Wilho Ilmari, Hannu Leminen and Ilmari Unho, all of whom were associated with either Suomi-Filmi or Suomen Filmiteollisuus at the time. The high-level visit took them to studios in Babelsberg, Munich and Vienna, and culminated in watching the brand-new melodrama *Die goldene Stadt* (1942) with not only the director Veit Harlan and the star Kristina Söderbaum but also the Minister of Propaganda Joseph Goebbels, who after the screening invited the Finnish delegation to his home.[59]

Among the terms of the peace agreement with the Soviet Union in September 1944 was that Finland should expel all German troops from its territory, which resulted in the Lapland War between Finland and Germany (September 1944–April 1945). With the peace agreement with the Soviets, the political situation turned upside down almost overnight. German newsreels were banned and replaced with American and Soviet ones.[60] Relations were established with Soviet filmmakers, and already in early 1945, Vsevolod Pudovkin visited Finland, meeting not only people from the film industry but also high-level politicians like the future presidents J. K. Paasikivi and Urho Kekkonen.[61]

The two contending organisations united again, as the Finnish Film Chamber decided in January 1945 to readmit as members those individuals and companies that had departed three years earlier. Suomen Filmiteollisuus was accepted as a member in May 1945, but Suomi-Filmi, having been more active in the Film Union, had to wait until the following year. Rannikko was finally re-elected as a member of the board in 1947.[62] Suomi-Filmi and Adams-Filmi were also on the blacklist established by the Americans, who were now the major provider of raw film stock. Suomi-Filmi was only able to survive its post-war crisis by replacing its board of directors, including Orko and Schreck. While Orko soon regained, and actually strengthened, his position in the company, Schreck stepped down, sold his shares and returned to banking.[63] The once pro-German Suomi-Filmi adapted itself to the new political situation, which later culminated in the large-scale co-production of the epic *Sampo* with the Soviets in 1959.[64]

## Notes

1. Ensio Hiitonen: 'Elokuva taloudellisena, poliittisena ja sivistyksellisenä tekijänä', *Kansan Lehti* 6 April 1943.
2. Ilmari Unho: 'Valtio ja elokuva', *Suomen Kinolehti* 12/1945: 171.

3. Pantti 2000: 129–32.
4. Ibid.: 132.
5. Ilmari Unho: 'Valtio ja elokuva', *Suomen Kinolehti* 12/1945: 171.
6. Uusitalo 1965: 157.
7. Sedergren and Kippola 2009: 109–13.
8. Ibid.: 157–8.
9. Ibid.: 158.
10. Uusitalo et al. 1992: 482.
11. Uusitalo et al. 1991: 100.
12. See, for example, Martti Savo: 'Skandaali', *Kansan Uutiset* 9 October 1960.
13. Heikki Eteläpää: 'Rahalla saa, autolla pääsee', *Uusi Suomi* 9 October 1960.
14. I. H.: 'Italialaisen filmin hyviä anteja', *Maaseudun Tulevaisuus* 31 August 1961.
15. Martti Savo: 'Rohkeita Hetkiä', *Kansan Uutiset* 27 August 1961.
16. Uusitalo et al. 1991: 559–60.
17. Nenonen 1999: 25–66.
18. Ibid.: 121–32.
19. Sedergren 2006: 15–17.
20. Ibid.: 15–17.
21. Sedergren 1999: 50–1.
22. Ibid.: 64.
23. Sedergren 2006: 22.
24. Sedergren 1999: 64–5.
25. Sedergren 2006: 14–7.
26. Sedergren 1999: 65–7.
27. Ammondt 1980: 145–6.
28. H. K.: 'Uppsluppen inhensk lustspelspremiär', *Hufvudstadsbladet* 18 October 1937.
29. 'Niskavuoren naiset', Censorship decision document 11 January 1938. State Board of Film Classification Collection, Helsinki: National Archives.
30. Appeal Board of Film Classification meeting 12 January 1938. State Board of Film Classification Collection, Helsinki: National Archives.
31. 'Riita Niskavuoren naiset -elokuvasta päättynyt', *Helsingin Sanomat* 13 January 1938. The subsequent prints for domestic markets, too, included the censured scene.
32. 'Elokuvakahnaukset', *Ilta-Sanomat* 12 January 1938.
33. Y.: 'Niskavuoren naiset', *Uusi Suomi* 17 January 1938.
34. See Koivunen 2003: 273–5.
35. U. T.: 'Suomi-Filmin Niskavuoren naiset', *Ajan Suunta* 17 January 1938.
36. Lehtisalo 2016: 126–7.
37. Sedergren 1999: 73–8.
38. Sedergren 2006: 73–82.
39. Sedergren 1999: 11.
40. Ibid.: 11–13.
41. 'Valtion suhde elokuvaan', *Elokuva* 4/1929: 3.
42. An undated letter [1929] from the General Headquarters (Dision 4) to the State Film Censorship Board. State Board of Film Classification Collection, Helsinki: National Archives.

43. Sedergren and Kippola 2009: 365–81.
44. Salmi 1991: 24; Mäkinen 1999.
45. Olavi Linnus: 'Filmi sodassa', *Suomen Kinolehti* 3/1941: 102–3.
46. Thompson 1985: 118–28.
47. Martin 2007: 32.
48. Soila 1998: 60–1.
49. Martin 2007.
50. The 'separate war' thesis remained central in Finnish post-war historiography. See Kivimäki 2011: 1–46.
51. Y. Rannikko: 'Maamme elokuvatoiminta tilastojen valossa 1945', *Elokuvateatteri - Suomen Kinolehti* 2/1946: 4–7.
52. Sedergren 1999: 206–7.
53. Even decades later, Orko, though not denying his pro-German sentiments, still emphasised the availability of raw film stock as the main reason for the film dispute. Mäkinen 1999.
54. A. L.: 'Kotimaisen filmiteollisuuden raakafilmin puute uhkaava', *Aamulehti* 19 November 1944.
55. Sedergren 1999: 207–13.
56. Suomi-Filmi's board meeting 29 May 1942. Suomi-Filmi Collection, Helsinki: National Audiovisual Archive.
57. Vaakamestari: 'Eräiden ulkomaisten filmien esittämistä koskevat erimielisyydet', *Elokuvateatteri* 6–7/1942: 9–10. See Martin 2007.
58. Matti Schreck: 'Filmi ja nykyaika', *Suomen Kinolehti* 7–10/1942: 125.
59. Stewen 2008: 318–27.
60. Sedergren 1999: 217.
61. 'Elokuva on nykyajan maailman mahtitekijä, sanoi Pudovkin', *Suomen Kinolehti* 1–3/1945: 34–5.
62. Sedergren 1999: 217.
63. Uusitalo 1994: 208–10.
64. Laine and Salmi 2009.

# Chapter 8

# Epilogue

What happened to the Finnish film studios and the studio system? A sense of crisis had manifested itself from time to time long before the 1960s. As we have seen in this book, the film industry was hit by various kinds of crises through the decades, some of which were internal, some external and some both. The early 1930s crisis can clearly be characterised as having both external factors including the general recession and the coming of recorded sound and internal ones such as the power struggle within Suomi-Filmi. The difficulties encountered by the film industry during and immediately after World War II were also varied in nature. In addition to the obvious obstacles caused by the state of war (difficulties in international trade, the scarcity of raw film stock and other materials), the film industry created its own internal crisis over its stance towards American films.

The actual structural crisis that led to the gradual breakdown of the studio system is usually dated to the late 1950s, with a more specific turning point in 1957–8, when the majors started laying off their staff and reducing their feature film production. Discussions about the crisis in domestic filmmaking had, however, been going on for nearly a decade. Although the actual term 'crisis' was often used both in the early and the late 1950s, the meaning, or at least the emphasis, of the word was different. Generally, while in the early 1950 critics and other commentators from outside or on the outskirts of the film industry perceived the crisis in terms of quality, film producers laid stress on taxation and other economic factors. The most comprehensive and talked-about debate on the crisis was organised by the left-wing newspaper *Vapaa Sana* in early 1952. The introduction to the first part of the debate read:

> Of all domestic arts, cinema is the one that has lately been the focus of attention. This is because complaints about a crisis of domestic film have risen from two directions. Whereas film critics as well as the

more enlightened sectors of the audience confirm the unsound artistic quality of film production time after time, the film producers complain that financial difficulties, the rise of production costs, taxation and competition from foreign popular films, will become a death trap for domestic cinema, and that it is only a matter of time before it is revealed whether it will be able to exist at all.[1]

The multi-part series of interviews featured representatives of various interest groups, including critics, producers, directors, screenwriters, cinematographers, state officials and ordinary cinemagoers. Interestingly, even if critics were clearly the accusing and producers the defending party in this debate, they shared some of the ideas. Taxation was considered unfairly high, while a lack of high-quality scripts was seen to hinder the development of domestic cinema. Directors, actors and cinematographers complained about overproduction and the hasty working pace as well as about the lack of decent scripts. Screenwriters, being blamed by all of the other groups, were discontented with their fees and their inability to participate in the making of films. Finally, the state representatives claimed that there were not enough discerning viewers and that the penalty tax was thus necessary; otherwise, producers might give in to bad taste.[2] Overall, the debate developed into a series of vicious circles, where each party blamed the other for the situation, in terms of both quality and economics.

A similar tension prevailed a few years later, in 1955 and 1956, when the trade journal *Kinolehti* organised a series of round-table discussions over the state of domestic cinema. Screenwriters,[3] set designers[4] and directors[5] still complained about hastiness and working conditions, whereas producers concentrated on taxation, rising production costs and the small size of the domestic audience. The growing gap between the participants' perspectives was commented on by the moderator of the closing discussion between producers:

> One would have wished that producers could have spared a word or two for film *art* and the creative work behind it, a word for *its* challenges from the producer's perspective – not only for financial problems. *Those* are the things we already know about. One might even suspect that the producers, wallowing in their money problems, have had no time ... even to read the reports about the previous discussions about domestic cinema.[6]

From 1957 on, however, discussions about the crisis of domestic cinema in *Kinolehti* were more often only about money. The issue of quality was still there, but in an acute situation where studios were laying of their staff, structural problems predominated, at least for a moment. The sense of structural crisis was summed up in a 1959 article by the new editor of *Kinolehti*, Helge Miettunen, who started with alarming words about the future of domestic film production:

> Indeed, it has been a long journey. Yet, now we have to ponder whether this journey was meant to be enduring and continuing, or rather just a passing stage of Finnish culture. It is quite obvious that the end point is in sight, unless things start to happen.[7]

However, Miettunen ended his article in a slightly optimistic tone. After commenting on the inconsistency of the state's film politics, culminating in the tax exemption for domestic films in 1958, which was absolutely too late, he proposed a potential remedy: following the Swedish model and refunding part of the stamp taxes to producers as subsidies. Even if Miettunen emphasised the cultural and artistic value of domestic film production, at this point its whole existence depended on the willingness of the state to lend a helping hand.[8]

Two years later, in 1961, when Jörn Donner published his epoch-making manifesto 'Finnish Cinema Year Zero', the emphasis was different again: 'Let us put the economics of Finnish cinema aside for a moment and start by discussing the real reason for the crisis: the films themselves, and the competence that these films manifest.'[9] The tone differed from the previous crisis talk in *Kinolehti* not only because Donner wrote more as a critic and less as an aspiring filmmaker, but also because in 1961 it might have seemed that film production was thriving again. On the one hand, after the reduction in the number of premieres in the late 1950s, Suomen Filmiteollisuus again had twelve opening nights in 1960, and another eleven in 1961. On the other hand, at the moment Donner wrote his manifesto, it was finally announced that the first state prizes for cinema would be awarded in 1961.[10] For a brief moment, it may have seemed possible and even probable that a new mode of production was on the way, combining old studio-based practices and new subsidised funding methods.

Yet, Donner was clearly aware of the structural changes that were taking place not only in film production but also in society at large. This was evident especially in his critique of the major studios' stubborn willingness to keep on pleasing everyone at the same time. As we have seen, this objective was based on the assumption, expressed by Mäkelä in 1952, that, because of the limited size of the domestic markets, it was impossible to make films for segmented audiences. In Donner's view, pleasing everyone had become a conceptual impossibility: in their effort to appeal to everyone, such 'family films' usually ended up appealing to no one. Therefore, there was no sense in complaining about the situation. On the contrary, according to Donner, it was precisely the attempts to please everyone that made it impossible to deal with the real contradictions in contemporary society. And, conversely, as long as the films could not get a grip on real social problems, they would not please anybody.[11]

If a unified national audience had ever existed outside the declarations by producers, by the 1960s it was quite clear to everyone that this was an illusion. An unforeseen wave of urbanisation and suburbanisation took place in the 1950s and 1960s.[12] At the same time, the few existing surveys about cinemagoing showed that young and urban audiences favoured European (especially in downtown Helsinki) and American films (especially in suburbs and smaller towns), whereas domestic films were preferred in the countryside and in some working-class districts of the cities.[13] In this situation, it was increasingly difficult to make films that would appeal to all of these preferences. As cinema audiences were getting younger, and as rural cinemas were closing down, the old strategies of the major studios were falling through.

As a result, even if the youth film was Mäkelä's central example of the impossibility of making targeted films in Finland, with their last efforts all three majors ended up attempting to address the young, urban audiences. Suomi-Filmi tried with a youthful Schlager film, *Swinging Youth* (1961), which was the penultimate feature film directed by Valentin Vaala (Figure 8.1), and with New Wave–oriented episodic films like *Happy Games* (1964). Fennada, too, made a Schlager film (*Hit Parade*, 1959) and co-produced with the Swedish Sandrew Film Jörn Donner's Antonioni-influenced *Adventure Starts Here* (1965). Suomen Filmiteollisuus made attempts not only with Schlager films (*Stardust*, 1961) but also with Eddie Constantine–like adventure films (*No Bodies in the Bedroom*, 1959; *Playing a Hard Game Up North*, 1959)[14] and sensationalist youth problem films (*Nina and Erik*, 1960; *The Gang*, 1963)[15].

With a few exceptions, such as the first three detective films in the Inspector Palmu series, *Inspector Palmu's Error* (SF 1960), *Gas Inspector Palmu!* (Fennada 1961) and *The Stars Will Tell, Inspector Palmu* (Fennada 1962), the post-crisis films were no longer profitable, and it became inevitable that the majors had to give up their feature film staff. The two-and-a-half-year actors' strike that started in 1963 was by no means a cause

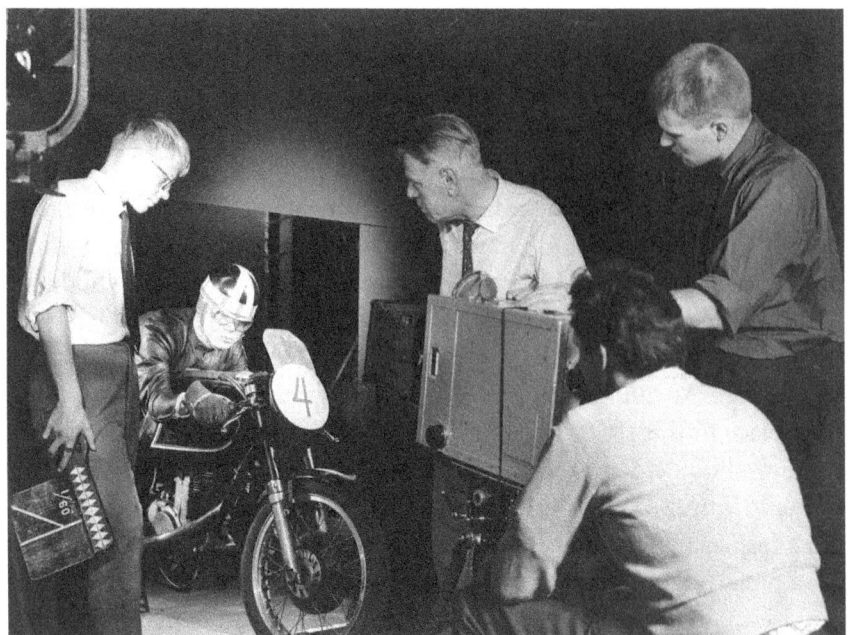

**Figure 8.1** *Swinging Youth* (1961): Suomi-Filmi's attempt at a youth film. Valentin Vaala (centre) prepares for a motorcycle rear projection scene.

of the crisis, which had begun years earlier, but it did deal one of the final death blows to the majors. For example, a fourth Inspector Palmu film had already been scripted by Mika Waltari, but since professional actors were an essential ingredient in the Palmu films, the film was never shot.[16]

It would be an exaggeration to claim that the early 1960s witnessed a complete break with the past and that one mode of film production was all at once replaced with another. First, as we have seen, independent and package-produced films were already being made during the studio years, with neither permanent studio nor staff, and each production put together separately. Second, there were powerful producers and long-lasting production companies even after the studio era. Examples of these are Pertti 'Spede' Pasanen, who through several companies bearing his name produced more than forty quickly made popular comedies between 1964 and 1998, very much in the tradition of Särkkä, and Jörn Donner, who produced or co-produced more than thirty feature films between 1967 and 2017 through his company Jörn Donner Productions, seeking for a 'third way' mode of production somewhere between commercial studio filmmaking and subsidised independent production.[17] Third, even if a generational change did take place in filmmaking during the 1960s, it was not a total one. Some of the key directors of both popular (Spede Pasanen) and art cinema (Mikko Niskanen, Jaakko Pakkasvirta) of the 1960s generation started their film careers as actors in the major studios; Niskanen even directed his first three films for Suomen Filmiteollisuus and Fennada. Some of the most important studio directors like Matti Kassila and Edvin Laine, for their part, continued making films for decades, even if sporadically and in different circumstances. And fourth, although television was often pictured as an enemy of cinema, there was a certain continuity between studio filmmaking and television. Many of the studio professionals were employed by television, many of the television genres originated from cinema, and filmmakers like Spede Pasanen and Mikko Niskanen moved smoothly between film and television.

Yet, notwithstanding such continuities, filmmaking after the early 1960s was different from what it had been during the studio decades. Full-service houses with permanent studios and staff were replaced mainly with a practice that resembles the package-unit system Janet Staiger describes in the Hollywood context.[18] Each film production was put together separately, and even the long-lasting companies hired most of the crew for one production at a time. Funding for each film was raised separately as well, combining private and public money, channelled after 1969 by the Finnish Film Foundation. Filmmakers were mainly freelancers, and sound recording and post-production services were provided by specialised companies.

The mechanisms of public funding have gone through several changes over the past decades.[19] Especially in the 1970s and 1980s, the funding principles differed fundamentally from the box-office-centred thinking of the studio era. Subsidies were delivered on the basis of the assumed quality of the project application (not without controversy though), with little interest in the popular appeal or marketing of the film. After a constant decrease in attendances and with a general shift towards neoliberal cultural politics, the Film Foundation's approach has gradually changed. In 1989, the Film Foundation, facing increasing budget responsibility, established a vacancy for a fiction film producer whose purpose was to invest in versatility, novelties and entertainment, and in that way find a renewed contact with audiences. With regard to subsidies, the focus was now on series and popular genres instead of the individual art films that were previously at the core. After this turning point, the public funding policy has adopted several practices that have their roots in the studio era. One-off payments have been replaced by phased forms of funding, starting with initial planning and screenwriting and then entering into shooting and post-production, and finally into marketing. The most fundamental difference between the first decades and the current state of public film funding is arguably in the emphasis given to marketing. In the 2000s, every feature film is supposed to have a target audience plan, a marketing plan and a publicity agent. If the marketing plan is successful, there is a good chance that the production company will be able to make new films – not unlike during the studio years.

Some of the renewed practices of the Film Foundation have deliberately been adapted from the studio decades. In general, studio-era cinema has anything but disappeared from our eyes. Specialised festivals have screened studio films since the 1990s. All of the surviving films by Suomi-Filmi, Suomen Filmiteollisuus and Fennada, as well as those of Teuvo Tulio, are available as complete DVD boxes. The Finnish Broadcasting Company has aired an old domestic film every working day for years, and hundreds of studio-era films can be watched online via the Elonet site run by the National Audiovisual Institute. Indeed, without the general interest in studio-era filmmaking, this book would not have come into being.

## Notes

1. 'Kotimaisen elokuvan kriisi vaatii vihdoinkin toimenpiteitä', *Vapaa Sana* 15 January 1952.
2. 'Kotimaisen elokuvan kriisi', *Vapaa Sana* 15 January, 19 January, 24 January, 26 January, 2 February, 5 February and 8 February 1952.
3. Maire Haahti: 'Suomalainen elokuva', *Kinolehti* 6/1955: 20–2.
4. Maire Haahti: 'Suomalainen elokuva', *Kinolehti* 2/1956: 6–8.
5. Maire Haahti: 'Suomalainen elokuva', *Kinolehti* 7–8/1955: 9–14.
6. Maire Haahti: 'Elokuvatuottajat ja suomalainen elokuva', *Kinolehti* 5/1956: 7–10. Italics in the original.
7. Helge Miettunen: 'Suomalainen elokuva ahdingossa', *Kinolehti* 2/1959: 3.
8. Ibid.: 4–5.
9. Donner 1961: 33.
10. Martti Savo: 'Kuka jakaa elokuvan 15 miljoonaa?', *Kansan Uutiset* 8 June 1961.
11. Donner 1961: 37, 46–8.
12. Valkonen, Alapuro, Alestalo, Jallinoja and Sandlund 1980: 205.
13. Hannikainen 1952: 45–7; Janne Hakulinen: 'Kuinka käydään elokuvissa ja mitä elokuvia katsotaan?', *Kinolehti* 2/1957: 6–7.

14. Seppälä 2019.
15. Römpötti 2019.
16. Kassila 2004: 301–3. At the time of writing this book, it was announced that the unused Palmu script will be made into a film after all, by the Finnish-born director Renny Harlin known for, for example, *Die Hard 2* (1990). *Helsingin Sanomat* 19 January 2021.
17. See Laine 2016: 173–6.
18. Bordwell, Staiger and Thompson 1985: 330–7.
19. See Kinnunen 1919.

# References

## Newspapers and periodicals

*Aamulehti* 1929, 1944
*Ajan Suunta* 1938
*Apu* 1974
*Elokuva* 1927–9, 1931
*Elokuva-Aitta* 1933, 1938, 1940, 1942–3, 1947
*Elokuvalukemisto* 1940
*Elokuvateatteri* 1942, 1944
*Elokuvateatteri – Suomen Kinolehti* 1946
*Filmiaitta* 1923, 1927, 1929
*Helsingin Sanomat* 1932, 1938–40, 2021
*Hufvudstadsbladet* 1937
*Ilta-Sanomat* 1938
*Kansan Lehti* 1943
*Kansan Uutiset* 1960–1
*Kauppalehti* 1921, 1936
*Kinolehti* 1951, 1955–7, 1959
*Maaseudun Tulevaisuus* 1961
*Opettajain Lehti* 1939
*Patenttirekisteri* 1932, 1937
*Rekisterilehti* 1920
*Seura* 1939
*SF-Uutiset* 1935, 1937–9, 1941, 1944
*Sisä-Suomi* 1927
*Suomen Kaupparekisteri* 1942
*Suomen Kinolehti* 1934, 1937, 1939, 1941–2, 1945
*Suomi-Filmin Uutisaitta* 1935, 1939–40
*Teatterimaailma* 1938
*Uusi Suomi* 1938, 1960, 1965
*Vapaa Sana* 1952

# Bibliography

Altman, Rick (1987), *The American Film Musical*, London: BFI Publishing.
Altman, Rick (1999), *Film/Genre*, London: BFI Publishing.
Ammondt, Jukka (1980), *Niskavuoren talosta Juurakon torppaan. Hella Wuolijoen maaseutunäytelmien aatetausta*, Helsinki: Gaudeamus.
Ascheid, Antje (2012), 'Germany', in Corey K. Creekmur and Linda Y. Mokdad (eds), *The International Film Musical*, Edinburgh: Edinburgh University Press, 45–58.
Aumont, Jacques (1987), *Montage Eisenstein*, translated by Lee Hildreth, Constance Penley and Andrew Ross, London: British Film Institute.
Bacon, Henry, Kimmo Laine and Jaakko Seppälä (2019), *ReFocus: The Films of Teuvo Tulio: An Excessive Outsider*, Edinburgh: Edinburgh University Press.
Bagh, Peter von (1991a), 'Risto Orko', *Filmihullu* 6/1991, 14–17.
Bagh, Peter von (1991b), *SF:n tarina*, television documentary, Yleisradio.
Bagh, Peter von (1992a), 'Oolannista Karjalaan', *Filmihullu* 4/1992, 37–9.
Bagh, Peter von (1992b), 'Rillumarei-elokuvat', in Kari Uusitalo et al. (eds), *Suomen kansallisfilmografia 4: 1948–1952*, Helsinki: Edita and Suomen elokuva-arkisto, 397–401.
Bagh, Peter von (1993a), *Suomi-Filmin tarina*, television documentary, Yleisradio.
Bagh, Peter von (1993b), *Fennadan tarina*, television documentary, Yleisradio.
Bagh, Peter von and Mauri Riikonen (1990), 'SF-elämää', *Filmihullu* 4/1990, 24–7.
Bordwell, David (2008), *Poetics of Cinema*, New York and London: Routledge.
Bordwell, David, Janet Staiger and Kristin Thompson (1985), *The Classical Hollywood Cinema. Film Style & Mode of Production to 1960*, London: Routledge.
Cagle, Chris (2014), 'Classical Hollywood, 1928–1946', in Patrick Keating (ed.), *Cinematography*, London and New York: I. B. Tauris, 34–59.
Donner, Jörn (1961), 'Suomalainen elokuva vuonna 0', in Aito Mäkinen (ed.), *Studio 6*, Helsinki: Suomen elokuva-arkisto, 17–58.
Donner, Jörn and Martti Savo (1953), *Filmipulmamme. Arenan poleeminen julkaisusarja 2*, Porvoo: Arena.
Dyer, Richard (1979), *Stars*, London: BFI Publishing.
Elo, Aarre (1996), *Elon aika*, Porvoo, Helsinki and Juva: WSOY.
Garncarz, Joseph (1999), 'Made in Germany: Multiple-Language Versions and the Early German Sound Cinema', in Andrew Higson and Richard Maltby (eds), *'Film Europe' and 'Film America'. Cinema, Commerce and Cultural Exchange 1920–1939*, Exeter: University of Exeter Press, 249–73.
Gomery, Douglas (1986), *The Hollywood Studio System*, London & Basingstoke: British Film Institute & MacMillan.
Gronow, Pekka (2002), 'Iskelmäelokuvien aika', in Kari Uusitalo et al. (eds), *Suomen kansallisfilmografia 6, 1957–1961*, Helsinki: Edita and Suomen elokuva-arkisto, 282–7.
Hakosalo, Heini (2008), 'Terve tendenssi: Hannu Lemisen probleemielokuvat sotienjälkeistä Suomea huoltamassa', in Kimmo Laine and Juha Seitajärvi (eds), *Valkoiset ruusut: Hannu Lemisen & Helena Karan elämä ja elokuvat*, Helsinki: Suomalaisen Kirjallisuuden Seura and Kansallinen audiovisuaalinen arkisto, 113–37.
Hällström, Roland af (1936), *Filmi – aikamme kuva. Filmin historiaa, olemusta ja tehtäviä*, Jyväskylä and Helsinki: Gummerus.

Halonen, Antti (1945), 'Elokuvamme tarvitsee sosiaalista uudistusta', in Toini Aaltonen (ed.), *Teatteri ja filmi*, Äänekoski: Kustannusosakeyhtiö Kirjamies, 115–19.
Hämäläinen, Pekka Kalevi (1968), *Kielitaistelu Suomessa 1917–1939*, Porvoo and Helsinki: WSOY.
Hannikainen, Marjetta (1952), *Elokuvissakäymisen sosiologisesta ja psykologisesta taustasta*, Helsinki: Helsingin yliopisto.
Hietala, Veijo (1992), 'Tuntematon sotilas Rovaniemen markkinoilla. Suomalaisen elokuvan lajityypit 1950-luvulla', in Anna Makkonen (ed.), *Avoin ja suljettu. Kirjoituksia 1950-luvusta suomalaisessa kulttuurissa*, Helsinki: Suomalaisen Kirjallisuuden Seura, 3–19.
Hietala, Veijo, Ari Honka-Hallila, Hanna Kangasniemi, Martti Lahti, Kimmo Laine and Jukka Sihvonen (1992), 'The Finn-between: Uuno Turhapuro, Finland's Greatest Star', in Richard Dyer and Ginette Vincendeau (eds), *Popular European Cinema*, London and New York: Routledge, 126–40.
Hillier, Jim (ed.) (1972), *New Cinema – Finland*, Helsinki: The Finnish Film Archive.
Hjort, Mette and Duncan Petrie (2007), 'Introduction' in Mette Hjort and Duncan Petrie (eds), *The Cinema of Small Nations*, Edinburgh: Edinburgh University Press, 1–19.
Honka-Hallila, Ari (1996), 'Äänielokuva tulee Suomeen', in Kari Uusitalo et al. (eds), *Suomen kansallisfilmografia 1, 1907–1935*, Helsinki: Edita and Suomen elokuva-arkisto, 463–9.
Hupaniittu, Outi (2013), *Biografiliiketoiminnan valtakausi. Toimijuus ja kilpailu suomalaisella elokuva-alalla 1900–1920-luvuilla*, Turku: Turun Yliopisto.
Hupaniittu, Outi (2015a), 'Suomalaisen elokuvan pientuottajat 1920–1930-luvuilla', in *Elonet – Kansallisfilmografia*, Helsinki: Kansallinen audiovisuaalinen instituutti, <http://www.elonet.fi/fi/kansallisfilmografia/suomalaisen-elokuvan-vuosikymmenet/1919-1929/suomalaisen-elokuvan-pientuottajat-1920-1930-luvuilla> (accessed 27 September 2020).
Hupaniittu, Outi (2015b), 'Gustaf Molin – Suomalaisen elokuva-alan unohdettu suuruus', in *Elonet – Kansallisfilmografia*, Helsinki: Kansallinen audiovisuaalinen instituutti, <https://elonet.finna.fi/Content/suomalaisen-elokuvan-vuosikymmenet?p=/1919-1929/gustaf-molin-suomalaisen-elokuva-alan-unohdettu-suuruus> (accessed 27 September 2020).
Hupaniittu, Outi (2018), 'Kuviteltu vuosien 1916–1918 katkos ja kesä 1918 – suomalaisen elokuva-alan varsinainen kohtalonhetki', *Lähikuva* 1/2018, 12–28.
Hupaniittu, Outi (2019a), 'Miten mahdoton onnistui? Suomen Filmiteollisuuden synnyn ja toiminnan taloudellinen perusta', in Kimmo Laine, Minna Santakari, Juha Seitajärvi and Outi Hupaniittu (eds), *Unelmatehdas Liisankadulla. Suomen Filmiteollisuus Oy:n tarina*, Helsinki: Suomalaisen Kirjallisuuden Seura, 20–52.
Hupaniittu, Outi (2019b), 'Televisiosopimus, verotarkastus ja konkurssi – Suomen Filmiteollisuuden loppu', in Kimmo Laine, Minna Santakari, Juha Seitajärvi and Outi Hupaniittu (eds), *Unelmatehdas Liisankadulla. Suomen Filmiteollisuus Oy:n tarina*, Helsinki: Suomalaisen Kirjallisuuden Seura, 324–35.
Ikonen, Ansa (1980), *Tähtiaika*, ed. Tuula Saarikoski, Helsinki: Weilin + Göös.
Jokinen, Osmo (1989), 'Pekka ja Pätkä valkokankaalla', in Kari Uusitalo et al. (eds), *Suomen kansallisfilmografia 5, 1953–1956*, Helsinki: Valtion painatuskeskus and Suomen elokuva-arkisto, 69–71.

Juva, Anu (2008), 'Hollywood-syndromi, jazzia ja dodekafoniaa. Elokuvamusiikin funktioanalyysi neljässä 1950- ja 1960-luvun vaihteen suomalaisessa elokuvassa, Åbo: Åbo Akademi University Press.

Kakko, Jorma (2019), 'Rillumarei ja musikaali', in Kimmo Laine, Minna Santakari, Juha Seitajärvi and Outi Hupaniittu (eds), Unelmatehdas Liisankadulla. Suomen Filmiteollisuus Oy:n tarina, Helsinki: Suomalaisen Kirjallisuuden Seura, 205–8.

Kalemaa, Kalevi (2008), Ensio Suominen – Kansallislavastaja, Helsinki: Like.

Karkama, Pertti (1994), Kirjallisuus ja nykyaika. Suomalaisen sanataiteen teemoja ja tendenssejä, Helsinki: Suomalaisen Kirjallisuuden Seura.

Kassila, Matti (1995), Mustaa ja valkoista, Helsinki: Otava.

Kassila, Matti (2004), Käsikirjoitus ja ohjaus: Matti Kassila, Helsinki: WSOY.

Kassila, Matti and Niko Jutila (2014), Härmän lumo ja voima. Etelä-Pohjanmaa elokuvissa, Helsinki: Avain.

Keto, Jaakko (1974), Elokuvalippujen kysyntä ja siihen vaikuttaneet tekijät Suomessa 1915–1972, Helsinki: The Helsinki School of Economics.

Kinnunen, Kalle (2019), Elokuvasäätiön tuella. Suomalaista elokuvaa tekemässä 1969–2019, Helsinki: Suomalaisen Kirjallisuuden Seura.

Kirjavainen, Sakari, Marja Pensala and Kati von Zansen (2013), Konnia ja huligaaneja. Elokuvasukupolvien kohtaamisia, Helsinki: Gaudeamus.

Kivimäki, Ville (2011), 'Introduction: Three Wars and their Epitaphs: The Finnish History and Scholarship of World War II', in Tiina Kinnunen and Ville Kivimäki (eds), Finland in World War II: History, Memory, Interpretations, Leiden and Boston, MA: Brill, 1–46.

Klemola, Pertti (2004), 'Suomalaisen elokuvan kultaiset vuodet. Valentin Vaala muistelee', in Kimmo Laine, Matti Lukkarila and Juha Seitajärvi (eds), Valentin Vaala, Helsinki: Suomalaisen Kirjallisuuden Seura, 286–305 (orig. 1965).

Koivunen, Anu (1995), Isänmaan moninaiset äidinkasvot. Sotavuosien suomalainen naisten elokuva sukupuoliteknologiana, Turku: Suomen elokuvatutkimuksen seura.

Koivunen, Anu (2003), Performative Histories, Foundational Fictions. Gender and Sexuality in Niskavuori Films, Helsinki: Finnish Literature Society.

Kolbe, Laura (1999), 'Suomalainen kaupunki. Historian hierarkioita ja modernia lähiöelämää', in Markku Löytönen and Laura Kolbe (eds), Suomi. Maa, kansa, kulttuurit, Helsinki: Suomalaisen Kirjallisuuden Seura, 156–70.

Koski, Markku (1977), 'Suomalaisen elokuvan kahdet kasvot', Filmihullu 1/1977, 20–2.

Koskimies, Rafael (1972), Suomen kansallisteatteri 2: 1917–1950, Helsinki: Otava.

Kuusela, A. M. Pertti (1976), Puoli vuosisataa filmiäänitekniikkaa Suomessa, Helsinki: Suomen Elokuvasäätiö.

Kärjä, Antti-Ville (2005), 'Varmuuden vuoksi omana sovituksena': Kansallisen identiteetin rakentuminen 1950- ja 1960-luvun taitteen suomalaisten elokuvien populaarimusiikillisissa esityksissä, Turku: k&h.

Laine, Edvin (1973), Asiat Halki, Helsinki: Kirjayhtymä.

Laine, Kimmo (1994), Murheenkryyneistä miehiä? Suomalainen sotilasfarssi 1930-luvulta 1950-luvulle, Turku: Suomen elokuvatutkimuksen seura.

Laine, Kimmo (1999), 'Pääosassa Suomen kansa'. Suomi-Filmi ja Suomen Filmiteollisuus kansallisen elokuvan rakentajina 1933–1939, Helsinki: Suomalaisen Kirjallisuuden Seura.

Laine, Kimmo (2012), 'Military Comedy, Censorship and World War II', *Journal of Scandinavian Cinema* 2: 3, 257–61.
Laine, Kimmo (2016), 'Popular Modernism', in Henry Bacon (ed.), *Finnish Cinema. A Transnational Enterprise*, London: Palgrave Macmillan, 171–84.
Laine, Kimmo (2019), 'Nyrki Tapiovaara: Between Avant-Garde and Mainstream Cinema', in Benedikt Hjartarson, Andrea Kollnitz, Per Stounbjerg and Tania Ørum (eds), *A Cultural History of the Avant-Garde in the Nordic Countries 1925–1950*, Amsterdam and New York: Rodopi/Brill, 548–59.
Laine, Kimmo and Silja Laine (2008), 'Näkemyksiä 1920-luvun elokuvan maaseudusta, kaupungista ja niiden välisistä suhteista', *Lähikuva* 1/2008, 8–25.
Laine, Kimmo and Hannu Salmi (2009), 'From Sampo to The Age of Iron – Cinematic Interpretations of the Kalevala', *Journal of Finnish Studies* 13:2, 73–84.
Laine, Silja (2011), *'Pilvenpiirtäjäkysymys'. Urbaani mielikuvitus ja 1920-luvun Helsingin ääriviivat*, Turku: k&h.
Lahtonen, Teemu and Anni Teppo (2020), 'Lapin noidat ja pohjoisen taika elokuvassa Valkoinen peura', *Lähikuva* 33:2, 61–9.
Lehtisalo, Anneli (2011), *Kuin elävinä edessämme. Suomalaiset elämäkertaelokuvat populaarina historiakulttuurina 1937–1955*, Helsinki: Suomalaisen Kirjallisuuden Seura.
Lehtisalo, Anneli (2016), 'Exporting Finnish Films', in Henry Bacon (ed.), *Finnish Cinema. A Transnational Enterprise*, London: Palgrave Macmillan, 115–38.
Leitch, Thomas (2010), 'Sequel-Ready Fiction. After Austen's Happily Ever After', in Carolyn Jess-Cooke and Constantine Verevis (eds), *Second Takes: Critical Approaches to the Film Sequel*, Albany, NY: Suny Press, 45–64.
Lindman, Åke (1992), *Åke ja hänen maailmansa*, ed. Heikki Eteläpää, Helsinki: Tammi.
Lounela, Pekka (2004), *Kohti arvoa ja ansiota. Suomen Näyttelijäliitto 1913–1975*, Helsinki: Like.
Mäkelä, Mauno (1996), *Kerrankin hyvä Kotimainen. Elokuvatuottajan muistelmat*, ed. Kalevi Koukkunen, Porvoo: WSOY.
Mäkinen, Aito (1999), *Ensimmäiset 100 vuotta*, television documentary, Filmitaito.
Malmberg, Tarmo (1975), 'Traditional Finnish Cinema: An Historical Overview', in Jim Hillier (ed.), *Cinema in Finland*, London: BFI Publishing, 1–11.
Martin, Benjamin George (2007), '"European Cinema for Europe!" The International Film Chamber, 1935–42', in David Welch and Roel Van de Winkel (eds), *Cinema and the Swastika. The International Expansion of Third Reich Cinema*, Basingstoke: Palgrave Macmillan, 25–41.
Nenonen, Markku (1999), *Elokuvatarkastuksen synty Suomessa (1907–1922)*, Helsinki: Suomen Historiallinen Seura.
Nestingen, Andrew (2014), 'Nordic Noir and Neo-Noir: The Human Criminal', in Homer B. Pettey and R. Barton Palmer (eds), *International Noir*, Edinburgh: Edinburgh University Press, 155–81.
Nevala, Maria-Liisa (2018), *Jack Witikka. Suomalaisen teatterin suurmies*, Helsinki: Minerva.
Nieminen, Outi (2004), *Rakennettu, markkinoitu, mainostettu. Suomi-Filmi Oy:n tuotantokoneisto ja julkisuuskuva vuosina 1933–1939*, unpublished MA thesis, Turku: University of Turku.

Nowell-Smith, Geoffrey (1996), 'General Introduction', in Geoffrey Nowell-Smith (ed.), *The Oxford History of World Cinema*, Oxford: Oxford University Press, xix–xxii.
Palo, Tauno (1969), *Käsi sydämellä*, ed. Aino Räty-Hämäläinen, Helsinki: Tammi.
Pantti, Mervi (2000), *'Kansallinen elokuva pelastettava'. Elokuvapoliittinen keskustelu kotimaisen elokuvan tukemisesta itsenäisyyden ajalla*, Helsinki: Suomalaisen Kirjallisuuden Seura.
Pennanen, Jukka and Kyösti Mutkala (1994), *Reino Helismaa. Jätkäpoika ja runoilija*, Porvoo, Helsinki and Juva: WSOY.
Pennanen, Riikka (2019), 'SF:n filmikoulu – kotimainen tähtitehdas', in Kimmo Laine, Minna Santakari, Juha Seitajärvi and Outi Hupaniittu (eds), *Unelmatehdas Liisankadulla. Suomen Filmiteollisuus Oy:n tarina*, Helsinki: Suomalaisen Kirjallisuuden Seura, 119–30.
Pettey, Homer B. and R. Barton Palmer (eds) (2014), *International Noir*, Edinburgh: Edinburgh University Press.
Riimala, Erkki (1998), *Valkokangasta vastapäätä. Teatteriprojektoreita Suomessa Filmiteknillisen lautakunnan (FTL) valvonnassa 1928–1978 äänielokuvan ensimmäisellä puolivuosisadalla*, Helsinki: Estrex.
Römpötti, Tommi (2012), *Vieraana omassa maassa. Suomalaiset road-elokuvat vapauden ja vastustuksen kertomuksina 1950-luvun lopusta 2000-luvulle*, Jyväskylä: Nykykulttuurin tutkimuskeskus.
Römpötti, Tommi (2019), 'Kriisi ja nuorisokuvan murros SF:n 1960-luvun elokuvissa – "mutta eräänä päivänä joudut kiinni ja vankilaan"', in Kimmo Laine, Minna Santakari, Juha Seitajärvi and Outi Hupaniittu (eds), *Unelmatehdas Liisankadulla. Suomen Filmiteollisuus Oy:n tarina*, Helsinki: Suomalaisen Kirjallisuuden Seura, 307–23.
Salmi, Hannu (1991), '"Pula-ajan kuva". Sota-ajan säännöstely ja Suomi-Filmin Poretta', *Lähikuva* 1/1991, 22–33.
Salmi, Hannu (2002), *Kadonnut perintö. Näytelmäelokuvan synty Suomessa 1907–1916*, Helsinki: Suomalaisen Kirjallisuuden Seura.
Santakari, Minna (2019a), 'Liisankadun studioilla kuvattua', in Kimmo Laine, Minna Santakari, Juha Seitajärvi and Outi Hupaniittu (eds), *Unelmatehdas Liisankadulla. Suomen Filmiteollisuus Oy:n tarina*, Helsinki: Suomalaisen Kirjallisuuden Seura, 113–18.
Santakari, Minna (2019b), 'SF:n elokuvien asut – suunnittelua, seksiä ja muodonmuutoksia', in Kimmo Laine, Minna Santakari, Juha Seitajärvi and Outi Hupaniittu (eds), *Unelmatehdas Liisankadulla. Suomen Filmiteollisuus Oy:n tarina*, Helsinki: Suomalaisen Kirjallisuuden Seura, 139–47.
Sedergren, Jari (1999), *Filmi poikki... Poliittinen elokuvasensuuri Suomessa 1939–1947*, Helsinki: Suomen Historiallinen Seura.
Sedergren, Jari (2006), *Taistelu elokuvasensuurista. Valtiollisen elokuvatarkastuksen historia 1946–2006*, Helsinki: Suomalaisen Kirjallisuuden Seura.
Sedergren, Jari and Ilkka Kippola (2009), *Dokumentin ytimessä. Suomalaisen dokumentti- ja lyhytelokuvan historia 1904–1944*, Helsinki: Suomalaisen Kirjallisuuden Seura.
Seitajärvi, Juha (2019), 'Helsinkiläiset kartanomiljööt SF-elokuvissa', in Kimmo Laine, Minna Santakari, Juha Seitajärvi and Outi Hupaniittu (eds), *Unelmatehdas Liisankadulla. Suomen Filmiteollisuus Oy:n tarina*, Helsinki: Suomalaisen Kirjallisuuden Seura, 92–112.

Seppälä, Jaakko (2012), *Hollywood tulee Suomeen. Yhdysvaltalaisten elokuvien maahantuonti ja vastaanotto kaksikymmentäluvun Suomessa*, Helsinki: Helsingin yliopisto, humanistinen tiedekunta.

Seppälä, Jaakko (2017), 'Following the Swedish Model: The Transnational Nature of Finnish National Cinema in the Early 1920s', *Kosmorama* #269 (www.kosmorama.org).

Seppälä, Jaakko (2019), 'SF:n kriisin ratkaisuyrityksenä Eddie Constantine -mukaelmat – "Nyrkeissä paukkuvaikutus ja donnilla hunajaääni sekä anteliaat kurvit kohdillaan"', in Kimmo Laine, Minna Santakari, Juha Seitajärvi and Outi Hupaniittu (eds), *Unelmatehdas Liisankadulla. Suomen Filmiteollisuus Oy:n tarina*, Helsinki: Suomalaisen Kirjallisuuden Seura, 294–306.

Sihvonen, Jukka (1987), *Kuviteltuja lapsia. Suomalaisen lastenelokuvan lapsikuvasta*, Helsinki: Valtion Painatuskeskus and Suomen elokuva-arkisto.

Soila, Tytti (1994), 'Five Songs of the Scarlet Flower', *Screen*, 35:3, 265–74.

Soila, Tytti (1998), 'Finland', in Tytti Soila, Astrid Söderbergh Widding and Gunnar Iversen, *Nordic National Cinemas*, London and New York: Routledge, 30–90.

Soila, Tytti (2019), 'Valtavirtoja ja pikku puroja – liikehdintää suomalaisten ja ruotsalaisten elokuvatuotantojen välillä', in Kimmo Laine, Minna Santakari, Juha Seitajärvi and Outi Hupaniittu (eds), *Unelmatehdas Liisankadulla. Suomen Filmiteollisuus Oy:n tarina*, Helsinki: Suomalaisen Kirjallisuuden Seura, 286–91.

Stewen, Kaarle (2008), 'Matka kolmanteen valtakuntaan 1942', in Kimmo Laine and Juha Seitajärvi (eds), *Valkoiset ruusut. Hannu Lemisen & Helena Karan elämä ja elokuvat*, Helsinki: Suomalaisen Kirjallisuuden Seura, 318–27.

Straubhaar, Joseph, Robert LaRose and Lucinda Davenport (2009), *Media Now: Understanding Media, Culture, and Technology*, Boston, MA: Wadsworth.

*Suomen tilastollinen vuosikirja* (1938), Helsinki: Tilastollinen päätoimisto.

Talvio, Raija (2015), *Filmikirjailijat. Elokuvakäsikirjoittaminen Suomessa 1931–1941*, Helsinki: Aalto-yliopisto.

Terttula, Eugen (1955), 'Severi Suhosesta Pekka Puupäähän', in Jörn Donner and Aito Mäkinen (eds), *Studio 1. Elokuvan vuosikirja 1955*, Helsinki: Studio, 59–67.

Terttula, Eugen (1957), 'Neorealismin perusrunko', in Aito Mäkinen and Bengt Pihlström (eds), *Studio 3. Elokuvan vuosikirja 1957*, Helsinki: Studio, 25–41.

Thompson, Kristin (1985), *Exporting Entertainment. America in the World Film Market 1907–1934*, London: BFI Publishing.

Todorov, Tzvetan (1980), *The Fantastic. A Structural Approach to a Literary Genre*, trans. Richard Howard, Ithaca, NY: Cornell University Press.

Toiviainen, Sakari (1975), *Uusi suomalainen elokuva – 60-luvun alusta nykypäivään*, Helsinki: Otava.

Toiviainen, Sakari (1986), *Nyrki Tapiovaaran tie*, Helsinki: VAPK and SEA.

Toiviainen, Sakari (1992), *Suurinta elämässä. Elokuvamelodraaman kulta-aika*, Helsinki: VAPK-Kustannus and Suomen elokuva-arkisto.

Toiviainen, Sakari (1993), 'Lankeemus ja pelastusarmeija: sodanjälkeinen ongelmaelokuva', in Kari Uusitalo et al. (eds), *Suomen kansallisfilmografia 3, 1942–1947*, Helsinki: Edita and Suomen elokuva-arkisto, 643–8.

Toiviainen, Sakari, Lauri Tykkyläinen and Peter von Bagh (1980), 'Kuvaajan matka menneeseen', *Filmihullu* 8/1980, 8–21.

Toiviainen, Sakari, Lauri Tykkyläinen and Peter von Bagh (1981), 'Kuvaajasta ohjaajaksi', *Filmihullu* 1/1981, 4–17.
Toni [Topo Leistelä and Nisse Hirn] (1950), *Haluatko elokuvanäyttelijäksi. Filmitietoa elokuvasta kiinnostuneille*, Hämeenlinna: Nide.
Töyri, Esko (1978), *Me mainiot löträäjät. Suomalaisen elokuvan raamikehitysvuodet 1920–1940*, Helsinki: Suomen elokuvasäätiö.
Töyri, Esko (1983), *Vanhat kameramiehet. Suomalaisen elokuvan kameramiehiä 1930–1950*, Helsinki: Suomen elokuvasäätiö.
Tulio, Teuvo (2002), 'Elämäni ja elokuvani', in Sakari Toiviainen (ed.), *Tulio: Levottoman veren antologia*, Helsinki: Suomalaisen Kirjallisuuden Seura, 23–157.
Tykkyläinen, Lauri (2004), 'Valentin Vaalan jäljillä', in Kimmo Laine, Matti Lukkarila, and Juha Seitajärvi (eds), *Valentin Vaala*, Helsinki: Suomalaisen Kirjallisuuden Seura, 17–31.
Uusitalo, Kari (1965), *Suomalaisen elokuvan vuosikymmenet. Johdatus kotimaisen elokuvan ja elokuva-alan historiaan 1896–1963*, Helsinki: Otava.
Uusitalo, Kari (1972a), *Eläviksi syntyneet kuvat. Suomalaisen elokuvan mykät vuodet 1896–1930*, Helsinki: Otava.
Uusitalo, Kari (1972b), *Kuusi vuosikymmentä suomalaista elokuvayritteliäisyyttä. Adams-Filmi Osakeyhtiö 1912–1972*, Helsinki: Adams-Filmi.
Uusitalo, Kari (1975), *T. J. Särkkä. Legenda jo eläessään*, Porvoo and Helsinki: WSOY.
Uusitalo, Kari (1981), *Suomen Hollywood on kuollut. Kotimaisen elokuvan ahdinkovuodet 1956–1963*, Helsinki: Suomen Elokuvasäätiö.
Uusitalo, Kari (1988), *Meidän poikamme. Erkki Karu ja hänen aikakautensa*, Helsinki: Valtion Painatuskeskus and Suomen elokuva-arkisto.
Uusitalo, Kari (1992), 'Fenn/adan lyhyt historia', *Filmihullu* 4/1992, 29–34.
Uusitalo, Kari (1994), *Kuvaus – kamera – käy! Lähikuvassa suomifilmit ja Suomi-Filmi Oy*, Helsinki: Suomen elokuvatutkimuksen seura and Kirjastopalvelu.
Uusitalo, Kari (1999), *Risto Orko. Suomi-Filmin 100-vuotias suurmies*, Helsinki: WSOY.
Uusitalo, Kari (2006), *Tarkastelua. Aarne Tarkas ja hänen elokuvansa*, Helsinki: Like.
Uusitalo, Kari (2011), *Pekat, Pekot ja Uunot. Suomalaiset sarjaelokuvat*, Vantaa: Avain.
Uusitalo, Kari et al. (1989), *Suomen kansallisfilmografia 5, 1953–1956*, Helsinki: Valtion Painatuskeskus and Suomen elokuva-arkisto.
Uusitalo, Kari et al. (1991), *Suomen kansallisfilmografia 6, 1957–1961*, Helsinki: Valtion Painatuskeskus and Suomen elokuva-arkisto.
Uusitalo, Kari et al. (1992), *Suomen kansallisfilmografia 4, 1948–1952*, Helsinki: Edita and Suomen elokuva-arkisto.
Uusitalo, Kari et al. (1993), *Suomen kansallisfilmografia 3, 1942–1947*, Helsinki: Painatuskeskus and Suomen elokuva-arkisto.
Uusitalo, Kari et al. (1995), *Suomen kansallisfilmografia 2, 1936–1941*, Helsinki: Painatuskeskus and Suomen elokuva-arkisto.
Uusitalo, Kari et al. (1996), *Suomen kansallisfilmografia 1, 1907–1935*, Helsinki: Edita and Suomen elokuva-arkisto.
Uusitalo, Kari et al. (1998), *Suomen kansallisfilmografia 7, 1962–1970*, Helsinki: Edita and Suomen elokuva-arkisto.
Valkonen, Tapani, Risto Alapuro, Matti Alestalo, Riitta Jallinoja and Tom Sandlund (1980), *Suomalaiset. Yhteiskunnan rakenne teollistumisen aikana*, Porvoo – Helsinki – Juva: WSOY.

# Select filmography

*Finlandia* (Finlandia, 1922). Directors: Erkki Karu and Eero Leväluoma. Producer: Erkki Karu. Production company: Suomi-Filmi.

*The Logroller's Bride* (Koskenlaskijan morsian, 1923). Director: Erkki Karu. Producer: Erkki Karu. Production company: Suomi-Filmi.

*The Fisherman of Storm Island* (Myrskyluodon kalastaja, 1924). Director: Erkki Karu. Producer: Erkki Karu. Production company: Suomi-Filmi.

*On the Highway of Life* (Elämän maantiellä, 1927). Directors: Kurt Jäger & Ragnar Hartwall. Producer: Gustaf Molin. Production Company: Komedia-Filmi.

*The Wide Road* (Laveata tietä, 1931). Director: Valentin Vaala. Producer: Armas Willamo Production company: Fennica.

*Superintendent of the Siltala Farm* (Siltalan pehtoori, 1934). Director: Risto Orko. Producers: Risto Orko & Väinö Mäkelä. Production company: Suomi-Filmi.

*The Scapegoat* (Syntipukki, 1935). Director: Erkki Karu. Producer: Erkki Karu. Production company: Suomen Filmiteollisuus.

*Surrogate Wife* (Vaimoke, 1936). Director: Valentin Vaala. Producer: Risto Orko. Production company: Suomi-Filmi.

*The Women of Niskavuori* (Niskavuoren naiset, 1938). Director: Valentin Vaala. Producer: Risto Orko. Production company: Suomi-Filmi.

*Stolen Death* (Varastettu Kuolema, 1938). Director: Nyrki Tapiovaara. Producer Erik Blomberg. Production company: Erik Blomberg Oy.

*February Manifesto* (Helmikuun manifesti, 1939). Directors: Toivo Särkkä and Yrjö Norta. Producer: T. J. Särkkä. Production company: Suomen Filmiteollisuus.

*Activists* (Aktivistit, 1939). Director: Risto Orko. Producer: Risto Orko. Production company: Suomi-Filmi.

*The Great Wrath* (Isoviha, 1939). Director: Kalle Kaarna. Producer: Kurt Jäger. Production company: Jäger-Filmi.

*The Vagabond's Waltz* (Kulkurin valssi, 1941). Director: Toivo Särkkä. Producer: T. J. Särkkä. Production company: Suomen Filmiteollisuus.

*The Suominen Family* (Suomisen perhe, 1941). Director: Toivo Särkkä. Producer: T. J. Särkkä. Production company: Suomen Filmiteollisuus.

*The Dead Man Falls in Love* (Kuollut mies rakastuu, 1942). Director: Ilmari Unho. Producer: Risto Orko. Production company: Suomi-Filmi.
*The Secret Weapon* (Salainen ase, 1943). Directors: Theodor Luts and Erkki Uotila. Producer: Theodor Luts. Production company: Fenno-Filmi.
*The Little Bride of the Garrison* (Varuskunnan pikku morsian, 1943). Director: Eero Levä. Producer: Kurt Nylund. Production company: Karhu-Filmi.
*The Way You Wanted Me* (Sellaisena kuin sinä minut halusit, 1944). Director: Teuvo Tulio. Producer: Teuvo Tulio. Production company: Oy Filmo.
*The Northern Express* (Pikajuna pohjoiseen, 1947). Director: Roland af Hällström. Producer: Yrjö Norta. Production company: Fenno-Filmi.
*Beautiful Vera* (Kaunis Veera, 1950). Director: Ville Salminen. Producer: T. J. Särkkä. Production company: Suomen Filmiteollisuus.
*At the Rovaniemi Fair* (Rovaniemen markkinoilla, 1951): Director: Jorma Nortimo. Producer: T. J. Särkkä. Production company: Suomen Filmiteollisuus.
*A Summer Night's Waltz* (Kesäillan valssi, 1951). Director: Hannu Leminen. Producer: Risto Orko. Production company: Suomi-Filmi.
*The White Reindeer* (Valkoinen peura, 1952). Director: Erik Blomberg. Producer: Aarne Tarkas. Production company: Junior-Filmi.
*Children of the Wilderness* (Putkinotko, 1954). Director: Roland af Hällström. Producer: Mauno Mäkelä. Production company: Fennada-Filmi.
*The Unknown Soldier* (Tuntematon sotilas, 1955). Director: Edvin Laine. Producer: T. J. Särkkä. Production company: Suomen Filmiteollisuus.
*A Man from this Planet* (Mies tältä tähdeltä, 1958). Director: Jack Witikka. Producer: Veikko Itkonen. Production company: Veikko Itkonen.
*Hit Parade* (Iskelmäketju, 1959). Director: Hannes Häyrinen. Producer: Mauno Mäkelä. Production company: Fennada-Filmi.
*The Glass Heart* (Lasisydän, 1959). Director: Matti Kassila. Producer: Matti Kassila. Production company: Kassila & Harkimo.
*Inspector Palmu's Error* (Komisario Palmun erehdys, 1960). Director: Matti Kassila. Producer: T.J. Särkkä. Production company: Suomen Filmiteollisuus.
*Here, beneath the North Star* (Täällä Pohjantähden alla, 1968). Director: Edvin Laine. Producer: Mauno Mäkelä. Production companies: Fennada-Filmi and Yleisradio (Finnish Broadcasting Company).

# Index

*65, 66 and I* (*66, 65 och jag*, 1936), 108

Aaltonen, Kosti, 58
*Activists* (*Aktivistit*, 1939), 20, 45, 55, 97, 100–2, 106, 113–14, 146, 160
Adams, Abel, 22, 35, 54, 57
Adams-Filmi, 9, 16, 21–2, 25–7, 31–6, 47–8, 50, 57, 59, 77, 164, 167
*Adventure in Morocco* (*Rantasalmen sulttaani*, 1953), 118
*Adventure Starts Here* (*Här börjar äventyret*, 1965), 173
Aho, Heikki, 39, 54, 83
Aho, Juhani, 54
Aho & Soldan, 39, 54, 83, 152
Alfthan, Dolly von, 50
Altman, Rick, 109–12
*Am I in a Harem?* (*Olenko mina tullut haaremiin?*, 1938), 96
*And Below Was a Fiery Lake* (*Ja alla oli tulinen järvi*, 1937), 139
*And Helena Plays on* (*Ja Helena soittaa*, 1952), 138
*Anja, Come Back Home!* (*Anja tule kotiin*, 1944), 116
*Anna-Liisa* (*Anna-Liisa*, 1922), 100, 105, 131
*Anu and Mikko* (*Anu ja Mikko*, 1955), 80
Antonioni, Michelangelo, 173

*Apple Falls, The* (*Omena putoaa*, 1952), 104
*Arctic Fury* (*Aila – Pohjolan tytär*, 1951), 6, 62
*Are They Guilty?* (*Syyllisiäkö?*, 1938), 115–16, 145
Arvelo, Ritva, 79
*As Dream and Shadow* (*Kuin uni ja varjo*, 1937), 102
*At the Rovaniemi Fair* (*Rovaniemen markkinoilla*, 1951), 62, 99, 117–19, 122, 138
Atelier Apollo, 8
Autio, Fiinu, 80

Bagh, Peter von, 118
*Ballad* (*Ballaadi*, 1944), 114
*Barren Tree, The* (*Hedelmätön puu*, 1947), 116
Bauer, Charles, 78, 140
*Beautiful Inkeri and the Railwayman* (*Ratavartijan kaunis Inkeri*, 1950), 144
*Beautiful Regina of Kaivopuisto* (*Kaivopuiston kaunis Regina*, 1941), 108, 114
*Beautiful Vera* (*Kaunis Veera*, 1950), 80, 90, 138
*Before the Face of the Sea* (*Meren kasvojen edessä*, 1926), 34–5, 67n

Bergman, Ingmar, 1, 6
Bergman, Ingrid, 1
Bergroth, Kersti, 79, 137
*Between Two Dances* (*Kahden tanssin välillä*, 1930), 16
*Big Hit Parade, The* (*Suuri sävelparaati*, 1959), 52
*Big Sleep, The* (1946), 156
Bio-Kuva, 47
Blomberg, Erik, 26, 30, 45, 54–6, 61–4, 82
*Blue Shadow, The* (*Sininen varjo*, 1933), 40–1
*Boys, The* (*Pojat*, 1963), 25
*Bride Springs a Surprise, The* (*Morsian yllättää*, 1941), 104, 137–8
*Bringing Up Father* (comic strip), 41
Brodén, Georg, 19
Buñuel, Luis, 54

Canth, Minna, 131
Capra, Frank, 137
*Car Girls* (*Autotytöt*, 1960), 154
*Catherine and the Count of Munkkiniemi* (*Katariina ja Munkkiniemen kreivi*, 1943), 108, 114, 146
*Caught and Held Fast* (*Kiinni on ja pysyy*, 1955), 99
*Cavalcade* (1933), 113
*Chien andalou, Un* (1929), 54
*Children of the Wilderness* (*Putkinotko*, 1954), 27, 100, 139
Chorell, Walentin, 153
Clair, René, 109
Cocteau, Jean, 54
*Conscript Hero* (*Sankarialokas*, 1955), 139
Constantine, Eddie, 173
*Cowherd, Maid and Housewife* (*Paimen, piika ja emäntä*, 1938), 87
*Creeping Danger* (*Hiipivä vaara*, 1944), 46–7, 50
*Cross of Love* (*Rakkauden risti*, 1946), 116, 142
Cruze, James, 43
Czech cinema, 142

Dahlström, Nils, 18–19, 74–5
Dali, Salvador, 54
Danish cinema, 1, 59
*Dance over the Graves, The* (*Tanssi yli hautojen*, 1950), 24, 100
*Dangerous Freedom* (*Vaarallista vapautta*, 1962), 52–3
*Dark Eyes* (*Mustat silmät*, 1929), 33, 38–40
*Dead Man Falls in Love, The* (*Kuollut mies rakastuu*, 1942), 138
*Dean's Honeymoon Travels, The* (*Rovastin häämatkat*, 1931), 42
*Decoy, The* (*Houkutuslintu*, 1946), 48–9, 116, 144
*Destiny Guides Our Way* (*Kohtalo johtaa meitä*, 1945), 51
*Die goldene Stadt* (1942), 167
*Die Hard 2* (1990), 177n
*Doll Merchant, The* (*Nukkekauppias ja kaunis Lilith*, 1955), 51
Donner, Jörn, 103, 134–5, 172–4
*Dressed Like Adam and a Bit Like Eve Too* (*Aatamin puvussa ja vähän Eevankin*, 1931), 42
Dreyer, Carl Theodor, 1
*Dynamite Girl* (*Dynamiittityttö*, 1944), 138

*Ecstasy* (*Ekstase*, 1933), 142
Eisenstein, Sergei, 141
*Elokuva*, 34–5, 37–8, 161
*Elokuva-Aitta*, 17, 35, 115, 120, 123
*Elokuvateatteri*, 165–6
*Eloseppo*, 54
Elstelä, Ossi, 74, 84, 110
Eriksen, Leif, 44
*Evacuated* (*Evakko*, 1956), 80
*Everybody's Love* (*Kaikki rakastavat*, 1935), 20, 86, 136
*Eyes in the Dark* (*Silmät hämärässä*, 1952), 52

Fager, Karl, 9, 14–15, 34
Family Suominen series, 79, 95, 125–6, 137

*Farmer's Daughter, The* (1947), 127n
Faustman, Erik 'Hampe', 116
*February Manifesto* (*Helmikuun manifesti*, 1939), 45, 55, 80, 97, 100–2, 106, 113–16, 145–6, 160
Fennada-Filmi, 3–4, 9, 13–14, 24–8, 31–2, 47–50, 62, 65–8, 71, 73–4, 76–8, 80, 86, 119–23, 129–30, 138–9, 144, 146–7, 173, 175–6
Fenno-Filmi, 10, 25–7, 32–3, 46–50, 61, 77, 130, 144
Fennica, 10, 33, 38–42, 130
*Ferryboat Romance* (*On lautalla pienoinen kahvila*, 1952), 138
*Fight over the Heikkilä Mansion, The* (*Taistelu Heikkilän talosta*, 1936), 26, 54, 57
*Filmi-Aitta*, 35–7, 84
*Filmi-Kuva*, 50
Filmivalmistamo, 50
*Finlandia* (*Finlandia*, 1922), 16–17, 37, 161
Finlandia-Filmi, 8
Finnish Broadcasting Company (YLE), 25, 28, 53, 176
Finnish Film Foundation, 11, 175–6
*Fisherman of Storm Island, The* (*Myrskyluodon kalastaja*, 1924), 133–4
Fock, Marie-Louise, 60
Fogelberg, Ola, 126
Forsman, Felix, 76, 140–1, 143
Forssell, Kyllikki, 79, 85
*Forward – Toward Life* (*Eteenpäin – elämään*, 1939), 115
French cinema, 6, 78, 103, 115, 139–43, 147
Frische, Axel, 108
*From the Land of the Kalevala* (*Kalevalan mailta*, 1935), 42–3

*Gabriel, Come Back* (*Gabriel, tule takaisin*, 1951), 104
*Gang, The* (*Jengi*, 1963), 154, 173
Garbo, Greta, 1

*Gas Inspector Palmu!* (*Kaasua, komisario Palmu*, 1961), 123, 173
German cinema, 6, 15, 35, 105, 121, 142, 151, 163–7
*Girl and Her Hat, A* (*Tyttö ja hattu*, 1961), 121
*Girl in the Barracks, The* (*Tyttö saapuu kasarmiin*, 1956), 139
*Girl from Muhos, The* (*Muhoksen Mimmi*, 1952), 118
*Girl Goes Out into the World, The* (*Tyttö astuu elämään*, 1943), 161
*Girl of the Week* (*Viikon tyttö*, 1946), 79
*Glass Heart, The* (*Lasisydän*, 1959), 10, 30, 33, 51, 64–6
*God's Doom* (*Jumalan tuomio*, 1939), 115
Goebbels, Joseph, 167
*Gold Candlestick, The* (*Kultainen kynttilänjalka*, 1946), 49
*Gone with the Wind* (1939), 5
*Great Gabbo, The* (1929), 43
*Great Wrath, The* (*Isoviha*, 1939), 45, 113, 160
*Green Chamber of Linnais, The* (*Linnaisten vihreä kamari*, 1945), 114
*Green Gold* (*Vihreä kulta*, 1939), 88
*Green Pastures, The* (1933), 156
Grosset, Raimond, 78, 140
Gunnari, Olavi, 54
*Gypsy Charmer, The* (*Mustalaishurmaaja*, 1929), 39–41

*Halli's Johnny* (*Hallin Janne*, 1949), 49
Hällström, Roland af, 7–8, 28, 49, 77, 132–4
Hamberg-Studio, 46
*Happy Games* (*Onnelliset leikit*, 1964)
Harkimo, Osmo, 62, 65–6, 76, 81–2, 90
Harlan, Veit, 167
Harlin, Renny, 177n
*Haunted Inn, The* (*Kummituskievari*, 1954), 119
Häyrynen, Hannes, 91
*Head of the House Plays the Accordion, The* (*Isäntä soittaa hanuria*, 1949), 64–5

*Hei, Trala-lala-lalaa* (*Hei, rillumarei!*, 1954), 119
Helismaa, Reino, 74, 99, 105, 117–18, 120, 122, 125–6, 144
*Helter-Skelter* (*Mullin mallin*, 1961), 52, 122
*Here, beneath the North Star* (novel), 28, 122
*Here, beneath the North Star* (*Täällä Pohjantähden alla*, 1968), 28, 122
Hietala, Veijo, 104
Hiitonen, Ensio, 149, 165
*Hilma's Name Day* (*Hilmanpäivät*, 1954), 24, 137
Hirn, Nisse, 83–4
Hirvonen, Armas, 78
*Hit Parade* (*Iskelmäketju*, 1959), 120–1, 173
Hollywood cinema, 5–7, 13, 30, 35–6, 43, 70, 74, 78, 87, 98–100, 103–4, 109–12, 115, 156, 164, 175
*Horse Swindler* (*Hevoshuijari*, 1943), 160–1
*Hulda from Juurakko* (*Juurakon Hulda*, 1937), 104, 127n, 157
*Hulda from Juurakko* (play), 127n, 157
Hupaniittu, Outi, 8–9, 22, 35
Huttunen, Jaakko, 75

Ikävalko, Jorma, 117
Ikonen, Ansa, 79, 86–7, 91, 106, 109
Ilmari, Wilho, 84, 143, 167
Ilomäki, Tapio, 44
*In the Beginning Was an Apple* (*Se alkoi omenasta*, 1962), 57
*In the Grip of Passion* (*Intohimon vallassa*, 1947), 60
*In the Shadow of the Prison Bars* (*Ristikon varjossa*, 1945), 116
*Inspector Palmu's Error* (*Komisario Palmun erehdys*, 1960), 66, 123–4, 173
*It Happened in Ostrobothnia* (*Lakeuksien lukko*, 1951), 112
*It Happened in Ostrobothnia* (novel), 112

Itkonen, Veikko, 10, 32–3, 49–53, 57
*It's Up to Us* (*Meiltähän tämä käy*, 1973), 122

Jäger, Kurt, 15, 33–8, 42–6, 71
Jäger-Filmi, 10, 33, 42–6, 113, 160, 164
Jännes, Paavo, 81
Jarva, Risto, 135
Järviluoma, Artturi, 136
Järvinen, Waldemar, 71
*Johan* (*Johan*, 1921), 131
Johansson, Ivar, 61
Jokela, Leo, 123
*Joseph of Ryysyranta* (*Ryysyrannan Jooseppi*, 1955), 27
Joutseno, Lea, 74, 79, 84, 137, 166
*Juha* (*Juha*, 1937), 30, 53–4
Junior-Filmi, 62–5
Jurkka, Jussi, 65, 86

Kaarna, Kalle, 44
Kaipainen, Eino, 48
Kakko, Jorma, 109
*Kalevala* (epic), 43, 112
Kallio, Kyösti, 102
Kansatieteellinen Filmi, 152
Kara, Helena, 80–1, 84, 166
Karhi, Maija, 86
Karhu-Filmi, 31–2, 108, 153, 164
Kari, Eino, 46, 49, 143–4
Karipää, Eija, 50–1
Kärki, Toivo, 66, 117–18, 126
Karu, Elli, 76
Karu, Erkki, 4, 14–18, 21–3, 33–7, 71, 74–6, 130–2, 134, 136
Kassila, Matti, 26, 30, 51, 62–6, 77–8, 93n, 112, 122–3, 137, 144, 175
Kataja, Väinö, 105, 131
Kaurismäki, Aki, 1
Käyhkö, Kauko, 118
Kekkonen, Urho, 167
*Kevätkatsaus* (1939), 102
Kianto, Ilmari, 27
*Killers, The* (1946), 156
*King of Karmankolo, The* (*Karmankolon kuningas*, 1937), 104, 130

*King of Poets and the Bird of Passage, The* (*Runon kuningas ja muuttolintu*, 1940), 114
*King of Sweden in Finland, The* (*Ruotsin kuningas Suomessa*, 1925), 34
*King of the Village Streets* (*Kyläraittien kuningas*, 1945), 48–9
*King's Street* (*Kungsgatan*, 1943), 60
Kinosto, 27, 47, 77
Kippola, Ilkka, 8
Kivi, Aleksis, 131
Kivijärvi, Erkki, 132
Klein, Amanda Ann, 111–12
Koivunen, Anu, 116, 134, 146
Komedia-Filmi, 10, 33–8, 42, 84, 132
Korhonen, Aku, 91
Koski, Markku, 97
Kumpulainen, Unto, 143
Kuosmanen, Mirjami, 61–4
Kurjensaari, Matti, 54
Kurkvaara, Maunu, 51, 154
Kuusela, Armi, 52
Kuusla, Matti, 52

Laakso, Uuno, 91
Lahyn-Filmi, 42
Laine, Edvin, 49, 77, 84, 86, 143, 175
Lehtonen, Joel, 27
Leinonen, Artturi, 112
Leistelä, Topo, 83–4
Leminen, Hannu, 26–7, 74, 83–4, 140, 162, 167
Leppänen, Glory, 79
Leväluoma, Eero, 49
*Lichtspiel Schwarz-Weiss-Grau* (1930), 54
Liemola, Lasse, 121
Lindelöf, Oscar, 39
Lindman, Åke, 89
Linna, Väinö, 24, 28, 122
Linnanheimo, Regina, 39, 60, 81, 142, 166
Linnankoski, Johannes, 57, 69n, 105
Linnus, Olavi, 162
Lintonen, Pentti, 83
*Little Bride of the Garrison, The* (*Varuskunnan pikku morsian*, 1943), 31–2, 108, 153

*Little Matti Out in the Wide World* (*Pikku-Matti maailmalla*, 1947), 116
Lloyd, Frank, 113
Lloyd, Harold, 40
*Log Drivers, The* (play), 44, 105
*Log Drivers, The* (*Tukkijoella*, 1928), 105
*Log Drivers, The* (*Tukkijoella*, 1937), 44, 105
*Log Drivers, The* (*Tukkijoella*, 1951), 105, 139
*Logroller's Bride, The* (*Koskenlaskijan morsian*, 1923), 100, 102, 105, 131
*Logroller's Bride, The* (*Koskenlaskijan morsian*, 1937), 100, 102, 105
*Logroller's Bride, The* (novel), 105, 131
Lohikoski, Armand, 6, 57–8, 80, 99
*Loveliest Girl in the World, The* (*Maailman kaunein tyttö*, 1953), 52
*Love's Sacrifice* (*Rakkautensa uhri*, 1945), 45–6, 116
Lubitsch, Ernst, 137
*Lumberjack's Bride, The* (*Tukkipojan morsian*, 1931), 42
Luts, Aksella, 47
Luts, Theodor, 46–9, 68n, 143–4
Lyyra-Filmi, 8

Machatý, Gustav, 142
McManus, George, 41
*Maid Silja, The* (novel), 51, 60
Mäkelä, Mauno, 4, 13, 26–8, 47–9, 59, 76–7, 80, 86, 92n, 119–20, 123, 145–7, 172–3
Mäkelä, Toivo, 65
Mäkelä, Väinö, 47, 77
*Man from Sysmä, The* (*Sysmäläinen*, 1938), 80
*Man from This Planet, A* (*Mies tältä tähdeltä*, 1958), 51–2
*Man's Rib* (*Miehen kylkiluu*, 1937), 80
Mannola, Pirkko, 121, 144
Markus, William, 6
*Marseillase, La* (1938), 113
Mattson, Ilmari, 71
Mattsson, Arne, 159

*Me and the Cabinet Minister* (*Minä ja ministeri*, 1934), 135
Miettunen, Helge, 172
*Milkmaid, The* (*Hilja – maitotyttö*, 1953), 24
*Millionare Recruit, The* (*Miljonäärimonni*, 1953), 139
Moholy-Nagy, László, 54
Molin, Gustaf, 34–6
*Moment's in the Night* (*Hetkiä yössä*, 1961), 154
Monark Film, 61
*Moonshiners, The* (*Salaviinanpolttajat*, 1907), 14
*Mr Coolman from the Wild West* (*Lännen lokarin veli*, 1952), 118, 153
*Mr Lahtinen Takes French Leave* (*Herra Lahtinen lähtee lipettiin*, 1939), 53, 141
Mustonen, Auvo, 83
*My Beloved Thief* (*Rakas varkaani*, 1957), 153–4

Naukkarinen, Lasse, 7–8, 135
Nevalainen, Esko, 65, 144
*Night Is Long, The* (*Yö on pitkä*, 1952), 64
*Nina and Erik* (*Nina ja Erik*, 1960), 173
Niskanen, Mikko, 25, 175
*No Bodies in the Bedroom* (*Ei ruumiita makuuhuoneeseen*, 1959), 173
Nordiska Biograf Kompaniet, 8
Norta, Yrjö, 23, 46, 48–9, 76, 143
Nortimo, Jorma, 49, 119, 143
*Northern Express, The* (*Pikajuna Pohjoiseen*, 1947), 48–9, 144
Nurkka, Tapio, 84
Nuorvala, Kaarlo, 123
Nylund, Kurt, 31

*Oh, Do You Remember...?* (*Oi, muistatkos...*, 1954), 105, 119
Oksanen, Kille, 58
*Olli Falls in Love* (*Suomisen Olli rakastuu*, 1944), 137
*Olli Pulls a Surprise* (*Suomisen Olli yllättää*, 1945), 116, 137

*On the Highway of Life* (*Elämän maantiellä*, 1927), 36–7, 132
*On the Roinila Farm* (*Roinilan talossa*, 1935), 22
*On the Way to Adventure* (*Matkalla seikkailuun*, 1945), 46
*One Man's Fate* (*Miehen tie*, 1940), 53, 61
*One Summer of Happiness* (*Hon dansade en sommar*, 1951), 159
Oravisto, Matti 91
Orko, Risto, 4, 6, 13–14, 18–20, 74–8, 81, 84, 135–8, 162, 167, 169n
*Orphan's Waltz, The* (*Orpopojan valssi*, 1949), 124
*Our Boys* (*Meidän poikamme*, 1929), 21, 151, 161
*Our Boys at Sea* (*Meidän poikamme merellä*, 1933), 21
*Our Boys in the Air – We on the Ground* (*Meidän poikamme ilmassa – me maassa*, 1934), 21–2
*Outlaw* (*Fredløs*, 1935), 59

Paasikivi, J. K., 167
Pacius, Fredrik, 114
*Päivän Elokuva*, 45
Pakarinen, Esa, 117–19, 122, 125–6, 144
Pakkala, Teuvo, 105
Pakkasvirta, Jaakko, 175
Palo, Tauno, 81, 87, 91, 106, 108–9
Pantti, Mervi, 150
Parvisfilmi, 62
Pasanen, Pertti 'Spede', 52, 123, 174–5
*Pekka and Pätkä on the Trail of the Abominable Snowman* (*Pekka ja Pätkä lumimiehen jäljillä*, 1954), 88
Pekka Puupää series, 66, 95, 99, 118, 125–6, 131, 137, 144, 146
Penttilä, Simo, 138
*Play for Me, Helena!* (*Soita minulle, Helena!*, 1948), 27
*Playing a Hard Game Up North* (*Kovaa peliä Pohjolassa*, 1959), 173
*Poretta, or the Emperor's New Points* (*Poretta eli keisarin uudet pisteet*, 1941), 109

Powell, Michael, 6, 62
Pöysti, Lasse, 86, 125
*Prelude to Ecstasy* (*Kuu on vaarallinen*, 1961), 159
*Price of One Night, The* (*Yhden yön hinta*, 1952), 24
Pudovkin, Vsevolod, 167
Pullinen, Eeva, 79
Puro, Teuvo, 9, 14, 34

*Queen of Spades, The* (*Patarouva*, 1959), 51

*Radio Commits a Burglary, The* (*Radio tekee murron*, 1951), 62, 66
*Radio Goes Mad, The* (*Radio tulee hulluksi*, 1952), 62–6
Raichi, Marius, 78, 140
Ranin, Matti, 123
Rannikko, Yrjö, 164–9
Rautavaara, Tapio, 85
*Red Line, The* (*Punainen viiva*, 1959), 66
*Regiment's Trouble-Boy, The* (*Rykmentin murheenkryyni*, 1938), 97, 103, 110, 116, 139
Renoir, Jean, 113
*Restaurant Patrons Seen through the Camera Lens* (*Ravintolayleisöä kameran silmin*, 1930), 40
Rinne, Jalmari, 82
Rinne, Joel, 81, 123
*Rob the Robber* (*Rosvo Roope*, 1949), 27
*Rock around the Clock* (1956), 121
Rodin, Gösta, 46
Rooney, Mickey, 125
*Ruined Youth* (*Tuhottu nuoruus*, 1947), 27, 116
Runeberg, Johan Ludvig, 108, 114
Ruutsalo, Eino, 154

Saarikivi, Orvo, 78, 162
*Safety Valve* (*Varaventtiili*, 1942), 137
*Säkkijärvi Polka* (*Säkkijärven polkka*, 1955), 80
Salmi, Hannu, 8
Salminen, Seere, 79, 125
Salminen, Ville, 74, 76, 80–1, 84, 90, 119
Salo, Jaakko, 66
*Sampo* (*Sampo*, 1959), 20, 167
Sandrew-Produktion, 61
*Sang d'un poète, Le* (1932), 54
Sari, Sirkka, 80
Särkkä, Margarita, 76
Särkkä, T. J., 4, 6, 13, 22–5, 49, 62, 64–6, 70, 74–8, 80–1, 83–4, 86, 97, 99, 106, 112–18, 120, 123, 125–6, 136, 143, 145, 153–4, 174
Savo, Martti, 103
*Say It in Finnish* (*Sano se suomeksi*, 1931), 42
*Scapegoat* (*Syntipukki*, 1935), 22–3
Schildt, Runar, 54–5
Schnéevoigt, George, 59
Schreck, Matti, 18–19, 74–5, 164, 166–7
*Scorned* (*Halveksittu*, 1939), 115–16, 145
Seabourne, Jon, 62
*Secret of the Summer Night, The* (*Suviyön salaisuus*, 1945), 104
*Secret Weapon, The* (*Salainen ase*, 1943), 46–7
Sedergren, Jari, 8, 155
Seikkula, Irma, 166–7
Seppälä, Jaakko, 105, 131–2
*Serenade with a War Trumpet* (*Serenaadi sotatorvella*, 1939), 97, 110
*Serenading Lieutenant* (*Serenaadiluutnantti*, 1949), 110
*Seven Brothers* (*Seitsemän veljestä*, 1939), 100
*SF Parade* (*SF-Paraati*, 1940), 109
SF-Uutiset, 21, 73, 97, 112–13, 130, 136, 141
*Shadows over the Isthmus* (*Varjoja Kannaksella*, 1943), 46
*Silja – Fallen Asleep When Young* (*Nuorena nukkunut*, 1937), 26, 59–60, 101
*Silja – the Maid* (*Silja – Nuorena nukkunut*, 1956), 51–2, 101
Sillanpää, F. E., 51, 60, 133
*Simo Hurtta* (*Simo Hurtta*, 1940), 45
*Sin of the Mistress of Yrjänä, The* (*Yrjänän emännän synti*, 1943), 61

*Singing Heart, The* (*Laulava sydän*, 1948), 116
Sipilä, Sirkka, 85
*Sixth Command, The* (*Kuudes käsky*, 1947), 116
Sjöberg, Alf, 6
Sjöström, Victor, 60
*Slaying of Elina, The* (*Elinan surma*, 1938), 45
Snellman, Jussi, 44
*Snow White and the Seven Loggers* (*Lumikki ja 7 jätkää*, 1953), 119
Söderbaum, Kristina, 167
Soila, Tytti, 131
Soini, Elsa, 79, 125
Soldan, Björn, 39, 54
*Soldier Boy's Sweethearts, The* (*Sotapojan heilat*, 1958), 139
*Something in People* (*Jokin ihmisessä*, 1956), 139, 144
*Song Hit Parade, A* (*Iskelmäkaruselli pyörii*, 1960), 121
*Song of the Blood-Red Flower, The* (novel), 57, 69n, 105–7
*Song of the City Outskirts* (*Laitakaupungin laulu*, 1948), 116–17
*Song of the Scarlet Flower, The* (*Laulu tulipunaisesta kukasta*, 1938), 57–8, 60–1, 69n, 106, 142
*Song of the Scarlet Flower, The* (*Sången om den eldröda blomman*, 1919), 60, 105–6, 131
*Sonja* (1943), 116
Soviet cinema, 6, 20, 160, 163, 167
*Star Reporters Are Coming, The* (*Tähtireportterit tulevat*, 1945), 51
*Stardom* (*Taape tähtenä*, 1962), 58
*Stardust* (*Tähtisumua*, 1961), 173
*Stars Will Tell, Inspector Palmu* (*Tähdet kertovat, komisario Palmu*, 1962), 123, 173
Stiller, Mauritz, 60, 105, 131
*Stolen Death* (*Varastettu kuolema*, 1938), 10, 30, 33, 45, 53–6, 112–14, 141
*Stranger Came into the House, A* (*Vieras mies tuli taloon*, 1938), 115–16

*Substitute Husband, The* (*Mieheke*, 1936), 140
*Summer Night's Waltz, The* (*Kesäillan valssi*, 1951), 20, 88
*Summery Fairy Tale* (*Suvinen satu*, 1925), 132, 134
Suomen Biografi, 16, 35, 40–1
Suomen Filmiteollisuus, 2–4, 9, 11n, 13–14, 21–8, 31–3, 45–6, 48–9, 51, 53, 61–6, 70–3, 75–8, 80–1, 83, 85–6, 89–90, 93n, 96–7, 100–2, 106, 108–9, 112–13, 115, 117–19, 123–6, 128n, 129–31, 136–9, 141–7, 153–4, 163, 167, 172–3, 175–6
*Suomen Kinolehti*, 145, 162–5, 171–2
Suomen Kuvatuote, 130
Suomi-Filmi, 1, 3–4, 7–9, 11n, 13–21, 23–8, 31–5, 37–8, 40–2, 44–51, 59–62, 64–5, 71–5, 77–81, 83–6, 88–90, 93n, 100, 102–3, 109, 112–13, 119, 126, 128n, 129–32, 134–43, 143, 146–7, 151–2, 157–9, 161–2, 164, 166–7, 170, 173–4, 176
*Suomi-Filmin Uutisaitta*, 71, 129
Suominen, Ensio, 28, 77
*Suominen Family, The* (*Suomisen perhe*, 1941), 125
*Superintendent of the Siltala Farm* (*Siltalan pehtoori*, 1934), 19, 82, 135–6
*Supreme Victory, The* (*Korkein voitto*, 1929), 16, 132
*Surrogate Wife* (*Vaimoke*, 1936), 20, 86, 104, 137
Svensk Filmindustri, 130
Svenska Bio, 9
Swedish cinema, 1–2, 6, 9, 42, 46, 57, 59–61, 105–6, 108–9, 116, 130–2, 159, 172–3
*Swinging Youth* (*Nuoruus vauhdissa*, 1961), 173–4
*Sylvi* (*Sylvi*, 1913), 14

Taide-Filmi, 34
Taini, Hanna, 39
*Tales of Ensign Stål, The* (epic), 108
Tallroth, Konrad, 9

Tanner, J. Alfred, 106, 124
Tapiovaara, Nyrki, 30, 53–6, 61, 112–13, 141–2, 154
Tarkas, Aarne, 62–4, 84
Temple, Shirley, 125
*Temptation* (*Kiusaus*, 1938), 26
*Ten Men from Härmä* (*Härmästä poikia kymmenen*, 1950), 112
Terttula, Eugen, 119
Tervapää, Juhani *see* Wuolijoki, Hella
*That's How It Is, Boys* (*Niin se on, poijaat!*, 1942), 162
Theel, Henry, 110, 144
*Those 45,000* (*Ne 45000*, 1933), 18
*Thus Was the Present Day Born* (*Näin syntyi nykypäivä*, 1951), 51
*To the Dark Continent* (*Matka mustien maanosaan*, 1952), 51
Toiviainen, Sakari, 55, 116
Toivonen, Ester, 21
*Tough Guy* (*Kovanaama*, 1954), 139
Töyri, Esko, 39–40, 44, 47–8, 82–3, 90, 120, 144
*Tracks of Sin, The* (*Synnin jäljet*, 1946), 116
*Transfigured Heart, The* (*Kirkastettu sydän*, 1943), 102
Trenker, Luis, 105
Tugai, Theodor *see* Tulio, Teuvo
Tulio, Teuvo, 19, 26–7, 30, 33, 38–41, 47, 49–50, 54–5, 57–63, 84, 130, 141–2, 176
Tuomi, Olavi, 76
Tuominen, Yrjö, 125
Turchányi, Oliver, 44
Tuukka, Martti, 14, 71
*Two Henpecked Husbands* (*Kaksi Vihtoria*, 1939), 53
*Two Old Lumberjacks* (*Kaksi vanhaa tukkijätkää*, 1954), 105

*Under the Roofs of Paris* (*Sous les toits de Paris*, 1930), 109
Unho, Ilmari, 77–8, 81, 84, 138, 150–1, 167
*Unknown Soldier, The* (*Tuntematon sotilas*, 1955), 5, 24, 88, 99, 106

*Unknown Soldier, The* (novel), 24
Uotila, Erkki, 49
Uuno Turhapuro series, 123
Uusitalo, Kari, 71, 122

Vaala, Valentin, 19–20, 33, 38–41, 57, 77–81, 84, 93n, 104, 130, 136–8, 140, 142, 157, 162, 173–4
*Vagabond King* (*Kuningas kulkureitten*, 1953), 108
*Vagabond's Girl, The* (*Kulkurin tyttö*, 1952), 108
*Vagabond's Mazurka* (*Kulkurin masurkka*, 1958), 108
*Vagabond's Waltz, The* (*Kulkurin valssi*, 1941), 23, 106–8, 114, 146
Väinän Filmi, 47, 59, 87, 164
Valentino, Rudolph, 39–40
Valkama, Reino, 81
Valkeala, Pentti, 90
Valtonen, Hilja, 137
Vartiainen, Toini, 85
*Verlorene Sohn, Der* (1934), 105
Vettenranta, Esko, 48
Viljanen, Emil, 47
Viljanen, Eva-Lisa, 54
*Village Shoemakers, The* (*Nummisuutarit*, 1923), 100–1, 131
*Village Shoemakers, The* (*Nummisuutarit*, 1938), 100–1
*Village Shoemakers, The* (*Nummisuutarit*, 1957), 20, 100–1
Virta, Olavi, 85
*Visit of the Swedish Royal Couple* (*Ruotsin kuningasparin vierailu*, 1925), 34
*VMV6* (*VMV6*, 1936), 136
*Vodka, Mr Palmu* (*Vodkaa, komisario Palmu*, 1969), 123

Wager, Leif, 166–7
Waltari, Mika, 26, 106, 122–4, 133, 147n, 174
*War Profiteer Kaiku's Disrupted Summer Vacation* (*Sotagulashi Kaiun häiritty kesäloma*, 1920), 15

Way You Wanted Me, The (*Sellaisena kuin sinä minut halusit*, 1944), 10, 30, 33, 49, 57–61, 142
We Songsters (*Vain laulajapoikia*, 1951), 109–10
We're All Guilty (*Olemme kaikki syyllisiä*, 1954), 139, 144
We're Coming Back (*Me tulemme taas*, 1953), 105
What a Night! (*Mikä yö!*, 1945), 32
When Father Has Toothache (*Kun isällä on hammassärky*, 1923), 132
When Father Wants to (*Kun isä tahtoo*, 1935), 41
White Heat (1949), 156
White Reindeer, The (*Valkoinen peura*, 1952), 10, 30, 33, 61–4
White Roses (*Valkoiset ruusut*, 1943), 114
Wide Road, The (*Laveata tietä*, 1931), 40–2, 132
Wild Generation (*Kuriton sukupolvi*, 1957), 121–2
Willamo, Armas, 39–40
With Serious Intent (*Tositarkoituksella*, 1943), 79
Witikka, Jack, 6, 51–2, 62
Women of Niskavuori, The (*Niskavuoren naiset*, 1938), 75, 80, 157–9
Women of Niskavuori, The (play), 75, 92n, 157
World War I, 36, 112, 150
World War II, 3, 5, 19–20, 23–4, 31, 45, 50, 53, 57, 61, 96–7, 111, 149, 152–5, 159–60, 162, 164–7, 170
Wuolijoki, Hella, 75, 92n, 127n, 157

Yager's Bride, A (*Jääkärin morsian*, 1931), 42
Yager's Bride, A (*Jääkärin morsian*, 1938), 20, 112–13
Yes and Right Away (*Jees ja just*, 1943), 162–3
Youth in a Fog (*Nuoruus sumussa*, 1946), 116
You've Gone into My Blood (*Olet mennyt minun vereeni*, 1956), 57

EU representative:
Easy Access System Europe
Mustamäe tee 50, 10621 Tallinn, Estonia
Gpsr.requests@easproject.com

www.ingramcontent.com/pod-product-compliance
Lightning Source LLC
Chambersburg PA
CBHW071844230426
43671CB00012B/2061